A Handbook to

BIBLICAL HEBREW

A Handbook to
Biblical Hebrew

An Introductory Grammar

Page H. Kelley

Terry L. Burden

Timothy G. Crawford

WILLIAM B. EERDMANS PUBLISHING COMPANY
GRAND RAPIDS, MICHIGAN

Printed in the United States of America

00 99 98 97 96 95 94   10 9 8 7 6 5 4 3 2 1

ISBN 0-8028-0828-X

CONTENTS

CONTENTS

PREFACE

There are arguments both for and against the publication of a handbook such as this. On the negative side, making an answer key available to students might tempt some of them to use it as a substitute for having to find the answers on their own. This would diminish the teaching value of the exercises. On the other hand, even the most conscientious students will sometimes be in doubt about the correctness of their answers to the exercises. Ideally, their work should be monitored on a regular basis, but time restraints and other factors often make this impractical. Still, it is poor pedagogy to make assignments in the exercises and then fail to provide the opportunity for students to check their work and correct their errors. This is why a number of users of the *Grammar* have requested the preparation of a handbook such as this. It is hoped that providing this help will enable students to resolve their individual problems at home, thus freeing up valuable class time for matters of broader concern.

Requests for the handbook have come from yet another group of users. It is made up of students who for one reason or another are studying Hebrew on their own. The *Grammar* was designed primarily for use in a classroom setting, but these persons, whether by choice or necessity, are using it to teach themselves. The handbook should make their private study of the language far more effective.

The purpose of the handbook is to facilitate the use of the *Grammar*, but not to revise it or to make it into a more advanced textbook. Revisions and corrections are made directly to the text of the *Grammar* itself, each time it is reprinted. This ongoing process of revision has been made possible by the willingness of users to share their suggestions and by the availability of modern computer technology. The text of the *Handbook* has been coordinated with that of the third printing of the *Grammar*.

The lessons in the handbook follow the same order as those in the *Grammar*. Each handbook lesson may contain some or all of the following sections:

Answer Key

All exercises requiring written answers are supplied with an answer key. A few exercises at the beginning of the *Grammar* are omitted because they require oral instead of written answers.

Footnotes

The answer keys are footnoted where grammatical and syntactical problems exist. Footnotes are kept to a minimum to avoid tiresome explanations of the obvious. The student is sometimes referred to relevant sections of the *Grammar* for additional information. There may also be cross references to related sections of the *Handbook*.

Additional Helps

Various types of practical helps are included from time to time under this heading. Suggestions are offered for expediting the student's progress in the language. Important historical data are occasionally highlighted.

Suggestions for Further Testing

Sample tests on the various lessons of the *Grammar* are provided here. They represent the accumulated experience of a number of persons who have taught the course. The tests may be copied and used as written, or adapted in any way the teacher may choose. These sample tests have not been supplied with answer keys.

Dr. Terry L. Burden and Dr. Timothy G. Crawford have assisted in the preparation of the *Handbook*. Both have had classroom experience in the teaching of the *Grammar*. They have given invaluable assistance in the format and content of this book. Dr. Burden has also been responsible for providing a camera-ready manuscript for the publication. These two deserve much of the credit for whatever usefulness the *Handbook* may have.

Page H. Kelley
Spring, 1994

LESSON I

Answer Key
(Cf. *G*, pp. 4f.)

[Note: References to the *Grammar* are abbreviated as *G*; those to the *Handbook* appear as *H*.]

I.3 Transliterate the following verse (Ezek. 38:12, one of twenty-six verses containing all the letters of the alphabet).

לשלל שלל ולבז בז להשיב ידך על חרבות נושבת ואל עם

מאסף מגוים עשה מקנה וקנין ישבי על טבור הארץ

lšll šll vlvz bz lhšyv ydkh ʿl ḥrvvt[a] nvšvt vʾl ʿm

mʾsf mgvym ʿśh mqnh vqnyn yšvy[a] ʿl ṭbvr hʾrṣ

I.5 Locate and identify all the final forms of letters that occur in the verse above.

ידך, ך final kǎf; עם, ם final mēm; מאסף, ף final pēʾ

מגוים, ם final mēm; וקנין, ן final nûn; הארץ, ץ final ṣādê

I.6 Transliterate the Hebrew names for all consonants as they appear in *G*, 1.8, pp. 2f.

(1) אלף ʾlf	(6) וו vv	(11) כף kf	(16) עין ʿyn	(21) שׂין śyn[a]	
(2) בית byt[a]	(7) זין zyn	(12) למד lmd	(17) פא pʾ	שׁין šyn[a]	
(3) גימל gyml	(8) חית ḥyt	(13) מם mm	(18) צדי ṣdy	(22) תו tv	
(4) דלת dlt	(9) טית ṭyt	(14) נון nvn[a]	(19) קוף qvf[a]		
(5) הא hʾ	(10) יוד yvd[a]	(15) סמך smkh	(20) ריש ryš		

I.7 Certain letters are similar in form and thus easily confused. Examine the following letters and learn to identify each by name.

(1) בּ, כּ, פּ (bêt, kăf, pē')

(2) ף, ק (final pē', qōf)

(3) גּ, נ (gîmĕl, nûn)

(4) ך, ן (final kăf, final nûn)

(5) ד, ר (dálĕt, rēš)

(6) ו, ז, י (vāv, zắyĭn, yôd)

(7) ם, ס (final mēm, sắmĕkh)

(8) ט, מ (ṭêt, mēm)

(9) ה, ח, ת (hē', ḥêt, tāv)

(10) ע, צ, ץ ('ăyĭn, ṣắdê, final ṣắdê)

I.8 Certain letters sound alike. Learn to identify these letters by name.

(1) ס, שׂ – S, as in Set (sắmĕkh, śîn)

(2) כּ, ק – K, as in Keep (kăf, qôf)

(3) ט, תּ – T, as in Tall (ṭêt, tāv)

(4) בּ, ו – V, as in Vine (bêt, vāv)

(5) ח, כ – CH, as in BaCH (ḥêt, kăf)

(6) א, ע – Silent letters ('ălĕf, 'ăyĭn)

I.9 What do the letters in each of the following groups have in common?

(1) ת פ כ ד ג ב (These six consonants are called the BeGaD KeFaT letters and may be written either with or without the dagesh lene, depending upon whether or not they are preceded by a vowel. Cf. *G*, 1.9, p. 3; *G*, 6, p. 12.)

(2) ב כ פ (These are the only BeGaD KeFaT letters whose pronunciations in Modern Hebrew are softened when they occur without a dagesh lene. Cf. *G*, 1.9, p. 3.)

(3) ך ם ן ף ץ (These are the forms taken by the letters כ מ נ פ צ when they occur as final consonants in a word. Cf. *G*, 1.11, p. 3.)

(4) א ה ח ע ר (א, ה, ח, ע, and sometimes ר, are classified as gutturals. Cf. *G*, 1.12, p. 3.)

I.10 Transliterate the following proper names and try to identify them from their consonantal forms. A reference is given to indicate where each may be found in the Hebrew Bible.

(1) בית לחם (Mic. 5:1; Eng. 5:2)
byt lḥm / Bethlehem[b]

(2) בלק (Num. 22:2)
blq / Balak

(3) בנימין (Gen. 42:4)
bnymyn / Benjamin

(4) גד (Gen. 30:11)
gd / Gad

(5) גלגל (Josh. 5:9)
glgl / Gilgal

(6) גשן (Gen. 46:28)
gšn / Goshen

(7) דוד (1 Sam. 16:23)
dvd / David

(8) הגר (Gen. 16:1)
hgr / Hagar

(9) חזקיה (2 Kgs. 18:1)
ḥzqyh / Hezekiah

(10) כנען (Gen. 12:5)
knʿn / Canaan

(11) ישראל (Gen. 35:10)
yśrʾl / Israel

(12) כלב (Num. 13:6)
klv / Caleb

(13) לאה (Gen. 29:16)
lʾh / Leah

(14) לבן (Gen. 24:29)
lvn / Laban

(15) משה (Exod. 2:10)
mšh / Moses

(16) נבכדנאצר (2 Kgs. 24:1)
nvkhdnʾṣr / Nebuchadnezzar

(17) נתן (2 Sam. 7:3)
ntn / Nathan

(18) סדם (Gen. 13:13)
sdm / Sodom

(19) עשו (Gen. 25:25)
ʿśv / Esau

(20) פארן (Deut. 1:1)
pʾrn / Paran

(21) קדש (Gen. 14:7)
qdš / Kadesh

(22) רבקה (Gen. 22:23)
rvqh / Rebecca

(23) רחל (Gen. 29:6)
rḥl / Rachel

(24) אברהם (Gen. 17:5)
ʾvrhm / Abraham

(25) שרה (Gen. 17:15)
śrh / Sarah

(26) שדרך (Dan. 1:7)
šdrkh / Shadrach

(27) שכם (Judg. 9:6)
škm / Shechem

(28) שלמה (2 Sam. 12:24)
šlmh / Solomon

(29) שם (Gen. 9:23)
šm / Shem

(30) שפן (2 Kgs. 22:9)
šfn / Shaphan

(31) תל אביב (Ezek. 3:15)
tl ʾvyv / Tel-abib

(32) תמר (Gen. 38:6)
tmr / Tamar

3

Footnotes

(a) In this first lesson, vāv is consistently transliterated as "v" and yôd as "y," although this produces some rather strange combinations of letters. In subsequent lessons it will become apparent that certain letters, especially vāv and yôd, represent consonants only when they begin a word or a new syllable within a word. Otherwise, they stand as component parts of long vowels and are known grammatically as *matres lectionis* (cf. *G*, pp. 6, 7, 18, 437). Understanding the frequent function of these letters as vowels, or vowel indicators, will greatly facilitate their transliteration.

(b) The English language takes certain liberties with Hebrew proper names. First, the English language capitalizes proper names, although there are no capital letters in Hebrew. Second, English translations sometime make a single name from a compound name, as in "Bethlehem." Third, the English language frequently anglicizes the spelling of Hebrew names, as in "Rebecca."

Additional Helps

The Origin and Early History of Biblical Hebrew

Hebrew belongs to the Semitic family of languages, a classification based on the cultural-linguistic elements of Genesis 10:21-31. Semitic languages are usually divided according to their geographical distribution into Northeast Semitic, Northwest Semitic, and Southwest Semitic. Northeast Semitic consists mainly of Akkadian, which in turn is divided into two dialects, Babylonian and Assyrian. Northwest Semitic is comprised of Amorite (known mainly from proper names), Ugaritic (known from the Ras Shamra tablets, discovered in 1929), Canaanite (known from inscriptions), Moabite (known almost exclusively from the Mesha stele), Hebrew, and Aramaic. Southwest Semitic includes Classical Arabic (the language of the Quran), Southern Arabic (known from inscriptions), and Ethiopic.

Before they arrived in Canaan, the Hebrews probably spoke a form of proto-Aramaic. Having settled in Canaan, they borrowed and adapted its language, although it is not known how much time was required for this process to be completed. Indications of the Canaanite origin of Hebrew are obvious. The Bible itself describes the language as "the language of Canaan" (Isa. 19:18). Elsewhere it is described as "Judahite," i.e., as the language spoken by the inhabitants of Judah (2 Kgs. 18:26, 28; Neh. 13:24). The earliest known use of the term "Hebrew" to designate the language is in the Prologue to Sirach (c. 180 B.C.E.). In Rabbinical writings it is often referred to simply as "the sacred language."

During the Babylonian exile and the following centuries, Hebrew was gradually replaced by Aramaic as the everyday language of the people. Still, Hebrew remained the literary language of the Jews. Among the late books of the Hebrew Bible, Esther and Ecclesiastes show rather strong Aramaic influence. Portions of Ezra and Daniel are actually written in Aramaic, at least in the form in which they have survived. A late variety of Hebrew mixed with Aramaic and variously know as Mishnaic, Rabbinic, or Tannaitic Hebrew is preserved in the Mishna, the oldest part of the Talmud, and in other Rabbinic writings.

In recent times Hebrew has been resurrected as the language of the new State of Israel. However, Israeli Hebrew is significantly different from Biblical Hebrew, especially in its vocabulary, grammar, and syntax.

Biblical Hebrew reflects the history of the Hebrew people and their interactions with their neighbors. It does this by the use of loan words and phrases characteristic of neighboring languages as well as by the physical appropriation of neighboring scripts. Though the books of the Hebrew Bible were largely edited under the influence of southern (i.e., Judean) editors (either in pre-exilic Judah or during the Exile) other influences also survive. For example, the difficult text of Hosea has long been regarded as "corrupt" because of its divergence from standard Hebrew word forms, syntax, etc. However, more recently some scholars have suggested that these difficulties are due rather to dialect and that Hosea reflects the northern (i.e., Israelite) dialect of the time (cf. Judg. 12:6).

The Hebrew Bible is largely grammatically uniform considering the vast centuries involved in its composition, but significant differences appear between the various documents. The time factor in the development of the language appears most dramatically when comparing earlier books (Samuel and Kings) with the latter books (Ecclesiastes, Esther, Ezra, Nehemiah, and Chronicles).

Suggestions for Further Testing

1. Five letters take different forms when they are final in a word. Write each of these, first in its regular and then in its final form.

    (a) _____ _____   (b) _____ _____   (c) _____ _____

    (d) _____ _____   (e) _____ _____

2. Write the six BeGaD KeFaT letters, first with and then without a dagesh lene.

    (a) _____ _____   (b) _____ _____   (c) _____ _____

    (d) _____ _____   (e) _____ _____   (f) _____ _____

3. Write the five letters that are classified as gutturals.

   (a) _____ (b) _____ (c) _____ (d) _____ (e) _____(sometimes)

4. Use the space above each letter in the following verse (Ezek. 38:12) to number the letter according to its alphabetical order. Repeated letters should be numbered alike. The same is true of regular and final forms of certain letters. Remember that שׁ and שׂ are also numbered alike (cf. *G*, 1.3, p. 2).

לשלל שלל ולבז בז להשיב ידך על חרבות נושבת ואל

עם מאסף מגוים עשה מקנה וקנין ישבי על טבור הארץ

5. From your study of the Glossary (cf. *G*, pp. 424ff.), define the following terms.

   1)   Alphabet
   (2)   Aramaic
   (3)   BeGaD KeFaT Consonants
   (4)   Dagesh Lene
   (5)   Hebrew Language
   (6)   Semitic Languages
   (7)   TANAKH

LESSON II

Answer Key
(Cf. *G*, pp. 9ff.)

II.3 The following combinations of Hebrew letters and vowels sound like English words with which you are familiar. However, the combinations for the most part have no meaning in Hebrew. See if you can discover an English word that matches each of the sounds.

(1)	אֶג	ʾĕg	"egg"	(21)	יֵשׁ	yĕś	"yes"
(2)	אָר	ʾār	"are"	(22)	קֵק	kēq	"cake"
(3)	בֵּית	bêt	"bait"	(23)	כֹּר	kōr	"core"
(4)	בִּיד	bîd	"bead"	(24)	כִּיל	kîl	"keel"
(5)	בּוֹת	bôt	"boat"	(25)	לֶת	lĕt	"let"
(6)	בֻּל	bŭl	"bull"	(26)	לִין	lîn	"lean"
(7)	בֹּן	bōn	"bone"	(27)	מֶט	mĕṭ	"met"
(8)	גֻּן	gŭn	"gun"	(28)	מִין	mîn	"mean"
(9)	גֵּיט	gêṭ	"gate"	(29)	מֶן	mĕn	"men"
(10)	דֶן	dĕn	"den"	(30)	נִיד	nîd	"need"
(11)	דוֹר	dôr	"door"	(31)	נֹת	nōt	"note"
(12)	הֵיט	hêṭ	"hate"	(32)	נֻט	nŭṭ	"nut"
(13)	הַג	hŭg	"hug"	(33)	סֵף	sēf	"safe"
(14)	הוֹל	hôl	"hole"	(34)	סוּן	sûn	"soon"
(15)	וִיל	vîl	"veal"	(35)	פֵּיא	pê'	"pay"
(16)	וֶת	vĕt	"vet"	(36)	פֶּט	pĕṭ	"pet"
(17)	טָר	ṭār	"tar"	(37)	רוּת	rût	"root"
(18)	טוּל	ṭûl	"tool"	(38)	שֹׂל	śōl	"sole"
(19)	יֶט	yĕṭ	"yet"	(39)	שֹׁל	šōl	"shoal"
(20)	יוּס	yûs	"use"	(40)	תּוּל	tûl	"tool"

II.4 We learned that י and ו can function not only as consonants but also as vowels (*matres lectionis*). See if you can determine which of the following words use ו as a consonant and which use it as a vowel. (Cf. *G*, p. 6)

(1) לוּן (a) <u>V</u> (3) וְשֵׁם (b) <u>C</u> (5) מָוֶת <u>C</u> (7) וַיְהִי <u>C</u>

(2) רוּת <u>V</u> (4) וַיְהִי <u>C</u> (6) בּוֹשׁ <u>V</u> (8) קוּם <u>V</u>

7

II.5 See if you can determine which of the following words employ י as a consonant and which employ it as a vowel.

(1) יָד ___C___   (3) אִישׁ(c) ___V___   (5) בֵּית ___V___

(2) יוֹם ___C___   (4) אִישׁ(d) ___C___   (6) שִׂים ___V___

II.6 Point the following words (supply them with vowels) by consulting a dictionary or word list. (Cf. G, pp. 374ff.)

(1) אֲדָמָה(e)   (3) חֲלוֹם   (5) חֲמוֹר   (7) נַחֲלָה

(2) אֱלֹהִים   (4) חֲלִי   (6) חֲצִי   (8) עֲרָבָה

II.7 Listed below are the letters of the alphabet written in their full Hebrew forms. Transliterate the Hebrew names for these letters and practice pronouncing them.

Example: אָלֶף, 'ắlĕf; בֵּית, bêt; etc. [The accent mark used in אָלֶף and elsewhere in this list is explained in G.8.1(1), p. 16.]

(1)	אָלֶף	'ắlĕf	(9)	טֵית	têt	(17)	פֵּא	pē'
(2)	בֵּית	bêt	(10)	יוֹד	yôd	(18)	צָדֵי	ṣắdê
(3)	גִּימֶל	gîmĕl	(11)	כַּף	kăf	(19)	קוֹף	qôf
(4)	דָּלֶת	dắlĕt	(12)	לָמֶד	lắmĕd	(20)	רֵישׁ	rêš
(5)	הֵא	hē'	(13)	מֵם	mēm	(21)	שִׂין	śîn
(6)	וָו	vāv	(14)	נוּן	nûn	(21)	שִׁין	šîn
(7)	זַיִן	zắyĭn	(15)	סָמֶךְ	sắmĕkh	(22)	תָּו	tāv
(8)	חֵית	ḥêt	(16)	עַיִן	'ắyĭn			

II.8 Here is a similar list of the vowels. Transliterate these and practice pronouncing them.

(1)	קָמֵץ	qắmĕṣ(f)	(7)	חִירֶק	ḥîrĕq
(2)	פַּתַח	pắtăḥ(f)	(8)	חוֹלֶם	ḥôlĕm
(3)	צֵרֵי	ṣērê	(9)	חוֹלֶם וָו	ḥôlĕm vāv
(4)	צֵרֵי יוֹד	ṣērê yôd	(10)	קָמֵץ חָטוּף	qắmĕṣ ḥắṭûf
(5)	סֶגוֹל	sⁿgôl	(11)	שׁוּרֶק	šûrĕq
(6)	חִירֶק יוֹד	ḥîrĕq yôd	(12)	קִבּוּץ	qĭbbûṣ

8

II.9 Transliterate the proper names listed below and practice pronouncing them in Hebrew.

(1)	בֵּית לֶחֶם	bêt léḥĕm	(13)	עֵשָׂו	ʿēśāv
(2)	גָּד	gād	(14)	פָּארָן	pāʾrān
(3)	גֹּשֶׁן	gōšĕn	(15)	קָדֵשׁ	qādēš
(4)	דָּוִד	dāvĭd	(16)	רָחֵל	rāḥēl
(5)	הָגָר	hāgār	(17)	שָׂרָה	śārāh
(6)	כְּנַעַן	kᵉnáʿăn	(18)	שְׁכֶם	šᵉkhĕm
(7)	כָּלֵב	kālēv	(19)	שְׁלֹמֹה	šᵉlōmōh
(8)	לֵאָה	lēʾāh	(20)	שֵׁם	šēm
(9)	לָבָן	lāvān	(21)	שָׁפָן	šāfān
(10)	מֹשֶׁה	mōšĕh	(22)	תֵּל אָבִיב	tēl ʾāvîv
(11)	נָתָן	nātān	(23)	תָּמָר	tāmār
(12)	סְדֹם	sᵉdōm	(24)	יִשְׂרָאֵל	yĭśrāʾēl

Footnotes

(a) Vāv functions as a *vowel* when it occurs immediately after a consonant and is pointed either as šûrĕq (וּ) or ḥólĕm vāv (וֹ). Examples in this exercise are לוּן, בּוֹשׁ, רוּת, and קוּם.

(b) Vāv functions as a *consonant* when it occurs at the beginning of a word or a new syllable within a word. In all such cases, vāv must be written with an accompanying vowel, which may be either a half-vowel or a full vowel. Examples in this exercise of vāvs that begin words are וְשֵׁם, וִיהִי, and וַיְהִי. An example of vāv at the beginning of a new syllable with a word is found in מָוֶת. The division of words into syllables will be studied later in Lesson IV (cf. G.12, pp. 19ff.).

(c) Yôd functions as a *vowel* when it occurs in a median or final position in a word and is written without an accompanying vowel. In this situation yôd combines with the full vowel written beneath the preceding consonant and forms a diphthong. The vowels that may occur with diphthongal yôd are páṭăḥ (sometimes lengthened to qắmĕṣ), sᵉgôl, ṣērê, and ḥírĕq. The resultant dipthongs are יַ, יָ, יֶ, יֵ, and יִ. Examples in this exercise of yôd functioning as a *vowel* are אִישׁ, בֵּית, and שִׂים. Other examples are צָדִי, צֵרֵי, and שִׁין.

9

(d) Yôd functions as a *consonant* when it stands at the beginning of a word or a new syllable within a word. In all such cases yôd must be followed immediately by its supporting vowel. Usually this is a full vowel, but it may also be a half-vowel. Examples in this exercise of yôd as a *consonant* are יָד, יוֹם, and יֵשׁ. Other examples are יְאוֹר (with half-vowel), יַיִן (twice), and בַּיִת (median yôd beginning a new syllable). The constant factor in all these examples is that yôd is always followed immediately by a vowel.

(e) Compound shevas occur almost exclusively with gutturals.

(f) In Modern Hebrew, no appreciable difference is made between the pronunciation of pǎtǎḥ and of qǎměṣ. For our purpose, however, pǎtǎḥ will be transcribed as "ă" and qǎměṣ as "ā" (cf. *G*.2.2, p. 7). This will enable students to reconstruct Hebrew words with greater accuracy when words occur with either pǎtǎḥ or qǎměṣ.

Suggestions for Further Testing

1. Transliterate the names for the letters of the alphabet, marking accented syllables where indicated, and supplying the vowels with appropriate accent marks. In the second blank give the consonant that each name designates. Hint: the first letter of the name designates the consonant.

		Name	*Consonant*			*Name*	*Consonant*
(1)	אָלֶף	___	___	(13)	מֵם	___	___
(2)	בֵּית	___	___	(14)	נוּן	___	___
(3)	גִּימֶל	___	___	(15)	סָמֶךְ	___	___
(4)	דָּלֶת	___	___	(16)	עַיִן	___	___
(5)	הֵא	___	___	(17)	פֵּא	___	___
(6)	וָו	___	___	(18)	צָדֵי	___	___
(7)	זַיִן	___	___	(19)	קוֹף	___	___
(8)	חֵית	___	___	(20)	רֵישׁ	___	___
(9)	טֵית	___	___	(21)	שִׁין	___	___
(10)	יוֹד	___	___		שִׂין	___	___
(11)	כַּף	___	___	(22)	תָּו	___	___
(12)	לָמֶד	___	___				

2. Transliterate the names for the vowels and write the vowels as they occur in the Hebrew Bible.

		Name	*Vowel*			*Name*	*Vowel*
(1)	קָמֶץ	___	___	(7)	חִירֶק	___	___
(2)	פַּתַח	___	___	(8)	חוֹלֶם	___	___
(3)	צֵרֵי	___	___	(9)	חוֹלֶם וָו	___	___
(4)	צֵרֵי יוֹד	___	___	(10)	קָמֶץ חָטוּף	___	___
(5)	סֶגּוֹל	___	___	(11)	שׁוּרֶק	___	___
(6)	חִירֶק יוֹד	___	___	(12)	קֻבּוּץ	___	___

3. Indicate which of the following words employ yôd as a consonant (C) and which employ it as a vowel (V).

(1)	אֲנִי	( )	(5)	הָיָה	( )	(9)	כִּי	( )
(2)	בְּרִית	( )	(6)	יוֹם	( )	(10)	מִי	( )
(3)	בֵּין	( )	(7)	זַיִן	( )	(11)	שְׁנַיִם	( )
(4)	דַּי	( )	(8)	יְשׁוּעָה	( )	(12)	שִׁית	( )

4. Indicate which of the following words employ vāv as a consonant (C) and which employ it as a vowel (V).

(1)	אוֹר	( )	(5)	גּוּר	( )	(9)	וָבֹהוּ	( )
(2)	גּוֹאֵל	( )	(6)	וְנָבִיא	( )	(10)	סוּס	( )
(3)	תִּקְוָה	( )	(7)	הוּא	( )	(11)	קוּם	( )
(4)	תּוֹרָה	( )	(8)	וְהָאָרֶץ	( )	(12)	שָׁלוֹם	( )

5. From your study of the Glossary (cf. *G*, pp. 424ff.), define the following terms:

(1) Compound Sheva
(2) Diphthong
(3) Half–Vowel
(4) Masoretes
(5) Masoretic Text
(6) Matres Lectionis
(7) Munah
(8) Pointed Text
(9) Scriptio Plena
(10) Transliteration

LESSON III

(Cf. *G*, pp. 14f.)

III.1 There are BeGaD KeFaT letters in all the words listed below. Add a dagesh lene wherever it belongs in one of these letters. Please note that the shevas are all silent. (Cf. *G*.1.9, p. 3.)

(1)	אֶכְתֹּב	(5)	דְּבַר	(9)	מִשְׁכָּב	(13)	פָּנִים
(a)	אֶכְתֹּב		דְּבַר		מִשְׁכָּב		פָּנִים
(2)	בֶּגֶד	(6)	יִגְדַּל	(10)	קָדוֹשׁ	(14)	נֶפֶשׁ
(b)	בֶּגֶד		יִגְדַּל				
(3)	בַּיִת	(7)	כֶּסֶף	(11)	מִשְׁפָּט	(15)	תּוֹרָה
	בַּיִת		כֶּסֶף		מִשְׁפָּט		תּוֹרָה
(4)	גָּדוֹל	(8)	מִדְבַּר	(12)	נָבִיא	(16)	תִּכְתֹּב
(c)	גָּדוֹל		מִדְבַּר				תִּכְתֹּב

III.2 Underscore the words in the following list which contain a dagesh forte.

(1)	אַתָּה(d)	(4)	הִנֵּה	(7)	כִּסֵּא	(10)	שִׁשִּׁי
(2)	גִּבּוֹר	(5)	חַיָּה	(8)	מִשְׁפָּט	(11)	תְּמוּנָה
(3)	דִּבֶּר	(6)	יַרְדֵּן(e)	(9)	שִׁבֵּר	(12)	תְּפִלָּה

III.3 Transliterate the words listed above and practice pronouncing them.

(1)	ʾăt tāh	(5)	hăy yāh	(9)	šĭb bēr
(2)	gĭb bôr	(6)	yăr dēn	(10)	šĭš šî
(3)	dĭb bēr	(7)	kĭs sēʾ	(11)	tᵉmû nāh
(4)	hĭn nēh	(8)	mĭš paṭ	(12)	tᵉfĭl lāh

III.4 Exodus 3:1 is reproduced here.

וּמֹשֶׁה הָיָה רֹעֶה אֶת־צֹאן יִתְרוֹ חֹתְנוֹ
כֹּהֵן מִדְיָן וַיִּנְהַג אֶת־הַצֹּאן אַחַר
הַמִּדְבָּר וַיָּבֹא אֶל־הַר הָאֱלֹהִים חֹרֵבָה:

(1) Copy the three words in which all the letters are gutturals.

(a) רֹעֶה (b) אַחַר (c) הַר

(2) Copy the three pairs of words linked together by măqqếfs.

(a) אֶל־הַר (b) אֶת־הַצֹּאן (c) אֶת־צֹאן

(3) Copy the word that has both a dagesh lene and a dagesh forte, indicating which is which.

הַמִּדְבָּר   מּ – dagesh forte,   בּ – dagesh lene

(4) Copy the word that contains a compound sheva.

הָאֱלֹהִים

III.5   Genesis 2:3 is reproduced here.

וַיְבָרֶךְ אֱלֹהִים אֶת־יוֹם הַשְּׁבִיעִי
וַיְקַדֵּשׁ אֹתוֹ כִּי בוֹ שָׁבַת מִכָּל־
מְלַאכְתּוֹ אֲשֶׁר־בָּרָא אֱלֹהִים לַעֲשׂוֹת׃

(1) Copy the two words that contain both a silent sheva and a vocal sheva.

(a) וַיְבָרֶךְ[f]   ךְ silent sheva;   יְ vocal sheva

(b) מְלַאכְתּוֹ[g]   כְ silent sheva;   מְ vocal sheva

(2) Copy the word that is marked as the direct object of the verb.

אֶת־יוֹם

(3) Copy the three words that contain dagesh fortes.

(a) מִכָּל (b) וַיְקַדֵּשׁ (c) הַשְּׁבִיעִי

(4) Copy the four words that contain compound shevas.

(a) לַעֲשׂוֹת (b) אֱלֹהִים (c) אֲשֶׁר (d) אֱלֹהִים

(5) Copy the three words that contain BeGaD KeFaT letters with dagesh lenes.

(a) בָּרָא (b) מְלַאכְתּוֹ (c) כִּי

Footnotes

(a) Since beginning students may still have difficulty distinguishing between silent and vocal shevas, students are informed that all shevas in Exercise III.1 are silent. Whenever a BeGaD KeFaT letter stands other than at the beginning of a word and is immediately preceded by a consonant with a silent sheva, it must be

13

pointed with a dagesh lene. The rule applies in this exercise to III.1(1), (6), (8), (9), (11), and (16).

(b) A BeGaD KeFaT letter that stands at the beginning of a word, and is therefore not preceded by a consonant with a vowel, must be pointed with dagesh lene [cf. III.1(2), (3), (4), (5), (7), (13), (15), (16)].

(c) A BeGaD KeFaT letter immediately preceded by a consonant with a vowel (half-vowel or full vowel) must be written without a dagesh lene. [Cf. III.1(1) כ and ב, (2) ג and ד, (3) ת, (4) ד, (5) ב, (6) ג, (7) ף, (8) ד, (9) ב, (10) ד, (12) ב, (14) פ, (16) כ and ב.]

(d) A consonant that is doubled by a dagesh forte must stand immediately after a consonant pointed with a full vowel. A half-vowel, whether simple or compound, does not permit a dagesh forte (or dagesh lene) in the following consonant.

(e) The silent sheva under ר (cf. G, 7, p. 13) causes a dagesh lene to be placed in the following ד, a BeGaD KeFaT consonant. The same is true of פ in III.2(8).

(f) Since the dagesh lene has dropped out of ב, a BeGaD KeFaT letter, the sheva under yôd must be vocal rather than silent.

(g) Since ת, another BeGaD KeFaT letter, has a dagesh lene, the sheva under the preceding consonant must be silent rather than vocal.

Suggestions for Further Testing

1. Transliterate the following words and supply the appropriate vowel accents.

(1)	אֶכְתֹּב	_____	(9)	מִשְׁכָּב	_____
(2)	בֶּגֶד	_____	(10)	קָדוֹשׁ	_____
(3)	בַּיִת	_____	(11)	מִשְׁפָּט	_____
(4)	גָּדוֹל	_____	(12)	נָבִיא	_____
(5)	דָּבָר	_____	(13)	פָּנִים	_____
(6)	יִגְדַּל	_____	(14)	נֶפֶשׁ	_____
(7)	כֶּסֶף	_____	(15)	תּוֹרָה	_____
(8)	מִדְבָּר	_____	(16)	תִּכְתֹּב	_____

2. The following words designate parts of the body. Transliterate each word (Column 1) and enter its meaning (Column 2) from the vocabulary list beginning on page 374 of the *Grammar*.

		(1)	(2)
(1)	אֹזֶן	_____	_____
(2)	אֶצְבַּע	_____	_____
(3)	בֶּטֶן	_____	_____
(4)	בֶּרֶךְ	_____	_____
(5)	בָּשָׂר	_____	_____
(6)	חֵק	_____	_____
(7)	יָד	_____	_____
(8)	כַּף	_____	_____
(9)	לֵב	_____	_____
(10)	לָשׁוֹן	_____	_____
(11)	עַיִן	_____	_____
(12)	רֹאשׁ	_____	_____

3. Define the following terms based on definitions in the Glossary (cf. *G*, pp. 424ff.).

   (1) Conjunctive Dagesh Forte
   (2) Dagesh Forte
   (3) Full Vowel
   (4) Maqqef
   (5) Sign of the Direct Object
   (6) Silent Sheva
   (7) Simple Sheva

LESSON IV

Answer Key
(Cf. *G*, pp. 21f.)

IV.1 Turn to Genesis 1:1–5 in a Hebrew Bible and copy the words in each verse that are accented with an ʾắtnāḥ or with a sĭllûq.

Example: Verse 1: אֱלֹהִים (ʾắtnāḥ), הָאָרֶץ (sĭllûq)

2: תְהוֹם (ʾắtnāḥ), הַמָּיִם(a) (sĭllûq)

3: אוֹר (ʾắtnāḥ), אוֹר (sĭllûq)

4: טוֹב (ʾắtnāḥ), הַחֹשֶׁךְ (sĭllûq)

5: לַיְלָה(b) (ʾắtnāḥ), אֶחָד (sĭllûq)

IV.2 The following words have been divided into syllables. Tell what kind of vowel each has (long or short). Caution: Be careful to distinguish between long "*a*," qắmĕṣ, and short "*o*," qắmĕṣ-ḥāṭûf.

Example: חָכְ/מָה

חָכְ – a closed syllable (C) with a short vowel (S) (because it is unaccented).

מָה – an open syllable (O) with a long vowel (L).

(1) חָכְ/מָה	(3) שֶׁל/מֹה	(5) פָּא/רָן	(7) יְרוּ/שָׁ/לַ/יִם	(9) וַנַּ/עֲשֶׂה
OL/CS	OL/OL	CL/OL	CS/OS/OL/OL	OS/OS

(2) מַלְ/כָּה	(4) דָּ/וִד	(6) מֹ/שֶׁה	(8) אֶ/עֱשֶׂה	(10) קְטֹל
OL/CS	CS/OL	OS/OL	OS/OS	CL/CS

IV.3 Divide the following words into syllables. Tell what kind of syllable each is (open or closed) and what kind of vowel each has (long or short).

(1) תִּכְ/תֹּב	(3) יָ/דַ/יִם(e)	(5) חָ/שֶׁךְ(f)	(7) יִ/שְׁבּוּ(h)	(9) שָׁ/לוֹם
CL/CS	CS/OS/OL	CS/OL	OL/OL	CL/OL

(2) כֻּלְ/לָה(d)(c)	(4) דְּרָ/כִים	(6) הֶ/עֱמִיד(g)	(8) בַּדְ/דָ/רֶךְ	(10) מִבְּ/בוֹא(j)(i)
CL/CS	CL/OL	CL/OS	CS/OS/CS	OL/CS

16

IV.4 There are four silent shevas and eleven vocal shevas in the following list of words. Locate and identify each of these.

(1) בְּרִית   בְּ vocal   (6) וְדִבַּרְתִּי[m]   רְ silent, וְ vocal

(2) נֶעֱבָד[k]   עֱ vocal   (7) תִּלְמְדִי[l]   מְ vocal, לְ silent

(3) עָבְדוּ   בְ vocal   (8) כְּכוֹכְבֵי[m]   כְ vocal, כְּ vocal

(4) יִכְתְּבוּ[l]   תְּ vocal, כְ silent   (9) בְּדָבְרִי[m]   בְ vocal, בְּ vocal

(5) לָךְ[f]   ךְ silent   (10) בְּגָדִים[m]   גְ vocal

IV.5 Take each word in Genesis 1:1, divide it into syllables, and describe each syllable according to the kind of syllable it is and the kind of vowel it has.

(1) בְּרֵא/שִׁית[j]   (3) אֱל/הִים   (5) הַשָּׁ/שָׁ/מַ/יִם   (7) הָאָ/רֶץ
     CL/OL   CL/OL   CS/OS/OL/CS   CS/OL/OL

(2) בָּ/רָא[j]   (4) אֵת   (6) וְאֵת
     OL/OL   CL   CL

Footnotes

(a) הַמָּיִם is the pausal form for הַמַּיִם (cf. *G*.8.3, p. 17).

(b) לָיְלָה is the pausal form for לַיְלָה (cf. *G*.8.3, p. 17).

(c) When a consonant is doubled by dagesh forte, the first of the doubled consonants ends the preceding syllable, thus making it a closed syllable, while the second initiates the following syllable, which may be either open or closed, depending on its structure.

There is an important exception to this rule. Whenever a yôd occurs with dagesh forte, the first of the doubled yôds combines with the vowel under the preceding consonant to form a diphthong, usually páṭâḥ yôd (יַ). This syllable remains open, since it ends in a vowel. [All diphthongs are long vowels.]

Examples: (1) הַי/יוֹם → הַיּוֹם   (3) אַי/יֶה → אַיֵּה
                CL/OL   OL/OL

(2) בְּלִי/יַעַל → בְּלִיַּעַל   (4) הַי/יִם → הַיִּם
          CS/OS/OL   CL/OL

(d) On final hē' with măppîq (ה) as a syllable–closing consonant, see *G*.11, pp. 18f., 436.

(e) The second syllable of this word is דְּ, which is allowed to stand as an open syllable with a short vowel because it bears the accent (cf. *G*.12.4, p. 20; also "Syllable," p. 444).

(f) Silent sheva in final kăf (ךְ) always indicates a closed syllable (cf. *G*.7, p. 13).

(g) The initial syllable הֶ is marked with the secondary accent mḗtĕg. The syllable is open and is allowed to stand with a short vowel because it is followed by a consonant supported by a vocal sheva (שְׁ) [cf. *G*.12.4(4), p. 21].

(h) The mḗtĕg beside qấmĕṣ marks it as a long vowel in an open syllable before a vocal sheva (שְׁ) [cf. *G*.9.2(3), p. 18].

(i) A dagesh forte in a BeGaD KeFaT letter hardens the sound just as if it were a dagesh lene. The resultant transliteration is mĭb-bō' [cf. *G*.6(3), p. 12].

(j) א never closes a syllable, either in the middle of a word or at the end (cf. *G*.10, p. 18).

(k) Compound shevas are always vocal (cf. *G*.3, pp. 8f.; also "Compound Sheva," p. 428).

(l) Whenever two shevas stand under adjacent consonants within a word, the first will be silent and the second vocal. Consequently, the syllable divider will be placed between these two consonants (cf. *G*.7, p. 13).

(m) Dagesh lene drops out of BeGaD KeFaT letters when these are preceded by a vowel, either full or half (cf. *G*.6, pp. 12f.).

Additional Helps

In regard to syllable division, my first Hebrew teacher advised students to start at the end of a word and work backward when they wished to divide the word into syllables. [Remember that there will be as many syllables as there are full vowels within a word and that every syllable must begin with a consonant (cf. *G*.12.2, p. 19).] Beginning at the end of a word, the student works backward to locate the first full vowel and the consonant that immediately precedes it. A divider is tentatively drawn before the consonant to mark the final syllable in the word. This process is then repeated to locate and mark the next syllable, and so on until the beginning of the word.

Take the word יִשְׂרָאֵל as an example. Its three full vowels, ṣērê, qāmĕṣ, and ḥîrĕq, indicate three syllables. The ṣērê is the first vowel from the end of the word and is preceded by א. This syllable can be identified as אֵל (יִשְׂרָ/אֵל). Since the accent falls on the final syllable of a word unless otherwise indicated (cf. *G.*2n., p. 6), אֵל stands as an accented, closed syllable and has a long vowel (cf. *G.*12.4, p. 20).

As one works backward in the word, the second full vowel is qāmĕṣ and its consonant ר (יִשְׂ/רָ/אֵל). רָ is an open, unaccented syllable with a long vowel.

The remaining full vowel is ḥîrĕq, preceded by yôd and followed by שׂ with a silent sheva (syllable divider). Thus יִשְׂ is a closed, unaccented syllable with a short vowel.

The approach to syllable division just explained becomes more complicated when vocal shevas (simple or compound) occur within a word. Here are some rules to follow whenever vocal shevas occur:

(1) A vocal sheva, whether simple or compound, stands only at the beginning and never at the end of a syllable (cf. *G.*12.3, pp. 19f.).

(2) Since a vocal sheva is only a half-vowel, it and its consonant alone do not constitute a syllable. Instead, they are joined to the following consonant pointed with a full vowel. The result is a single syllable beginning with a consonant and its half-vowel immediately followed by a second consonant and its full vowel.

Examples: (a)   בְּנֵי   - a single-syllable word
                  (OL)

           (b)   בְּרִית   - a single-syllable word
                  (CL)

           (c)   אֱל/הִים   - a two-syllable word
           (CL, OL)

(3) When two consonants with shevas stand next to each other within a word, the first sheva will be silent, thus marking the end of a closed syllable. The second sheva will be vocal, marking the beginning of the next syllable.

Examples: (a) יִשְׁ/מְרוּ   (b) בַּל/עֲדֵי
               OL/CS   OL/CS

(4) If a sheva occurs beneath a consonant that is doubled by dagesh forte, the pattern of syllable division is the same as that discussed under (2). The doubled consonant is divided into two and the division into syllables is drawn between the two. The first syllable will be closed and will have a short vowel. The second of the two consonants will be pointed with a vocal sheva and will attach itself to the following syllable.

Examples: (a) קִטְּלִי → קִטְ/טְלִי   (b) שִׁמְּרוּ → שִׁמְ/מְרוּ
                   OL/CS   OL/CS

Suggestions for Further Testing

1. Each of the following words has a consonant doubled by a dagesh forte. Rewrite the word with the doubled consonant repeated, divide the word into syllables, and indicate whether a syllable is open (O) or closed (C), and whether it has a long (L) or short (S) vowel.

Example: קָטֵל → קַט/טֵל
CL/CS

(1) הַשָּׁמַיִם

(2) בַּדֶּרֶךְ

(3) וַתְּהִי

(4) וַתִּשְׁמֹר

(5) יִקְטְלוּ

(6) הַמְּאֹרֹת

(7) הַמִּדְבָּר

(8) אִשָּׁה

(9) הַפְּרִי

(10) בְּדַבְּרִי

2. From your study of the Glossary (cf. *G*, pp. 424ff.), define the following terms:

(1) Accented Syllable
(2) Accents
(3) ʾAtnaḥ
(4) Meteg
(5) Silluq
(6) Syllable
(7) Tone Syllable

LESSON V

Answer Key
(Cf. *G*, pp. 26f.)

V.2 Prefix the definite article to the following words.

(1)	יָד	הַיָּד[a]	(7)	עָשָׁן	הֶעָשָׁן[d]	(13)	הֵיכָל	הַהֵיכָל[f]
(2)	יְאֹר	הַיְאֹר[b]	(8)	אֶרֶץ	הָאָרֶץ[e]	(14)	הַר	הָהָר[e]
(3)	מִדְבָּר	הַמִּדְבָּר[a]	(9)	עַם	הָעָם[e]	(15)	גַּן	הַגַּן[e]
(4)	בַּיִת	הַבַּיִת[a]	(10)	חֶרֶב	הַחֶרֶב[f]	(16)	חַג	הֶחָג[d]
(5)	אִשָּׁה	הָאִשָּׁה[c]	(11)	רוּחַ	הָרוּחַ[g]	(17)	הָרִים	הֶהָרִים[d]
(6)	עֵת	הָעֵת[c]	(12)	בְּרִית	הַבְּרִית[a]	(18)	רֹאשׁ	הָרֹאשׁ[c]

V.3 Divide the following words into syllables and specify whether the syllables are open (O) or closed (C), and whether their vowels are long (L) or short (S).
Example: הַחֹשֶׁךְ – 1st. syllable (הַח) is closed (ח is doubled by implication) and has a short vowel (CS). 2nd. syllable (ח) is open and has a long vowel (OL). 3rd. syllable (שֶׁךְ) is closed and has a short vowel (CS).

(1)	הַחֹשֶׁךְ	הַח/ח/שֶׁךְ[f]	(6)	הָאֱלֹהִים	הָ/אֱלֹ/הִים
		CS/OL/CS			CL/OL/OL
(2)	הֶעָשִׁיר	הֶ/עָ/שִׁיר[h]	(7)	הַשֵּׁם	הַשׁ/שֵׁם
		CL/OL/OS			CL/CS
(3)	הַנָּבִיא	הַנ/נָ/בִיא	(8)	הַיּוֹם	הַי/יוֹם[i]
		OL/OL/CS			CL/OL
(4)	הָאָדוֹן	הָ/אָ/דוֹן	(9)	הַמִּצְוָה	הַמ/מִצְ/וָה[j]
		CL/OL/OL			OL/CS/CS
(5)	הֶעָנָן	הֶ/עָ/נָן[h]	(10)	הַדְּבָרִים	הַד/דְבָ/רִים
		CL/OL/OS			CL/OL/CS

V.4 All the words in the preceding exercise have the definite article. Be prepared to explain why each article was given the form that it has.

(1)	הַחֹשֶׁךְ	Cf. *G*.14.3(2)(a), pp. 24f.
(2)	הֶעָשִׁיר	Cf. *G*.14.3(2)(c), p. 24.
(3)	הַנָּבִיא	Cf. *G*.14.3(1), p. 24.
(4)	הָאָדוֹן	Cf. *G*.14.3(2)(b), p. 25.
(5)	הֶעָנָן	Cf. *G*.14.3(2)(c), p. 24.
(6)	הָאֱלֹהִים	Cf. *G*.14.3(2)(b), p. 25.
(7)	הַשֵּׁם	Cf. *G*.14.3(1), p. 24.
(8)	הַיּוֹם	Cf. *G*.14.3(1), p. 24.
(9)	הַמִּצְוָה	Cf. *G*.14.3(1), p. 24.
(10)	הַדְּבָרִים	Cf. *G*.14.3(1), p. 24.

V.5 Mark the words in the following list that are feminine.(k)

(1)	אוֹר		(7)	חֹשֶׁךְ		(13)	שָׁלוֹם	
(2)	אֶרֶץ	Fem.	(8)	חֶרֶב	Fem.	(14)	בְּרִית	Fem.
(3)	אִישׁ		(9)	רֹאשׁ		(15)	רוּחַ	Fem.
(4)	אִשָּׁה	Fem.	(10)	עִיר	Fem.	(16)	אָדָם	
(5)	בַּת	Fem.	(11)	הַר		(17)	מֶלֶךְ	
(6)	בֵּן		(12)	שָׁנָה	Fem.	(18)	בַּיִת	

V.6 Complete the writing of the definite article with the following nouns.

(1)	הָאָרֶץ	הָאָרֶץ	(7)	הַיְאֹר	הַיְאֹר	(13)	הָרֹאשׁ	הָרֹאשׁ
(2)	הַיּוֹם	הַיּוֹם	(8)	הֶעָנָן	הֶעָנָן	(14)	הַשָּׁלוֹם	הַשָּׁלוֹם
(3)	הַצֹּאן	הַצֹּאן	(9)	הָהָר	הָהָר	(15)	הַלֵּב	הַלֵּב
(4)	הָאֹהֶל	הָאֹהֶל	(10)	הָאֱלֹהִים	הָאֱלֹהִים	(16)	הָעִיר	הָעִיר
(5)	הָעָם	הָעָם	(11)	הַבְּרִית	הַבְּרִית	(17)	הַבַּיִת	הַבַּיִת
(6)	הֶחָג	הֶחָג	(12)	הָעֵת	הָעֵת	(18)	הַשָּׁנָה	הַשָּׁנָה

Footnotes

(a) On the pointing of the definite article before non–gutturals, cf. *G*.14.3(1), p. 24.

(b) The dagesh forte is frequently omitted from yôd when yôd is supported by vocal sheva [cf. *G*.14.3(3), p. 25].

(c) On the pointing of the definite article before the gutturals א, ע, and ר, cf. *G*.14.3(2)(b), p. 25.

(d) On the pointing of the definite article before הָ, and before unaccented הָ or עָ, cf. *G*.14.3(2)(c), p. 25.

(e) On the internal vowel changes that take place when the definite article is prefixed to certain words, cf. *G*.14.3(4), p. 26.

(f) ה and ח are doubled by implication after the definite article and occur without the dagesh forte [cf. *G*.13.1, p. 23; 14.3(2)(a), pp. 24f.].

(g) On the function of pătăḥ furtive before the final gutturals ה, ח, and ע, cf. *G*.13.2, p. 23.

(h) Segôl in this pointing of the article is apparently a short vowel in an open, unaccented syllable, which would be an exception to the rule previously stated, that an open, unaccented syllable must have a long vowel (cf. *G*.12.4, p. 20). However, older grammarians pointed out that under certain circumstances segôl is interchangeable with "a" class vowels. For example, the pausal forms of certain words (cf. *G*.8.3, p. 17) may occur with either segôl or qāmeṣ in their accented syllables (cf. חֶרֶב/חָרֶב, אֶרֶץ/אָרֶץ). In all likelihood, therefore, the segôl in הֶעָנָן and similar words should be regarded as a long vowel, which is what is expected in an open, unaccented syllable.

(i) Whenever yôd occurs with dagesh forte, the first of the doubled yôds unites with the vowel immediately preceding it to form a diphthong. The syllable remains open since it ends in a vowel.

(j) Vāv stands after a consonant that closes the preceding syllable, as indicated by its silent sheva. Vāv, therefore, functions as a regular consonant and not as a vowel. The final syllable would be transliterated as *vāh*. It is an open syllable since it ends in ה without a măppîq (cf. *G*.11, pp. 18f.).

(k) For the gender of nouns, see the vocabulary list in the *Grammar*, pp. 347ff. All masculine nouns are unmarked; all feminine nouns are marked with (f) placed before their translations.

Suggestions for Further Testing

1. Vocabulary Review: In each of the following groups there are three words. Circle the word that is least like the other two.

   (1) אֶרֶץ בְּרִית יָם   (4) אָחוֹת לֵב רוּחַ

   (2) יָם מַיִם הַר   (5) חֹשֶׁךְ אוֹר חֶרֶב

   (3) אֵם עוֹף בַּת   (6) שָׁנָה אָחוֹת אָח

   (7) בַּיִת גַּן קוֹל

2. A few nouns undergo internal vowel changes when prefixed with the definite article. Write the correct form for each of the following with the definite article.

   (1) אֶרֶץ   (3) הַר   (5) עַם

   (2) גַּן   (4) חַג

3. Prefix the definite article to the following words:

   (1) אוֹר   (5) רֹאשׁ   (9) מַיִם

   (2) אִישׁ   (6) בֵּן   (10) שֵׁם

   (3) אֱלֹהִים   (7) יָם   (11) חֶרֶב

   (4) עִיר   (8) לֵב   (12) חֹשֶׁךְ

4. Divide the following words into syllables, indicating whether individual syllables are open (O) or closed (C) and whether their vowels are long (L) or short (S).

   (1) בְּרֵאשִׁית   (6) הַיַּיִן

   (2) בָּרָא   (7) כִּסֵּא

   (3) בְּתוּלָה   (8) מְסִלָּה

   (4) גּוֹאֵל   (9) מִשְׁכָּב

   (5) דֶּרֶךְ   (10) נַחֲלָה

5. From your study of the Glossary (cf. *G*, pp. 424ff.), define the following terms:

   (1) Definite Article   (4) Mappiq
   (2) Definite/Indefinite Noun   (5) Patah Furtive
   (3) Gutturals   (6) Particle

LESSON VI

Answer Key
(Cf. *G*, pp. 33ff.)

VI.1 Prefix the preposition לְ to the following words, first without the article, then with it. Make the necessary changes where BeGaD KeFaT letters are involved. Translate both forms of each word.

Example: בֵּן – לְבֵן to a son   הַבֵּן – לַבֵּן to the son

(1)	שָׁלוֹם	לְשָׁלוֹם	for peace	הַשָּׁלוֹם → לַשָּׁלוֹם	for the peace
(2)	דָּבָר	לְדָבָר(a)	for a word	הַדָּבָר(b) → לַדָּבָר	for the word
(3)	רוּחַ	לְרוּחַ	for a spirit	הָרוּחַ → לָרוּחַ	for the spirit
(4)	אִשָּׁה	לְאִשָּׁה	for a woman	הָאִשָּׁה → לָאִשָּׁה	for the woman
(5)	פְּרִי	לִפְרִי(a)	for fruit	הַפְּרִי(b) → לַפְּרִי	for the fruit
(6)	בְּרִית	לִבְרִית(a)	for a covenant	הַבְּרִית(b) → לַבְּרִית	for the covenant
(7)	מָקוֹם	לְמָקוֹם	to a place	הַמָּקוֹם → לַמָּקוֹם	to the place
(8)	אֱמֶת	לֶאֱמֶת	for truth	הָאֱמֶת → לָאֱמֶת	for the truth
(9)	הֵיכָל	לְהֵיכָל	to a temple	הַהֵיכָל(c) → לַהֵיכָל	to the temple

VI.2 Prefix the preposition מִן to the following words.

(1)	בַּיִת	מִבַּיִת		(10)	רֹאשׁ	מֵרֹאשׁ
(2)	הַבַּיִת	מִן־הַבַּיִת		(11)	אֶרֶץ	מֵאֶרֶץ
(3)	אֱמֶת	מֵאֱמֶת		(12)	הָאָרֶץ	מִן־הָאָרֶץ
(4)	אִשָּׁה	מֵאִשָּׁה		(13)	חֹשֶׁךְ	מֵחֹשֶׁךְ
(5)	יְרוּשָׁלַיִם	מִירוּשָׁלַיִם(d)		(14)	הַחֹשֶׁךְ	מִן־הַחֹשֶׁךְ
(6)	אֱלֹהִים	מֵאֱלֹהִים		(15)	הָעִיר	מִן־הָעִיר
(7)	פְּרִי	מִפְּרִי		(16)	הַהֵיכָל	מִן־הַהֵיכָל
(8)	יָד	מִיָּד		(17)	רוּחַ	מֵרוּחַ
(9)	הַר	מֵהַר		(18)	הָרוּחַ	מִן־הָרוּחַ

VI.3 Place the vav conjunction on the following words or phrases and give a translation of each completed form.

Example: וּבְשֵׁם ,בְּשֵׁם and by a name

(1)	בְּשֵׁם	וּבְשֵׁם	and by a name
(2)	כְּדָבָר	וּכְדָבָר	and like a word
(3)	כַּדָּבָר	וְכַדָּבָר	and like the word
(4)	בְּרִית	וּבְרִית(e)	and a covenant
(5)	לִבְרִית	וְלִבְרִית	and for a covenant
(6)	יְהוּדָה	וִיהוּדָה(f)	and Judah
(7)	בִּיהוּדָה	וּבִיהוּדָה(e)	and in Judah
(8)	אֱמֶת	וֶאֱמֶת	and truth
(9)	מֵאֱמֶת	וּמֵאֱמֶת(e)	and from truth
(10)	לָאִשָּׁה	וְלָאִשָּׁה	and for the woman
(11)	בַּהֵיכָל	וּבַהֵיכָל(e)	and in the temple
(12)	מִמֶּלֶךְ	וּמִמֶּלֶךְ(e)	and from a king
(13)	מִן־הָעֵץ	וּמִן־הָעֵץ(e)	and from the tree
(14)	פְּרִי	וּפְרִי(e)	and fruit
(15)	לְשָׁלוֹם	וּלְשָׁלוֹם(e)	and for peace
(16)	אֱלֹהִים	וֵאלֹהִים(g)	and God
(17)	בַּלֵב	וּבַלֵב(e)	and in the heart
(18)	הַשָּׁנָה	וְהַשָּׁנָה	and the year

VI.4 Translate the following phrases:

(1)	אִישׁ וְאִשָּׁה	a man and a woman
(2)	שָׁלוֹם בָּאָרֶץ	peace in the land
(3)	הָאוֹר וְהַחֹשֶׁךְ	the light and the darkness
(4)	בֵּין הָאוֹר וּבֵין הַחֹשֶׁךְ	between the light and between the darkness
(5)	יוֹם וָלַיְלָה	day and night
(6)	בַּיּוֹם וּבַלַּיְלָה	in the day and in the night
(7)	אָדָם וֵאלֹהִים	man and God
(8)	מִיָּם וּמֵאֶרֶץ	from sea and from land
(9)	אֶל־יְרוּשָׁלַיִם	to Jerusalem
(10)	פְּרִי מִן־הָעֵץ	fruit from the tree
(11)	בָּעִיר וּבַהֵיכָל	in the city and in the temple
(12)	בָּאָדָם וּבֵאלֹהִים	with man and with God

26

(13)	אֵצֶל הָהָר	beside the mountain
(14)	עַד־הָעֶרֶב	until the evening
(15)	יָד וָשֵׁם	a hand and a name
(16)	שָׁלוֹם וֶאֱמֶת	peace and truth
(17)	טוֹב וָרָע	good and evil
(18)	מִבֵּן וּמִבַּת	from a son and from a daughter

VI.5 Translate the following clauses.

Example:	אֵין פְּרִי בַּגָּן	There is no fruit in the garden.
(1)	אֵין אִשָּׁה בַּבַּיִת	There is no woman in the house.
(2)	אֵין אִישׁ בָּעִיר	There is no man in the city.
(3)	אֵין בֵּן לָאָדָם	There is no son for the man[h].
(4)	אֵין בְּרִית עִם־הָעָם	There is no covenant with the people.
(5)	אֵין שָׁלוֹם בָּאָרֶץ	There is no peace in the land.
(6)	הָעִיר עַל־הָהָר	The city (is) upon the mountain.
(7)	אֵין בַּת לָאִשָּׁה	There is no daughter for the woman[i].
(8)	אֵין אוֹר לָעָם	There is no light for the people[j].
(9)	הַגָּן אֵצֶל הַבַּיִת	The garden (is) beside the house.
(10)	טוֹב הָאוֹר מִן־הַחֹשֶׁךְ	The light (is) better than the darkness.
(11)	טוֹב הַיּוֹם מִן־הַלַּיְלָה	The day (is) better than the night.
(12)	אֵין מַיִם בַּמָּקוֹם	There is no water in the place.

Footnotes

(a) A BeGaD KeFaT letter must be written without dagesh lene when a vowel stands immediately before it (cf. *G*.6, pp. 12f.).

(b) Whenever a consonant pointed with a dagesh has a vowel immediately preceding it, the dagesh must be classified as a dagesh forte (cf. *G*.6, pp. 12f.).

(c) For a summary of the rules governing the pointing of the definite article, see "Definite Article," *G*, pp. 429f.

(d) For the rule governing the writing of מִן before an initial yod pointed with a simple (vocal) sheva, cf. *G*.15.3(2), p. 30.

(e) Before **בּ**, **מ**, **פּ**, and any consonant supported by a simple sheva, except the consonant yod (cf. *G*.16.3, p. 31), the vav conjunction will be written as šureq (**וּ**) (cf. *G*.16.2, p. 31).

Older grammarians sometimes used a mnemonic device to assist students further in learning the above rule regarding **וּ**. The mnemonic device consisted of the nonsense word **בּוּמֵף**, transliterated as BuMP, which was designed to remind students that before the "BuMP" letters (**בּ**, **מ**, and **פּ**) vav conjunction was pointed as **וּ**. Students were also to remember that **וּ** occurs before initial consonants supported by simple shevas.

(f) **וִיהוּדָה** is the final form that emerged from a three–step process. First, the vav conjunction (**וְ**) prefixed to the proper name **יְהוּדָה**, "Judah," resulted in the form **וְיְהוּדָה**. Second, since two vocal shevas could not stand together, the initial one had to be raised to a ḥireq, leading to the form **וִיְהוּדָה** [cf. *G*.15.1(2), p. 28]. Third, since yod was immediately preceded by ḥireq, the two united to form a diphthong (**יִ**). Thus yod ceased to function as a consonant and became part of a diphthong. The vocal sheva beneath it was no longer necessary and so dropped out. The final form became **וִיהוּדָה**.

(g) For an explanation of this unusual form, cf. *G*.16.6, p. 32.

(h) A more idiomatic translation would read, "The man has no son."

(i) A more idiomatic translation: "The woman has no daughter."

(j) A more idiomatic translation: "The people have no light."

Suggestions for Further Testing

1. Circle the word that is least like the other two in each of the following groups.

(1)	יֵשׁ	לֹא	אֵין
(2)	לַיְלָה	עֶרֶב	יוֹם
(3)	עֵץ	רֹאשׁ	פְּרִי
(4)	אָב	עַם	לִפְנֵי
(5)	אִישׁ	אָדָם	טוֹב

2. Translate the following clauses with אֲשֶׁר, "who, which, what":

(1)	הַהֵיכָל אֲשֶׁר בַּמָּקוֹם
(2)	הַהֵיכָל אֲשֶׁר לֵאלֹהִים
(3)	הַדָּבָר אֲשֶׁר בַּלֵּב
(4)	הַיּוֹם אֲשֶׁר בַּשָּׁנָה
(5)	הַבֵּן אֲשֶׁר לָאָב
(6)	הַמַּיִם אֲשֶׁר בַּיָּם
(7)	הַחֹשֶׁךְ אֲשֶׁר בַּלַּיְלָה
(8)	הָאוֹר אֲשֶׁר בַּבֹּקֶר
(9)	הָרוּחַ אֲשֶׁר בָּאָרֶץ
(10)	הַבַּת אֲשֶׁר בַּבַּיִת

3. Match each of the phrases with its correct translation. Students should be able to complete this exercise even though it contains a few new words.

(1) (   ) וְאִישׁ אֵין בָּאָרֶץ — (A) For there is no food and no water. (Num. 21:5)

(2) (   ) יֵשׁ יְהוָה בַּמָּקוֹם הַזֶּה — (B) There was no king in Israel. (Judg. 17:6)

(3) (   ) יֶשׁ־לָנוּ אָב זָקֵן — (C) There was no sword in David's hand. (1 Sam. 17:50)

(4) (   ) וְלֶחֶם אֵין בְּכָל־הָאָרֶץ — (D) The LORD is in this place. (Gen. 28:16)

(5) (   ) אֵין מֶלֶךְ בְּיִשְׂרָאֵל — (E) [Saying] "Peace, peace," when there is no peace. (Jer. 6:14)

(6) (   ) כִּי אֵין לֶחֶם וְאֵין מַיִם — (F) But there was no breath (spirit) in them. (Ezek. 37:8)

(7) (   ) כִּי אֵין הַלֶּחֶם עוֹד בָּעִיר — (G) And there is not a man on earth. (Gen. 19:31)

(8) (   ) וְרוּחַ אֵין בָּהֶם — (H) Now there was no food (bread) in all the land. (Gen. 47:13)

(9) (   ) וְחֶרֶב אֵין בְּיַד־דָּוִד — (I) For there is no bread left in the city. (Jer. 38:9)

(10) (   ) שָׁלוֹם שָׁלוֹם וְאֵין שָׁלוֹם — (J) We have an old father. (Gen. 44:20)

4. From your study of the Glossary (cf. *G*, pp. 424ff.), define the following terms:

(1) Comparative Degree   (3) Proper Noun
(2) Noun   (4) Vav Conjunction

LESSON VII

Answer Key
(Cf. *G*, pp. 40ff.)

VII.1 Add the plural endings to the following words and indicate the gender of each.

(1)	אָב	אָבוֹת(a)	Masc.	(7)	הַר הָרִים	Masc.
(2)	אִשָּׁה	נָשִׁים(b)	Fem.	(8)	מֶלֶךְ מְלָכִים(d)	Masc.
(3)	בַּיִת	בָּתִּים(c)	Masc.	(9)	סוּס סוּסִים	Masc.
(4)	בֵּן	בָּנִים	Masc.	(10)	סוּסָה סוּסוֹת	Fem.
(5)	בַּת	בָּנוֹת	Fem.	(11)	סֵפֶר סְפָרִים(d)	Masc.
(6)	דָּבָר דְּבָרִים(d)	Masc.	(12)	רוּחַ רוּחוֹת(e)	Fem.

VII.2 Translate the following:

(1)	הָאֲנָשִׁים וְהַסּוּסִים	the men and the horses
(2)	הַמִּצְוֹת אֲשֶׁר בַּסֵּפֶר(f)	the commandments which (are) in the book
(3)	הַנָּשִׁים אֲשֶׁר בַּבַּיִת(f)	the women who (are) in the house
(4)	הַמְּלָכִים וְהַנְּבִיאִים	the kings and the prophets
(5)	הַבְּהֵמָה בַּשָּׂדֶה(g)	the cattle in the field
(6)	הֶעָרִים וְהֶהָרִים(h)	the cities and the mountains
(7)	הַבָּנוֹת וְהָאִמּוֹת	the daughters and the mothers
(8)	הַבָּתִּים בֶּעָרִים(h)	the houses in the cities
(9)	הַדֶּרֶךְ מִן־הָעִיר	the way from the city
(10)	הַיָּדַיִם וְהָרַגְלַיִם(i)	the hands and the feet

VII.3 Add the plural or dual endings to the following words and translate each plural or dual form.

(1)	אִישׁ	אֲנָשִׁים(d)(j)	men	(6)	כָּנָף	כְּנָפַיִם(i) (dual)	wings
(2)	אֵם	אִמּוֹת	mothers	(7)	עַיִן	עֵינַיִם(i) (dual)	eyes
(3)	אֶרֶץ	אֲרָצוֹת(d)	lands	(8)	עִיר	עָרִים(b)	cities
(4)	יָד	יָדַיִם(i) (dual)	hands	(9)	עֵץ	עֵצִים	trees
(5)	יוֹם	יָמִים	days	(10)	תּוֹרָה	תּוֹרוֹת	laws

30

VII.4 Translate the following:

(1)	הַמַּיִם בְּתוֹךְ הַיָּם	the water in the midst of the sea
(2)	הָעוֹף בַּשָּׁמַיִם	the bird in the sky
(3)	הָאָזְנַיִם וְהָעֵינַיִם	the noses and the eyes
(4)	הַבְּרִית עִם־הַמֶּלֶךְ	the covenant with the king
(5)	בָּנִים וּבָנוֹת	sons and daughters
(6)	הַמִּצְוֹת בַּתּוֹרָה	the commandments in the law
(7)	עָפָר מִן־הָאֲדָמָה	dust from the earth
(8)	בַּיּוֹם וּבַלַּיְלָה	in the day and in the night
(9)	הַשָּׁמַיִם וְהָאָרֶץ	the heavens and the earth
(10)	הַמְּלָכִים (k)מִירוּשָׁלַיִם	the kings from Jerusalem
(11)	הַנָּשִׁים וְהָאֲנָשִׁים	the women and the men
(12)	הַסּוּסִים וְהַסּוּסוֹת	the horses and the mares

VII.5 Circle the word that seems to be out of place in each of the following groups.

(1)	אָב	בֵּן	(סוּס)		(10)	(חֶרֶב)	חֹשֶׁךְ	אוֹר
(2)	יוֹם	לַיְלָה	(נֶפֶשׁ)		(11)	(לִפְנֵי)	אֵין	לֹא
(3)	בֵּין	(פְּרִי)	מִן		(12)	עִם	(מְאֹד)	אֵצֶל
(4)	(עֵץ)	בֹּקֶר	עֶרֶב		(13)	דָּבָר	קוֹל	(דֶּרֶךְ)
(5)	יָד	עַיִן	(עָפָר)		(14)	חַג	הֵיכָל	(אֲשֶׁר)
(6)	מַיִם	(יַבָּשָׁה)	יָם		(15)	מִצְוָה	(בְּתוֹךְ)	תּוֹרָה
(7)	אֲדָמָה	(שָׁמַיִם)	שָׂדֶה		(16)	(לֵב)	יִשְׂרָאֵל	יְהוּדָה
(8)	(אָדָם)	יְהוָה	אֱלֹהִים		(17)	רֹאשׁ	עַיִן	(רוּחַ)
(9)	עִיר	(אִשָּׁה)	הֵיכָל		(18)	(שֵׁם)	אִישׁ	אָדָם

Footnotes

(a) A few masculine nouns have plurals ending in וֹת, the usual ending for feminine plurals [cf. G.19.2(1)(b), p. 38].

(b) A few feminine nouns have plurals ending in ִים, the normal ending for masculine plurals [cf. G.19.2(2)(b), p. 39].

(c) The plural of בַּיִת is irregular. Other common nouns with irregular plurals include אָב, father, אָבוֹת, fathers; אָח, brother, אַחִים, brothers; בֵּן, son, בָּנִים, sons; בַּת, daughter, בָּנוֹת, daughters; פֶּה, mouth, פִּיּוֹת, mouths.

(d) A bisyllabic noun whose initial syllable is open will undergo certain internal vowel changes when pluralized.

First, the accent shifts to the newly created syllable containing the plural ending.

דְּבָרִים → דָּבָר

נְפָשׁוֹת → נֶפֶשׁ

אֲרָצוֹת → אֶרֶץ

Second, the open syllable at the beginning of the word, now two syllables removed from the accented (tone) syllable, is volatilized (reduced to a half-vowel) for phonetical reason (difficult to pronounce otherwise). Under non-gutturals the vowel is reduced to a simple sheva (ְ); under initial gutturals it becomes ḥatef-pataḥ

דְּבָרִים → דְּבָרִים

נְפָשׁוֹת → נְפָשׁוֹת

אֲרָצוֹת → אֲרָצוֹת

Third, since the syllable before the accented syllable is open and unaccented, it needs a long vowel (cf. *G*.12.4, p. 20). If the vowel is already long, it remains unchanged, but if the vowel is short (either pataḥ or segol), it is lengthened to qames.

דְּבָרִים → remains the same

נְפָשׁוֹת → נְפָשׁוֹת

אֲרָצוֹת → אֲרָצוֹת

Segholate nouns form one of the largest groups subject to these changes (cf. *G*.25.3, pp. 57f.).

Plural forms of bisyllabic adjectives are also formed in a similar manner [cf. *G*.20.3(2)(a)(*i*)(*ii*), pp. 44f.].

(e) The pataḥ furtive drops out before ח when רוּחַ is pluralized and ח is no longer final in רוּחוֹת (cf. *G*.13.2, p. 23).

(f) The verb "to be," though not written, is generally assumed in verbless clauses such as these.

(g) בְּהֵמָה is classified as a collective noun, one that is singular in form but either singular or plural in its use (cf. *G*, "Collective Nouns," p. 427).

(h) Before הָ, and before unaccented הָ or עָ, the ה of the definite article is pointed with a sᵉgol [cf. *G.*14.3(2)(c), p. 25].

(i) For the rules governing the dual form of nouns, cf. *G.*19.3, pp. 39f.

(j) The plural of אִישׁ, "man," is אֲנָשִׁים. The longer form of the plural, with a median נ, can be explained by its relationship to אֱנוֹשׁ, another similar word for "man."

(k) The form that the preposition מִן takes before words like יְרוּשָׁלַיִם is explained in *G.*15.2n., p. 30.

Additional Helps

1. At this stage in the study of Biblical Hebrew, teachers are perhaps unwise to assume that students have already mastered the Hebrew alphabet and the table of vowels. Drills should be devised to determine whether or not they have sharpened their skills. One such drill that has been helpful is to have the teacher "spell" orally a passage from the Hebrew Bible, perhaps Genesis 1:1ff., and then have students write what they hear. The teacher reads, "bet (with dagesh lene), simple sheva, reš, ṣere, 'alef, šin, ḥireq-yod, tav," after which the students should have written בְּרֵאשִׁית. This exercise can be varied by having students themselves turn to a verse in the Hebrew Bible and "spell" it, either orally or in writing.

2. By this time in the course students should have discovered and learned how to use the "Subject Index" at the back of the *Grammar*, pp. 448ff. For example, earlier in this lesson (cf. *H*, footnote (d), p. 32) reference was made to the *volatilization of vowels* in the formation of plural forms of bisyllabic nouns. Students who wish to know more about this subject should consult the "Subject Index," where on page 452 is found the entry, "Volatilization of vowels," with a list of the pages in the *Grammar* where the subject is mentioned.

Suggestions for Further Testing

1. Write the plural form for each of these words. [Review footnote (d), p. 32.]

(1) נֶפֶשׁ (f)   (5) דָּבָר

(2) אֶרֶץ (f)   (6) דֶּרֶךְ

(3) סֵפֶר   (7) בֹּקֶר

(4) מֶלֶךְ

2. Match the following:

(1) (　) דָּוִד מֶלֶךְ יִשְׂרָאֵל   (A) peace and truth

(2) (　) מֶלֶךְ מְלָכִים   (B) city of God

(3) (　) אֲנָשִׁים מִיהוּדָה   (C) from the city

(4) (　) אָבוֹת וּבָנִים   (D) David, king of Israel

(5) (　) בָּנִים וּבָנוֹת   (E) between men

(6) (　) שָׁלוֹם וֶאֱמֶת   (F) sons and daughters

(7) (　) רֹאשׁ הַשָּׁנָה   (G) king of kings

(8) (　) עִיר אֱלֹהִים   (H) fathers and sons

(9) (　) מִן־הָעִיר   (I) beginning (head) of the year

(10) (　) בֵּין אֲנָשִׁים   (J) men of (from) Judah

3. Translate the following:

(1) בֵּין הַיּוֹם וּבֵין הַלָּיְלָה (Gen. 1:14)

(2) בַּבַּיִת וּבַשָּׂדֶה (Gen. 39:5)

(3) אֵין שָׁלוֹם לְכָל־בָּשָׂר (Jer. 12:12)

(4) גַּם מֵעוֹף הַשָּׁמַיִם (Gen. 7:3)

(5) מִן־הַבָּתִּים וּמִן־הַשָּׂדֹת (Exod. 8:9)

(6) הָאֲנָשִׁים אֲשֶׁר בַּבָּתִּים (Judg. 18:22)

(7) בֵּין הַשָּׁמַיִם וּבֵין־הָאָרֶץ (2 Sam. 18:9)

(8) מִפְּרִי הָעֵץ אֲשֶׁר בַּגָּן (Gen. 3:3)

4. Define the following terms based on definitions given in the Glossary (cf. *G*, pp. 424ff.).

(1) Apocopation   (4) Number

(2) Collective Nouns   (5) Pausal Forms

(3) Gender   (6) Volatilization

LESSON VIII

Answer Key
(Cf. *G*, pp. 47ff.)

VIII.1 Each of the following entries contains an adjective. In the space marked (a) indicate whether the adjective is used attributively (A) or predicatively (P). In the space marked (b) give the gender of the adjective, and in (c) give its number.

Example:

מֵאֶרֶץ רְחוֹקָה from a distant land (Josh. 9:6)

    (a) ___A___   (b) ___fem.___   (c) ___sing.___

(1) נַעֲרָה קְטַנָּה⁽ᵃ⁾ a little maid (2 Kgs. 5:2)

    (a) ___A___   (b) ___fem.___   (c) ___sing.___

(2) בְּדֶרֶךְ יְשָׁרָה by a straight way (Ps. 107:7)

    (a) ___A___   (b) ___fem.___   (c) ___sing.___

(3) אֶבֶן גְּדוֹלָה a great stone (Josh. 24:26)

    (a) ___A___   (b) ___fem.___   (c) ___sing.___

(4) בַּיִת חָדָשׁ a new house (Deut. 22:8)

    (a) ___A___   (b) ___masc.___   (c) ___sing.___

(5) עִיר גְּדוֹלָה a great city (Josh. 10:2)

    (a) ___A___   (b) ___fem.___   (c) ___sing.___

(6) קָרוֹב הַיּוֹם⁽ᶜ⁾ The day is near. (Ezek. 7:7)

    (a) ___P___   (b) ___masc.___   (c) ___sing.___

(7) בְּרִית חֲדָשָׁה a new covenant (Jer. 31:31)

    (a) ___A___   (b) ___fem.___   (c) ___sing.___

(8) ^(b)נָשִׁים רַבּוֹת many women (Ezek. 16:41)

(a) ___A___ (b) ___fem.___ (c) ___plur.___

(9) ^(b)אֲבָנִים גְּדֹלוֹת great stones (Josh. 10:18)

(a) ___A___ (b) ___fem.___ (c) ___plur.___

(10) וְרוּחַ גְּדוֹלָה and a great wind (1 Kgs. 19:11)

(a) ___A___ (b) ___fem.___ (c) ___sing.___

(11) ^(c)טוֹבָה הָאָרֶץ מְאֹד מְאֹד The land was exceedingly good. (Num. 14:7)

(a) ___P___ (b) ___fem.___ (c) ___sing.___

(12) הַדֶּרֶךְ הַטּוֹבָה the good way (2 Chr. 6:27)

(a) ___A___ (b) ___fem.___ (c) ___sing.___

VIII.2 Underscore the correct adjectival form in each of the following entries.

(1) מֶלֶךְ (חֲדָשָׁה , חָדָשׁ) עַל־מִצְרָיִם a new king over Egypt (Exod. 1:8)

(2) כִּי אֵל (גָּדוֹל , גְּדוֹלָה) יְהוָה For the LORD is a great God. (Ps. 95:3)

(3) בְּיָד (חָזָק , חֲזָקָה) with a strong hand (Deut. 26:8)

(4) רוּחַ־(גְּדוֹלָה , גָּדוֹל) a great wind (Jon. 1:4)

(5) עִיר־(גְּדוֹלָה , גָּדוֹל) a great city (Jon. 3:3)

(6) אִישׁ (חֲכָמָה , חָכָם) מְאֹד an exceedingly wise man (2 Sam. 13:3)

(7) לֵב (חָכָם , חֲכָמָה) a wise heart (1 Kgs. 3:12)

(8) אִשָּׁה (חָכָם , חֲכָמָה) a wise woman (2 Sam. 14:2)

(9) אֲנָשִׁים (חֲכָמִים , חַכְמוֹת) wise men (Deut. 1:13)

(10) ^(b)נָשִׁים (רַבּוֹת , רַבִּים) many women (Judg. 8:30)

(11) ^(b)עָרִים (רַבּוֹת , רַבִּים) many cities (Zech. 8:20)

(12) (רַבּוֹת , רַבִּים) בָּנוֹת many daughters (Prov. 31:29)

VIII.3 Match the following:

(1) (I) מְלָכִים גְּדוֹלִים   (A) And the stone was great. (Gen. 29:2)

(2) (E) יָמִים רַבִּים   (B) a small city (Eccl. 9:14)

(3) (H) רָעָה רַבָּה   (C) many lands (Jer. 28:8)

(4) (R) אֶבֶן גְּדוֹלָה   (D) And the maiden was beautiful. (1 Kgs. 1:4)

(5) (Q) אֶרֶץ רְחוֹקָה   (E) many days (Gen. 21:34)

(6) (P) בָּנִים רַבִּים   (F) a beautiful woman (Prov. 11:22)

(7) (M) הָעִיר הַקְּרֹבָה   (G) a new spirit (Ezek. 11:19)

(8) (N) אֲבָנִים גְּדֹלוֹת (b)   (H) a great evil (Eccl. 2:21)

(9) (B) עִיר (a) קְטַנָּה   (I) great kings (Jer. 25:14)

(10) (C) אֲרָצוֹת רַבּוֹת   (J) an evil spirit (Judg. 9:23)

(11) (A) וְהָאֶבֶן גְּדֹלָה (c)   (K) many years (Neh. 9:30)

(12) (O) נַעֲרָה יָפָה   (L) a full (whole) year (Lev. 25:30)

(13) (F) אִשָּׁה יָפָה   (M) the near city (Deut. 21:3)

(14) (G) רוּחַ חֲדָשָׁה   (N) large stones (Josh. 10:18)

(15) (J) רוּחַ רָעָה   (O) a beautiful maiden (1 Kgs. 1:3)

(16) (L) שָׁנָה תְמִימָה   (P) many children (1 Chr. 4:27)

(17) (D) וְהַנַּעֲרָה יָפָה (c)   (Q) a distant land (2 Chr. 6:36)

(18) (K) שָׁנִים רַבּוֹת (b)   (R) a great stone (Josh. 24:26)

VIII.4 Fill in the blanks with the correct translation of the adjectives in the following examples.

(1) בָּתִּים רַבִּים גְּדֹלִים וְטוֹבִים   many houses ___great___ and ___good___ (Isa. 5:9)

(2) אִישׁ זָקֵן   an ___old___ man (Judg. 19:16)

(3) בַּדֶּרֶךְ הַטּוֹבָה וְהַיְשָׁרָה   in the ___good___ and the ___straight___ way (1 Sam. 12:23)

(4) בְּדֶרֶךְ רָע   into an ___evil___ way (Prov. 28:10)

(5)	בְּיָד חֲזָקָה	by a ___strong___ hand (Exod. 3:19)
(6)	מֶלֶךְ חָכָם	a ___wise___ king (Prov. 20:26)
(7)	שָׁלוֹם רָב	___great___ peace (Ps. 119:165)
(8)	עַם גָּדוֹל וָרָב	a people ___great___ and ___many___. (Deut. 2:10)
(9)	בָּנִים רַבִּים	___many___ children (1 Chr. 4:27)
(10)	כְּיוֹם מָר	as a ___bitter___ day (Amos 8:10)
(11)	נָשִׁים יָפוֹת	___beautiful___ women (Job 42:15)
(12)	אִשָּׁה חֲדָשָׁה	a ___new___ wife (Deut. 24:5)

Footnotes

(a) For the irregular forms of קָטֹן, "small," cf. G.20.3(2)(b), p. 45.

(b) A few masculine and feminine nouns seem to have abandoned their normal plural endings, with masculine plurals ending in וֹת and feminine plurals in יִם. [cf. G.19.2(1)(b) and (2)(b), pp. 38f.].

    However, plural adjectives accompanying these nouns appear with their normal gender endings, יִם. for those that modify or describe masculine plural nouns, and וֹת for those that modify or describe feminine plural nouns.

Examples:

אָבוֹת	"fathers"
אָבוֹת טוֹבִים	"good fathers"
נָשִׁים	"women"
נָשִׁים טוֹבוֹת	"good women"

(c) The verb "to be," though not written, may be assumed when adjectives are used in a predicative sense.

Suggestions for Further Testing

1. Each of the adjectival forms listed here fits into one (only one) of the blanks. Copy each in its correct position.

    גָּדוֹל   גְּדוֹלָה   הֶחָכָם   הַגָּדוֹל   הַגְּדוֹלָה

    חֲכָמִים   גְּדוֹלִים   גְּדוֹלוֹת   חָכָם   חָכְמָה

(1)	_____ הָאֵשׁ	the great fire (Deut. 5:22)
(2)	_____ הַבַּיִת	the great house (Amos 6:11)
(3)	_____ מְלָכִים	great kings (Jer. 27:7)
(4)	_____ וְהָאֶבֶן	And the stone was great. (Gen. 29:2)
(5)	_____ הַבַּיִת	The house is great. (2 Chr. 2:8)
(6)	_____ הֶעָרִים	The cities are great. (Num. 13:28)
(7)	_____ אֲנָשִׁים	wise men (Deut. 1:15)
(8)	_____ לֵב	a wise heart (Eccl. 8:5)
(9)	_____ הָאִישׁ	the wise man (Jer. 9:11)
(10)	_____ אִשָּׁה	a wise woman (2 Sam. 14:2)

2. Translate the following:

(1)	כִּי־גָדוֹל יְהוָה	(Exod. 18:11)
(2)	אִישׁ חָכָם מְאֹד	(2 Sam. 13:3)
(3)	טוֹב הַדָּבָר	(1 Kgs. 2:38)
(4)	עָרִים גְּדֹלֹת וְטֹבֹת	(Deut. 6:10)
(5)	מִן־הַיָּם הַגָּדֹל	(Num. 34:7)
(6)	בַּיִת־חָדָשׁ	(Deut. 20:5)
(7)	שָׁמַיִם חֲדָשִׁים	(Isa. 65:17)
(8)	קָרוֹב הַיּוֹם	(Ezek. 7:7)
(9)	אִישׁ יָפֶה	(2 Sam. 14:25)
(10)	אָחוֹת יָפָה	(2 Sam. 13:1)

3. From your study of the Glossary (cf. *G*, pp. 424ff.), define the following terms:

    (1) Agreement   (3) Gentilic Adjective

    (2) Attributive Adjective   (4) Predicate Adjective

LESSON IX

Answer Key
(Cf. *G*, pp. 54ff.)

IX.1 Complete the translation of the following entries by filling in the blanks.

(1) הַשָּׁנִים הַטּבֹת הָאֵלֶּה[a] ___these___ good years (Gen. 41:35)

(2) צַדִּיק אַתָּה ___you___ are righteous. (Jer. 12:1)

(3) כִּי מֶלֶךְ גָּדוֹל אָנִי[b] For ___I___ (am) a great King. (Mal. 1:14)

(4) לָעִיר הַגְּדוֹלָה הַזֹּאת to ___this___ great city (Jer. 22:8)

(5) כִּי־חֲזָקִים הֵמָּה For ___they___ (are) strong. (Judg. 18:26)

(6) חֲכָמִים אֲנַחְנוּ ___We___ (are) wise. (Jer. 8:8)

(7) כִּי־חָזָק הוּא For ___he___ (is) strong. (Num. 13:31)

(8) כִּי מָרִים הֵם For ___they___ (were) bitter. (Exod. 15:23)

(9) הָעִיר הַזֹּאת קְרֹבָה ___This___ city (is) near. (Gen. 19:20)

(10) וְאָנֹכִי נַעַר קָטֹן And ___I___ (am) a little child. (1 Kgs. 3:7)

IX.2 Underscore the correct pronominal form in the following entries.

(1) כִּי קָטֹן (הוּא / הִיא) For he (is) small. (Amos 7:2)

(2) כִּי קָשֶׁה (אַתְּ / אַתָּה[c]) that you (are) stubborn (Isa. 48:4)

(3) כִּי־יָפָה (הוּא / הִוא[d]) מְאֹד For she (was) very beautiful. (Gen. 12:14)

(4) יָפָה (אַתָּה / אַתְּ) You (are) lovely. (Song of Sol. 6:4)

(5) תָּמִים (אַתָּה / אַתְּ) You (were) perfect (blameless). (Ezek. 28:15)

(6) הַדָּבָר הָרָע (הַזֹּאת / הַזֶּה) this evil word (Exod. 33:4)

(7) (וְהוּא / וְהוּא) נַעַר And he (was) a lad. (Gen. 37:2)

(8) (זֶה / זֹאת) הַדָּבָר This (is) the word. (Num. 30:2)

(9) בַּיּוֹם (הַהוּא / הַהוּא) on that day (Gen. 15:18)

(10) בַּיּוֹם (הַזֹּאת / הַזֶּה) on this day (Gen. 7:11)

(11) כִּי (זֶה / זֹאת) הוּא For this (is) he. (1 Sam. 16:12)

(12) (הוּא / הִוא) הָעִיר הַגְּדֹלָה That (is) the great (chief) city. (Gen. 10:12)

40

IX.3 Each of the following entries contains either a personal or a demonstrative pronoun. In the space marked (a) indicate whether the pronoun is to be classified as personal (P) or as demonstrative (D). In the space marked (b), give the gender of the pronoun, and in (c) its number.

Example:

יְהוָה הוּא הָאֱלֹהִים(e)

The LORD, he (is) God. (1 Kgs. 18:39)

(a)   P

(b)   masc.

(c)   sing.

(1) לֹא בַשָּׁמַיִם הִוא

It (she) (is) not in the heavens. (Deut. 30:12)

(a)   P

(b)   fem.

(c)   sing.

(2) הַגּוֹי הַגָּדוֹל הַזֶּה(f)

this great nation (Deut. 4:6)

(a)   D

(b)   masc.

(c)   sing.

(3) זֶה הַיּוֹם

This (is) the day. (Judg. 4:14)

(a)   D

(b)   masc.

(c)   sing.

(4) כִּי אָנִי יְהוָה

For I (am) the LORD. (Exod. 7:5)

(a)   P

(b)   com.

(c)   sing.

(5) הָעָם הַזֶּה הָרָע

this evil people (Jer. 13:10)

(a)   D

(b)   masc.

(c)   sing.

(6) כַּדָּבָר הָרָע הַזֶּה

according to this evil word (Deut. 13:12)

(a)   D

(b)   masc.

(c)   sing.

Footnotes

(a) For irregular plural endings on certain nouns, cf. *G*.19.2(1)(b) and (2)(b), pp. 38f.

(b) אָנִי is the pausal form for אֲנִי (cf. *G*.8.3, p. 17; also *G*.68, pp. 240f.).

(c) אָתָּה is pausal (with ʾatnaḥ, אָתָּה [cf. MT in *Biblia Hebraica Stuttgartensia*]) for אַתָּה (cf. *G*.8.3, p. 17; *G*.68, pp. 240f.).

(d) The normal form for the third person feminine singular personal pronoun is הִיא, but throughout the Pentateuch vav replaces yod and the form becomes הוּא. It is still pronounced as if the vowel were a ḥireq-yod.

(e) For the translation of יְהוָה as LORD (all capital letters), cf. *G*16.6, p. 32.

(f) הַגּוֹי consists of the masculine noun גּוֹי, "nation, people," prefixed by the definite article. The noun alone would be transliterated as *gôy*. In modern Hebrew usage it is applied to all non-Jewish persons.

Suggestions for Further Testing

1. Translate the following:

   (1) כִּי אָדָם אֵין צַדִּיק בָּאָרֶץ (Eccl. 7:20)

   (2) אַבְרָהָם וְשָׂרָה זְקֵנִים (Gen. 18:11)

   (3) אֲנַחְנוּ אַחִים (Gen. 42:32)

   (4) מֶלֶךְ יִשְׂרָאֵל הוּא (1 Kgs. 22:32)

   (5) כִּי גָדוֹל הַיּוֹם הַהוּא (Jer. 30:7)

   (6) הַגּוֹי הַגָּדוֹל הַזֶּה (Deut. 4:6)

   (7) הָאֵשׁ הַגְּדוֹלָה הַזֹּאת (Deut. 5:22)

   (8) כַּדְּבָרִים הָאֵלֶּה (Gen. 24:23)

2. Match each word in the first two columns with its opposite or counterpart from the words in the last two columns.

(1) ( ) טוֹב	(8) ( ) יוֹם	(A) גָּדוֹל	(H) יֵשׁ
(2) ( ) זָקֵן	(9) ( ) קָטֹן	(B) אוֹר	(I) חָדָשׁ
(3) ( ) אָב	(10) ( ) אָדָם	(C) לַיְלָה	(J) אֵם
(4) ( ) אֵין	(11) ( ) רָחוֹק	(D) קָרוֹב	(K) רַע
(5) ( ) חֹשֶׁךְ	(12) ( ) פְּרִי	(E) עֵץ	(L) יַבָּשָׁה
(6) ( ) רֶגֶל	(13) ( ) בֵּן	(F) בַּת	(M) רֹאשׁ
(7) ( ) יָם	(14) ( ) רוּחַ	(G) בָּשָׂר	(N) אִשָּׁה

3. From your study of the Glossary (cf. *G*, pp. 424ff.), define the following terms:

   (1) Demonstrative Pronouns
   (2) Independent Pronouns

LESSON X

Answer Key
(Cf. *G*, pp. 65ff.)

X.1 Fill in the blanks in order to complete the following construct relationships:

(1) עַם^(a) הָאָרֶץ — the people of the earth (Jer. 37:2)

(2) בְּנֵי יִשְׂרָאֵל — the sons of Israel (Gen. 42:5)

(3) עָרֵי יְהוּדָה — the cities of Judah (2 Sam. 2:1)

(4) מֶלֶךְ יְרוּשָׁלַם — the king of Jerusalem (Josh. 10:1)

(5) אֶרֶץ יִשְׂרָאֵל — the land of Israel (1 Sam. 13:19)

(6) דֶּרֶךְ הַמִּדְבָּר — the way of the wilderness (Exod. 13:18)

(7) נֶפֶשׁ הָעָם — the soul of the people (1 Sam. 30:6)

(8) עַבְדֵי הַמֶּלֶךְ — the servants of the king (2 Sam. 16:6)

(9) עֶבֶד הָאֱלֹהִים^(b) — the servant of God (1 Chr. 6:34)

(10) בְּסֵפֶר^(c) תּוֹרַת מֹשֶׁה — in the book of the law of Moses (Josh. 8:31)

(11) בֵּית יִשְׂרָאֵל — the house of Israel (Exod. 16:31)

(12) דִּבְרֵי^(c) סֵפֶר הַתּוֹרָה — the words of the book of the law (2 Kgs. 22:11)

X.2 Translate the following:

(1) מִיַּד הָאִשָּׁה — from the hand of the woman (Gen. 38:20)

(2) יוֹם הַשַּׁבָּת — the day of the Sabbath (Exod. 20:11)

(3) בֶּן־אָדָם — son of man (Ezek. 2:1)

(4) מִבְּנֵי־הַנְּבִיאִים — from the sons of the prophets (2 Kgs. 2:7)

(5) וּמִבְּנֵי יִשְׂרָאֵל — and from the sons of Israel (1 Kgs. 9:22)

(6) בְּנוֹת^(c) אַנְשֵׁי הָעִיר — the daughters of the men of the city (Gen. 24:13)

(7) בְּשֵׁם הַמֶּלֶךְ — in the name of the king (Est. 3:12)

(8) רָאשֵׁי הֶהָרִים — the tops of the mountains (Gen. 8:5)

(9) וְאֵלֶּה^(d) מַלְכֵי הָאָרֶץ — and these (are) the kings of the land (Josh. 12:1)

43

(10) (c)בְּאֶרֶץ בְּנֵי יִשְׂרָאֵל   in the land of the sons of Israel
(Josh. 11:22)

(11) עַבְדֵי הַמֶּלֶךְ   the servants of the king (1 Sam. 22:17)

(12) (e)מֹשֶׁה עֶבֶד יְהוָה   Moses, servant of the LORD (Josh. 1:15)

[Watch for the proper names in #5, 10, and 12.]

X.4 Translate the following:

(1) כָּל־יְמֵי הָאָרֶץ   all the days of the earth (Gen. 8:22)

(2) דַּם־כָּל־בָּשָׂר   blood of all flesh (Lev. 17:14)

(3) וְלֹא בֶן־נָבִיא אָנֹכִי   And I (am) not a son of a prophet
(Amos 7:14)

(4) אִישׁ מִבְּנֵי יִשְׂרָאֵל   a man from the children of Israel
(Lev. 17:13)

(5) בְּהַר צִיּוֹן וּבִירוּשָׁלַם   on the mountain of Zion and in Jerusalem
(Isa. 10:12)

(6) שֵׁם אֵשֶׁת־אַבְרָם שָׂרָי   The name of Abraham's wife (was) Sarai.
(Gen. 11:29)

(7) וְאֵלֶּה שְׁמוֹת בְּנֵי יִשְׂרָאֵל   And these (are) the names of the children of
Israel (Exod. 1:1)

(8) אֶת־דֶּרֶךְ עֵץ הַחַיִּים   the way of the tree of life (Gen. 3:24)

(9) בְּתוֹרַת מֹשֶׁה עֶבֶד־הָאֱלֹהִים   in the law of Moses the servant of God
(Dan. 9:11)

(10) כִּי (f)בַת־מֶלֶךְ הִיא   for she (is) a daughter of a king
(2 Kgs. 9:34)

X.5 Match the following:

(1) (F) כְּכוֹכְבֵי הַשָּׁמַיִם   (A) For they (are) merciful kings.
(1 Kgs. 20:31)

(2) (E) בְּנוֹת אַנְשֵׁי הָעִיר   (B) the book of the law of
the LORD (2 Chr. 17:9)

(3) (Q) כִּי מִצְוַת הַמֶּלֶךְ הִיא   (C) The voice (is) the voice of Jacob.
(Gen. 27:22)

(4) (H) מִנְשֵׁי בְּנֵי־הַנְּבִיאִים   (D) and the houses of the kings of
Judah (Jer. 19:13)

(5) (R) וְזֹאת תּוֹרַת הָאָדָם   (E) the daughters of the men of
the city (Gen. 24:13)

(6) (L) זֹאת תּוֹרַת הַבָּיִת   (F) as the stars of the heavens
(Gen. 26:4)

(7) (B)	סֵפֶר תּוֹרַת יְהוָה	(G) in the way of the kings of Israel (2 Kgs. 8:18)
(8) (J)	דִּבְרֵי הַנָּבִיא הַהוּא	(H) from the wives of the sons of the prophets (2 Kgs. 4:1)
(9) (K)	דִּבְרֵי שָׁלוֹם וֶאֱמֶת	(I) men from the elders of Israel (Ezek. 14:1)
(10) (N)	לְכָל־זִקְנֵי הָאָרֶץ	(J) the words of that prophet (Deut. 13:4)
(11) (O)	וּדְבַר יְהוָה מִירוּשָׁלָם	(K) words of peace and truth (Est. 9:30)
(12) (P)	וְאֵלֶּה דִּבְרֵי הַסֵּפֶר	(L) This (is) the law of the house. (Ezek. 43:12)
(13) (I)	אֲנָשִׁים מִזִּקְנֵי יִשְׂרָאֵל	(M) concerning the houses of this city (Jer. 33:4)
(14) (M)	עַל־בָּתֵּי הָעִיר הַזֹּאת	(N) to all the elders of the land (1 Kgs. 20:7)
(15) (D)	וּבָתֵּי מַלְכֵי יְהוּדָה	(O) and the word of the LORD from Jerusalem (Isa. 2:3)
(16) (G)	בְּדֶרֶךְ מַלְכֵי יִשְׂרָאֵל	(P) And these (are) the words of the book. (Jer. 29:1)
(17) (A)	כִּי מַלְכֵי חֶסֶד הֵם	(Q) For it (is) the commandment of the king. (Isa. 36:21)
(18) (C)	הַקֹּל קוֹל יַעֲקֹב	(R) And this (is) the law of the man. (2 Sam. 7:19)

Footnotes

(a) A noun in the construct state never takes the definite article but is considered definite if the absolute noun that follows it has the definite article or is a proper name. All the examples in this exercise are definite.

(b) אֱלֹהִים is treated as a proper name when it refers to the God of Israel. It is classified as definite whether it stands with or without the definite article. Nouns in a construct relationship with it are translated with the definite article. The same rule applies to all the proper names.

(c) Two or more construct nouns may occur in the same construct relationship. The rule regarding definiteness applies to both of them: if the noun in the absolute state is indefinite, they are indefinite; if it is definite, they are definite.

(d) אֵלֶּה is the masculine or feminine plural demonstrative pronoun, translated "these" (cf. G.24.2, p. 53).

45

(e) An appositional phrase consisting of nouns forming a construct relationship often occurs after a proper noun and serves to define the proper noun more exactly. "Moses, servant of the LORD" tells us who Moses is. (Cf. 2 Chr. 29:27: "David, king of Israel"; 2 Sam. 6:16: "Michal, daughter of Saul.")

(f) A construct noun is indefinite when the absolute noun following it is indefinite.

(g) The noun חֶסֶד takes on the force of an adjective when used as the absolute noun in a construct relationship. For example, אַנְשֵׁי חֶסֶד (Isa. 57:1), "men of חֶסֶד" has been rendered "pious men" and "men of good faith." תּוֹרַת חֶסֶד (Prov. 31:26), "law of חֶסֶד," has been translated "kindly teaching." Examples of other nouns used in a similar way include the following:

(1) אִישׁ דְּבָרִים "a man of words," i.e., "an eloquent man" (Exod. 4:10)

(2) אַנְשֵׁי אֱמֶת "men of truth," i.e., "trustworthy men" (Exod. 18:21)

(3) שַׂר שָׁלוֹם "a prince of peace," i.e., "a peaceable ruler" (Isa. 9:5; Eng. 9:6)

(4) אַנְשֵׁי מִלְחָמָה "men of war," i.e., "trained warriors" (2 Chr. 8:9)

(5) אַנְשֵׁי הַשֵּׁם "men of the name," i.e., "renowned men" (Gen. 6:4)

(6) אֶרֶץ שָׁלוֹם "a land of peace," i.e., "a tranquil, safe land" (Jer. 12:5)

(7) אִישׁ דָּמִים "a man of bloods," i.e., "a bloodguilty man, a murderer" (2 Sam. 16:7)

Suggestions for Further Testing

1. Circle the word that does not belong to the category indicated.

(1)	parts of the body	יָד	לֵב	אֹהֶל	רֶגֶל
(2)	food and drink	מַיִם	אֶבֶן	פְּרִי	לֶחֶם
(3)	where people gather	יַיִן	יְרוּשָׁלַיִם	בַּיִת	עִיר
(4)	related to time	שָׁנָה	תְּהוֹם	עֵת	יוֹם
(5)	where things grow	מִדְבָּר	שָׂדֶה	יָם	מִשְׁפָּט
(6)	desirable qualities	חָזָק	חָכָם	קָשֶׁה	יָפֶה
(7)	living creatures	יַבָּשָׁה	בְּהֵמָה	סוּס	חַיָּה
(8)	related to obedience	מִצְוָה	תּוֹרָה	נַעֲרָה	בְּרִית
(9)	persons with a vocation	חֶרֶב	מֶלֶךְ	נָבִיא	מַלְכָּה
(10)	in liquid form	דָּם	יַיִן	מַיִם	עוֹף

2. Match the following:

(1) (   )   מְיַד אֱלֹהִים הִיא   (A) according to the commandment of
                                             Moses (2 Chr. 8:13)
(2) (   )   כִּי בֶן רִבְקָה הוּא   (B) stars of light (Ps. 148:3)
(3) (   )   זְקֵנִים וּזְקֵנוֹת   (C) For it (is) from the hand of God.
                                             (Eccl. 2:24)
(4) (   )   תּוֹרַת אֱמֶת   (D) according to the word of the LORD
                                             (Josh. 8:27)
(5) (   )   אֵשֶׁת־הָאִישׁ   (E) on the mountains of Israel
                                             (Ezek. 37:22)
(6) (   )   כּוֹכְבֵי אוֹר   (F) judgment of truth (Zech. 7:9)
(7) (   )   מִבְּנוֹת יִשְׂרָאֵל   (G) law of truth (Mal. 2:6)
(8) (   )   מִשְׁפַּט אֱמֶת   (H) the top (head) of the mountain
                                             (Exod. 19:20)
(9) (   )   כְּמִצְוַת מֹשֶׁה   (I) For he (was) the son of Rebecca.
                                             (Gen. 29:12)
(10) (   )   כִּדְבַר יְהוָה   (J) from the daughters of Israel
                                             (Deut. 23:18)
(11) (   )   בְּהָרֵי יִשְׂרָאֵל   (K) the man's wife (Gen. 20:7)
(12) (   )   רֹאשׁ הָהָר   (L) old men and old women (Zech. 8:4)

3. Translate the following:

(1)   וְגוֹי קָדוֹשׁ   (Exod. 19:6)
(2)   הֶעָרִים גְּדוֹלֹת מְאֹד   (Num. 13:28)
(3)   אֵין אֱמֶת וְאֵין חֶסֶד   (Hos. 4:1)
(4)   כַּדְּבָרִים הָאֵלֶּה   (Gen. 24:23)
(5)   לֹא אִישׁ דְּבָרִים אָנֹכִי   (Exod. 4:10)
(6)   וְאֵלֶּה שְׁמוֹת הָאֲנָשִׁים   (Num. 1:5)
(7)   כָּל־עָרֵי הַמְּלָכִים־הָאֵלֶּה (Josh. 11:12)
(8)   אִשָּׁה מֵאֶרֶץ מִצְרַיִם   (Gen. 21:21)
(9)   סֵפֶר הַבְּרִית   (Exod. 24:7)
(10) עַם אֱלֹהֵי אַבְרָהָם   (Ps. 47:10; Eng. 47:9)

4. From your study of the Glossary (*G*, pp. 424ff.), define the following terms:

(1) Absolute State   (4) Hapax Legomenon
(2) Construct Relationship   (5) Relative Pronoun
(3) Construct State

LESSON XI

Answer Key
(Cf. *G*, pp. 76ff.)

XI.1 Match the following:*

(1)	(H)	מִדַּרְכּוֹ הָרָעָה (a)	(A) I am your son. (Gen. 27:32)
(2)	(E)	גָּדוֹל שְׁמוֹ	(B) Our father is old. (Gen. 19:31)
(3)	(K)	כִּי־גָדוֹל אֱלֹהֵינוּ	(C) You are my God. (Ps. 31:15; Eng. 31:14)
(4)	(P)	בִּשְׁמִי הַגָּדוֹל (a)	(D) You are my father. (Ps. 89:27; Eng. 89:26)
(5)	(J)	וְתוֹרַת־יְהוָה אִתָּנוּ	(E) His name is great. (Ps. 76:2; Eng. 76:1)
(6)	(M)	תָּמִים דַּרְכּוֹ	(F) For the ways of the LORD are right. (Hos. 14:10; Eng. 14:9)
(7)	(N)	תָּמִים אַתָּה בִּדְרָכֶיךָ	(G) He is my brother. (Gen. 20:5)
(8)	(Q)	כִּי־יָשָׁר דְּבַר־יְהוָה	(H) from his evil way (Jer. 26:3)
(9)	(F)	כִּי יְשָׁרִים דַּרְכֵי יְהוָה	(I) For God is with us. (Isa. 8:10)
(10)	(B)	אָבִינוּ זָקֵן	(J) And the law of the LORD is with us. (Jer. 8:8)
(11)	(O)	יֶשׁ־לָנוּ אָב זָקֵן	(K) For our God is great. (2 Chr. 2:4)
(12)	(R)	אִישָׁהּ זָקֵן	(L) For I will be with you. (Gen. 26:24)
(13)	(C)	אֱלֹהַי (b) אַתָּה	(M) His way is perfect. (Ps. 18:31; Eng. 18:30)
(14)	(G)	אָחִי הוּא	(N) Perfect are you in your ways. (Ezek. 28:15)
(15)	(I)	כִּי עִמָּנוּ אֵל	(O) We have an old father. (Gen. 44:20)
(16)	(L)	כִּי־אִתְּךָ (c) אָנֹכִי	(P) by my great name (Jer. 44:26)
(17)	(A)	אֲנִי בִנְךָ	(Q) For the word of the LORD is upright. (Ps. 33:4)
(18)	(D)	אָבִי (b) אַתָּה (d)	(R) Her husband was old. (2 Kgs. 4:14)

*Note: The verb "to be" is so consistently assumed in verbless clauses that its various forms will no longer be set off in parentheses.

XI.2 Translate the following:

(1) אַתָּה אָבִינוּ You are our father. (Isa. 63:16)

(2) מִיַּד הָאִשָּׁה from the hand of the woman (Num. 5:25)

(3) בְּנֵי יִשְׂרָאֵל the sons of Israel (Josh. 9:26)

(4) בְּיַד עַמִּי יִשְׂרָאֵל by the hand of my people Israel (Ezek. 25:14)

(5) בְּיַד־נְבִיאֶיךָ by the hand of your prophets (Neh. 9:30)

(6) בְּיַד עֲבָדֶיךָ by the hand of your servants (Ezra 9:11)

(7) כִּי לִי(e) כָל־הָאָרֶץ For to me is all the earth. (Exod. 19:5)

(8) וְכָל־אַנְשֵׁי בֵיתוֹ and all of the men of his house (Gen. 17:27)

(9) וּדְבַר אֱלֹהֵינוּ and the word of our God (Isa. 40:8)

(10) אֱלֹהֵי אָבִי אַבְרָהָם the God of my father Abraham (Gen. 32:10; Eng. 32:9)

XI.3 Supply the correct pronouns in order to translate the following entries:

(1) יְהוָה צְבָאוֹת עִמָּנוּ The LORD of hosts is with ____us____. (Ps. 46:12; Eng. 46:11)

(2) בְּיַד עֲבָדָיו(f) הַנְּבִיאִים by the hand of ____his____ servants the prophets (2 Kgs. 24:2)

(3) מִימֵי אֲבֹתֵינוּ from the days of ____our____ ancestors (Ezra 9:7)

(4) לָכֶם וְלַאֲבוֹתֵיכֶם(g) to ____you____ and to ____your____ ancestors (Jer. 7:14)

(5) הֵמָּה וַאֲבוֹתָם ____they____ and ____their____ ancestors (Jer. 9:15; Eng. 9:16)

(6) אֱלֹהֵי אֲבוֹתֵיהֶם(g) the God of ____their____ ancestors (1 Chr. 5:25)

(7) כָל־בָּנָיו וְכָל־בְּנֹתָיו(h) all ____his____ sons and all ____his____ daughters (Gen. 37:35)

(8) מִפְּרִי יָדֶיהָ from the fruit of ____her____ hands (Prov. 31:31)

(9) וְהִנֵּה יָדִי עִמָּךְ Behold, ____my____ hand is with ____you____. (2 Sam. 3:12)

(10) הִנֵּה כָל־אֲשֶׁר־לוֹ(i) בְּיָדֶךָ(j) Behold, all that ____he____ has is in ____your____ hand. (Job 1:12)

(11) יָדַי וְרַגְלָי(k) ____my____ hands and ____my____ feet (Ps. 22:17; Eng. 22:16)

(12) אַתֶּם וּבְנֵיכֶם ____you____ and ____your____ sons (Deut. 12:12)

49

Footnotes

(a) A noun is definite when it has the definite article, is a proper name, is in the construct relationship with a definite noun, or has a pronominal suffix (cf. *G*.26.5, p. 63; *Glossary*, "Definite/Indefinite Noun," p. 430). The example here is of a noun made definite by its pronominal ending.

(b) אַתָּה is the pausal form (with silluq, אַתָּֽה [cf. MT in *Biblia Hebraica Stuttgartensia*]) for אַתָּ֫ה (cf. *G*.68, pp. 240f.).

(c) אָנֹכִי is the pausal form (with secondary accent, אָֽנֹכִי [cf. MT in *Biblia Hebraica Stuttgartensia*]) for אָנֹכִ֫י (cf. *G*.68, pp. 240f.).

(d) The word אָב, "father," exhibits forms that are easily confused. The singular construct is אֲבִי, "father of." When the first person singular pronominal suffix is added, the result is אָבִי, "my father" [cf. *G*.28.3(2), pp. 73.f.]. According to the way אָבִי is normally written, the final syllable is the accented syllable. Before the pausal form אַתָּה, however, the accent is pushed back to the initial syllable (אָ֫בִי). This was done to avoid juxtaposing two heavily accented syllables within a sentence. Such changes in accentuation are not uncommon in the Hebrew Bible.

(e) לִי is idiomatic for "mine," making it possible to translate: "For mine is all the earth."

(f) The transliteration (pronunciation) of עֲבָדָיו is ʿᵃvādāv. The final vav functions as a regular consonant, closing the final syllable (דָיו). The vowel is qameṣ–yod, a diphthong. All third masculine singular pronominal suffixes, when added to plural construct nouns, produce final closed syllables in a similar manner [cf. *H*.XI.3(7), p. 49].

(g) The secondary accent meteg may occur on long vowels in open syllables when the long vowels stand two or more syllables before the tone syllable of a word (cf. *G*.9.2, pp. 17f.).

(h) A BeGaD KeFaT letter loses its dagesh lene when placed immediately after a vowel (cf. *G*.6, pp. 12f.). The dagesh lene may be caused to drop out when a BeGaD KeFaT letter stands first in a word if the preceding word ends in a vowel. In the example taken from Genesis 37:35, כָל stands without a dagesh lene since, in the larger context of the sentence, it is preceded by a word with a final vowel (. . . . וַיָּקֻמוּ כָל־בָּנָיו). The preceding šureq causes kaf to drop its dagesh lene. The exercises throughout the *Grammar* contain many similar examples, because they faithfully reproduce the texts from which they were drawn.

(i) In this case כ appears without its dagesh lene because it comes immediately after a word ending in a final ה without mappiq, which means that the syllable is open [cf. *G*.12.4(4), p. 21]. The ṣere in הַנֵּה, therefore, is treated as preceding kaf and causing it to lose its dagesh lene.

(j) בְּיָדֶךְ, "in your hand," is the pausal form (with secondary accent, בְּיָדֶךְ [cf. MT in *Biblia Hebraica Stuttgartensia*]) for בְּיָדְךָ (cf. Exod. 13:9).

(k) רַגְלָי, "my feet," is the pausal form (with silluq, רַגְלָי [cf. MT in *Biblia Hebraica Stuttgartensia*]) for רַגְלַי (cf. Isa. 60:13). This word occurs more often with 'atnaḥ than with silluq (cf. *G*.8.3, p. 17).

Suggestions for Further Testing

1. Match the following:

(1) (   ) לִפְנֵי הָאֱלֹהִים
(A) his wife and his sons' wives (Gen. 7:7)

(2) (   ) אֱלֹהֵי אֲבוֹתֵיכֶם
(B) our sons and our daughters (Jer. 35:8)

(3) (   ) אִשְׁתְּךָ וּנְשֵׁי־בָנֶיךָ
(C) they and our ancestors (Neh. 9:16)

(4) (   ) אִשְׁתּוֹ וּנְשֵׁי־בָנָיו
(D) their wives and their daughters (Jer. 14:16)

(5) (   ) בָּנֵינוּ וּבְנֹתֵינוּ
(E) you and your sons (Deut. 12:12)

(6) (   ) אֶת־בָּנָיו וְאֶת־נָשָׁיו
(F) the God of their ancestors (1 Chr. 5:25)

(7) (   ) נְשֵׁיהֶם וּבְנֹתֵיהֶם
(G) your wife and your sons' wives (Gen. 6:18)

(8) (   ) בִּימֵי אֲבֹתֵיכֶם
(H) in the presence of God (Exod. 18:12)

(9) (   ) אֱלֹהֵי אֲבֹתֵיהֶם
(I) your brothers and your houses (Neh. 4:8)

(10) (   ) אַתֶּם וּבְנֵיכֶם
(J) the God of your ancestors (Exod. 3:13)

(11) (   ) הֵם וַאֲבֹתֵינוּ
(K) in the days of your ancestors (fathers) (Joel 1:2)

(12) (   ) אֲחֵיכֶם וּבָתֵּיכֶם
(L) his sons and his wives (Gen. 31:17)

2. Translate the following:

(1) וַיַּד אֱלֹהֵינוּ עָלֵינוּ (Ezra 8:31)

(2) יָדָיו עַל־יְדֵי הַמֶּלֶךְ (2 Kgs. 13:16)

(3) וְקוֹלוֹ כְּקוֹל מַיִם רַבִּים (Ezek. 43:2)

(4) הַבָּנוֹת בְּנֹתַי וְהַבָּנִים בָּנַי (Gen. 31:43)

(5) וְאֵלֶּה שְׁמוֹת בְּנֹתָיו (Num. 27:1)

(6) יְהוָה אֱלֹהֶיךָ עִמָּךְ (Deut. 2:7)

(7) כִּי אֲחִי אָבִיהָ הוּא (Gen. 29:12)

(8) הָאָרֶץ וְכָל־אֲשֶׁר בָּהּ (Deut. 10:14)

(9) אֲנִי וְכָל־הָעָם אֲשֶׁר אִתִּי (Josh. 8:5)

(10) הוּא וְכָל־הָעָם אֲשֶׁר עִמּוֹ (Gen. 35:6)

(11) אַתָּה וְהָעָם אֲשֶׁר אִתָּךְ (Judg. 9:32)

(12) לְךָ אֲנִי וְכָל־אֲשֶׁר־לִי (1 Kgs. 20:4)

3. Supply the correct pronouns in order to complete the translations.

(1) כַּסְפִּי וּזְהָבִי _____ silver and _____ gold (Joel 4:5; Eng. 3:5)

(2) אֶת־נָשַׁי וְאֶת־יְלָדַי _____ wives and _____ children (Gen. 30:26)

(3) בְּעָרֵיהֶם וּבְבָתֵּיהֶם in _____ cities and in _____ houses (Deut. 19:1)

(4) בַּת־אָבִי הוּא אַךְ לֹא בַת־אִמִּי _____ is the daughter of _____ father but not the daughter of _____ mother. (Gen. 20:12)

(5) לִי־הֶם _____ are _____. (Gen. 45:8)

(6) כִּי־עֲבָדַי הֵם For _____ are _____ servants. (Lev. 25:42)

(7) אֲשֶׁר אַתָּה בַּבַּיִת who were with _____ in the house (Gen. 27:15)

(8) לְכָל־עֲבָדָיו אֲשֶׁר־אִתּוֹ בִירוּשָׁלַם to all _____ servants who were with _____ in Jerusalem (2 Sam. 15:14)

(9) הִיא טוֹבָה לָךְ _____ is good to (for) _____. (Ruth 4:15)

(10) כִּי זְקֵנִים־הֵמָּה מִמֶּנּוּ For _____ were older than _____. (Job 32:4)

(11) צַדִּיק אַתָּה מִמֶּנִּי _____ are more righteous than _____. (1 Sam. 24:17)

(12) כִּי הוּא צַדִּיק בְּעֵינָיו For _____ was righteous in _____ (own) eyes. (Job 32:1)

LESSON XII

Answer Key
(Cf. *G*, pp. 89ff.)

XII.1 Write the Qal perfect inflection of מָשַׁל, "he ruled."

(1)	3 ms	מָשַׁל	he ruled		(6)	3 cp	מָשְׁלוּ	we ruled
(2)	3 fs	מָשְׁלָה	she ruled					
(3)	2 ms	מָשַׁלְתָּ	you ruled		(7)	2 mp	מְשַׁלְתֶּם	you ruled
(4)	2 fs	מָשַׁלְתְּ	you ruled		(8)	2 fp	מְשַׁלְתֶּן	you ruled
(5)	1 cs	מָשַׁלְתִּי	I ruled		(9)	1 cp	מָשַׁלְנוּ	we ruled

XII.2 Indicate beside each of the following verbs whether it is weak (W) or strong (S).

(1)	(W)	אָכַל	he ate		(10)	(S)	מָלַךְ	he reigned
(2)	(W)	בּוֹא	to go, enter		(11)	(S)	מָשַׁל	he ruled
(3)	(W)	בָּרָא	he created		(12)	(W)	נָתַן	he gave
(4)	(S)	גָּדַל	he was great		(13)	(W)	עָשָׂה	he did, made
(5)	(W)	יָדַע	he knew		(14)	(S)	קָטַל	he killed
(6)	(W)	יָשַׁב	he sat, dwelled		(15)	(W)	שִׂים	to put, place
(7)	(S)	כָּתַב	he wrote		(16)	(S)	שָׁכַב	he lay down
(8)	(S)	לָבַשׁ	he put on, wore		(17)	(W)	שָׁלַח	he sent
(9)	(W)	לָקַח	he took		(18)	(W)	שָׁמַע	he heard, obeyed

XII.3 Each of the following entries contains a Qal perfect form of a verb. Give the correct translation of the verb form by filling in the blank. In the space marked (a) give the person, gender, and number of the verb form; in the space marked (b) give its root.

Example:

וְאֶת־אֲשֶׁר בַּשָּׂדֶה לָקָחוּ (a) ___3 cp___

And that which was in the field they ___took___ . (b) לָקַח

(Gen. 34:28)

(1) וְלֹא־הָלְכוּ בְתוֹרָתִי (a) ___3 cp___

And they did not ___walk___ in my law. (Jer. 44:10) (b) הָלַךְ

(2) כִּי שָׁמַעְנוּ אֱלֹהִים עִמָּכֶם   (a)   1 cp

For we have __heard__ that God is with you. (Zech. 8:23)   (b)   שָׁמַע

(3) וְלַחֹשֶׁךְ קָרָא לָיְלָה(a)   (a)   3 ms

And to the darkness he __called__ night. (Gen. 1:5)   (b)   קָרָא

(4) כָּל־הָעָם אָמְרוּ אָמֵן(b)   (a)   3 cp

All the people __said__, "Amen!" (Deut. 27:15)   (b)   אָמַר

(5) אֵשׁ אֱלֹהִים נָפְלָה מִן־הַשָּׁמַיִם(c)   (a)   3 fs

The fire of God __fell__ from the heavens. (Job 1:16)   (b)   נָפַל

(6) בְּכָל־כֹּחִי עָבַדְתִּי אֶת־אֲבִיכֶן(d)   (a)   1 cs

With all my strength I __served__ your father. (Gen. 31:6)   (b)   עָבַד

(7) הָלְכוּ בְנֵי יִשְׂרָאֵל בַּמִּדְבָּר   (a)   3 cp

The people of Israel __walked__ in the wilderness.   (b)   הָלַךְ
(Josh. 5:6)

(8) מָצָאנוּ מָיִם   (a)   1 cp

We have __found__ water. (Gen. 26:32)   (b)   מָצָא

(9) אָהַבְתָּ רָע מִטּוֹב   (a)   2 ms

You __loved__ evil more than good. (Ps. 52:5; Eng. 52:3)   (b)   אָהַב

(10) עֲבָדִים מָשְׁלוּ בָנוּ   (a)   3 cp

Servants __ruled__ over us. (Lam. 5:8)   (b)   מָשַׁל

(11) וְשָׁמְרוּ בְנֵי־יִשְׂרָאֵל אֶת־הַשַּׁבָּת(e)   (a)   3 cp

And the people of Israel shall __keep__ the sabbath.   (b)   שָׁמַר
(Exod. 31:16)

(12) כַּסְפִּי וּזְהָבִי לְקַחְתֶּם(f)   (a)   2 mp

You have __taken__ my silver and my gold.   (b)   לָקַח
(Joel 4:5; Eng. 3:5)

XII.4 Complete the translation of each entry by supplying the missing pronouns.

(1) וְאֶת־קֹלוֹ שָׁמַעְנוּ(g) And __we__ heard __his__ voice. (Deut. 5:24)

(2) אֶת־קֹלְךָ שָׁמַעְתִּי בַגָּן(h) __I__ heard __your__ voice in the garden.
(Gen. 3:10)

(3) וְאָבִיו וְאִמּוֹ לֹא יָדְעוּ(i) But __his__ father and __his__ mother
did not know. (Judg. 14:4)

(4) לֹא שָׁמַרְתָּ אֶת־מִצְוַת יְהוָה אֱלֹהֶיךָ __You__ have not kept the
commandment of the LORD __your__ God. (1 Sam. 13:13)

(5) לֹא־שָׁמְרוּ תוֹרָתֶךָ(j) __They__ did not keep __your__ law. (Ps. 119:136)

(6) שָׁמַעְתִּי אֶת־תְּפִלָּתְךָ _____I_____ have heard ___your___ prayer.
(1 Kgs. 9:3)

(7) לֹא שָׁמַעְתָּ בְּקוֹל יְהוָה אֱלֹהֶיךָ ___You___ have not listened to
the voice of the LORD ___your___ God. (Deut. 28:45)

(8) וְלֹא שָׁמְעוּ בְּקוֹלִי And ___they___ have not listened to (obeyed)
___my___ voice. (Num. 14:22)

(9) וְלָקַחְתָּ אִשָּׁה לִבְנִי (e) And ___you___ shall take a wife for ___my___ son.
(Gen. 24:4)

(10) כִּי־אֹתוֹ אָהַב אֲבִיהֶם (k) For ___their___ father loved ___him___. (Gen. 37:4)

XII.5 Translate the following:

(1) כִּי שָׁמַע אֱלֹהִים אֶל־קוֹל הַנַּעַר — And God heard the voice of the boy. (Gen. 21:17)

(2) כֹּה־אָמַר יְהוָה אֱלֹהֵי יִשְׂרָאֵל — Thus says the LORD, the God of Israel. (Exod. 5:1)

(3) וּבִירוּשָׁלַם מָלַךְ עַל כָּל־יִשְׂרָאֵל (l) — And in Jerusalem he reigned over all Israel. (2 Sam. 5:5)

(4) וּלְכָל־בְּנֵי יִשְׂרָאֵל הָיָה אוֹר (m) — But to all the people of Israel there was light. (Exod. 10:23)

(5) וּמֹשֶׁה עָלָה אֶל־הָאֱלֹהִים (n) — And Moses went up unto God. (Exod. 19:3)

(6) כִּי־שָׁכַב דָּוִד עִם־אֲבֹתָיו — that David had lain down with his ancestors (1 Kgs. 11:21)

(7) וּדְבָרָיו שָׁמַעְתָּ מִתּוֹךְ הָאֵשׁ (o) — And you heard his words from the midst of the fire. (Deut. 4:36)

(8) לֹא שָׁמְרוּ בְּרִית אֱלֹהִים — They did not keep God's covenant. (Ps. 78:10)

(9) לֹא שָׁמְרוּ אֲבוֹתֵינוּ אֶת־דְּבַר יְהוָה — Our ancestors did not keep the word of the LORD. (2 Chr. 34:21)

(10) וְלֹא־שָׁמַע עַמִּי לְקוֹלִי — But my people did not listen to my voice. (Ps. 81:12; Eng. 81:11)

XII.6 Match the following:

(1) (J) אֹתִי שָׁלַח יְהוָה (p) — (A) And I shall lie down with my ancestors. (Gen. 47:30)

(2) (F) וַיהוָה פָּקַד אֶת־שָׂרָה (q) — (B) as a sign upon your hand (Exod. 13:9)

(3) (L) וְלַחֹשֶׁךְ קָרָא לָיְלָה (a) — (C) and the word of the LORD from Jerusalem (Isa. 2:3)

(4) (A) (e)וְשָׁכַבְתִּי עִם־אֲבֹתַי

(5) (G) כִּי־פָקַד יְהוָה אֶת־עַמּוֹ

(6) (B) לְאוֹת עַל־יָדֶךָ

(7) (K) כָּל־יְמֵי אָדָם

(8) (E) כִּדְבַר אִישׁ הָאֱלֹהִים

(9) (C) וּדְבַר יְהוָה (r)מִירוּשָׁלָם

(10) (H) דִּבְרֵי הַנָּבִיא הַהוּא

(11) (D) אֶת־סֵפֶר תּוֹרַת־יְהוָה

(12) (I) אֱלֹהֵי אֲבֹתֵינוּ

(D) the book of the law of the LORD (2 Chr. 34:14)

(E) according to the word of the man of God (2 Kgs. 5:14)

(F) The LORD visited Sarah. (Gen. 21:1)

(G) that the LORD had visited his people (Ruth 1:6)

(H) the words of that prophet (Deut. 13:4)

(I) the God of our ancestors (Deut. 26:7)

(J) The LORD sent me. (1 Sam. 15:1)

(K) all the days of Adam (Gen. 5:5)

(L) But the darkness he called night. (Gen. 1:5)

Footnotes

(a) וְלַחֹשֶׁךְ is made emphatic by being written before the verb (cf. *G*.32, p. 87). Students may gain new insight into the meaning of a text if they are sensitive to the use of inverted word order in Biblical Hebrew to achieve emphasis.

(b) כָּל־הָעָם is made emphatic by the inverted word order of the sentence.

(c) אִישׁ אֱלֹהִים is another example of inverted word order for emphasis.

(d) בְּכָל־כֹּחִי also uses inverted word order for emphasis.

(e) A perfect form of a verb, when prefixed with vav conjunction, will ordinarily be translated in the future tense [cf. *G*.31.1(4), p. 86].

(f) כַּסְפִּי וּזְהָבִי are made emphatic by being placed before the verb.

(g) וְאֶת־קֹלוֹ is another example of inverted word order, used for emphasis.

(h) אֶת־קֹלֶךָ is made emphatic by its position in the sentence.

(i) וְאָבִיו וְאִמּוֹ illustrates inverted word order for emphasis.

(j) תּוֹרָתֶךָ is the pausal form (with silluq, תּוֹרָתֶךָ) for תּוֹרָתְךָ (cf. *G*.8.2, 8.3, pp. 16f.). The dagesh lene has dropped out of the initial tav in this word because the preceding word ends in a vowel (וֹ) (cf. *G*.6, pp. 12f.).

(k) כִּי־אֹתוֹ is made emphatic by its position before the verb.

(l) וּבִירוּשָׁלַם is emphasized by the inverted word order.

(m) וּלְכָל־בְּנֵי יִשְׂרָאֵל is a vivid example of how words and phrases could be made emphatic by their position in a sentence. Try reading Hebrew with this in mind.

(n) וּמֹשֶׁה is highlighted by being placed before the verb.

(o) וּדְבָרָיו shifts emphasis to God's spoken words by its inverted position in the sentence.

(p) אֹתִי is the speaker's way of stressing his commission from the LORD. It is another instance of emphasis through dislocation.

(q) וַיהוָה stresses that the astounding thing to be communicated is that *the LORD* visited Sarah.

(r) On the unusual ending on יְרוּשָׁלַם, see *G*.12.2, p. 19.

Additional Helps

Those who have studied the *Grammar* up to this point should be prepared to make an analysis of Hebrew phrases, clauses, and sentences. A translation based upon this analysis should then be possible. The translation process involves examining each word, dividing it into its component parts, and identifying and explaining each part. All verb forms should be fully located. The examples given below suggest one way to analyze Hebrew sentences.

1. אֹתִי שָׁלַח יְהוָה (1 Sam. 15:1)

    (1) אֹתִי, the sign of the direct object, אֵת (cf. *G*.5, p. 12), plus first person pronominal suffix, which serves as the direct object, and is translated "me" (cf. *G*.27.2, p. 71). This word is made emphatic by its position in the sentence prior to the subject and verb (cf. *G*.32, p. 87).

    (2) שָׁלַח, a Qal perfect, third masculine singular, from the same root שָׁלַח, translated "he sent."

(3) יְהוָה, the divine name Yahweh, for which אֲדֹנָי (ʾĂdōnāy) is substituted in the pronunciation. יְהוָה is translated "LORD" (all capital letters) (cf. G.16.6, p. 32).

Translation:

אֹתִי שָׁלַח יְהוָה   "The LORD sent *me*."

2. וְאֵלֶּה שְׁמוֹת בְּנֵי יִשְׁמָעֵאל (Gen. 25:13)

(1) וְאֵלֶּה, the vav conjunction וְ ("and"), plus the demonstrative masculine (or feminine) plural pronoun, translated "and these" (cf. G.24.2, p. 53).

(2) שְׁמוֹת, a masculine plural construct noun, from the absolute שֵׁמוֹת, "names," translated "names of" [cf. G.26.4(2)(c), p. 61]. שְׁמוֹת is one of the several masculine plural nouns ending in וֹת, an ending normally used on feminine plural nouns [cf. G.19.2(1)(b), p. 38].

(3) בְּנֵי, the masculine plural construct noun, from בָּנִים, "sons," translated "sons of" [cf. G.26.4(2)(c), p. 61].

(4) יִשְׁמָעֵאל, the proper name "Ishmael," which has a quiescent (silent) א in its final syllable. Since a proper name is definite, all the nouns in a construct relationship with it are also definite (cf. G.26.5, p. 63).

Translation:

וְאֵלֶּה שְׁמוֹת בְּנֵי יִשְׁמָעֵאל   "And these (are) the names of the sons of Ishmael."

3. זָכַרְתִּי בַלַּיְלָה שִׁמְךָ יְהוָה (Ps. 119:55)

(1) זָכַרְתִּי, Qal perfect, first common singular, from זָכַר, "he remembered," translated "I remember." The position of זָכַרְתִּי illlustrates the normal word order for a Hebrew verbal sentence in which the verb appears first (cf. G.32, p. 87).

(2) בַלַּיְלָה, masculine singular noun (לַיְלָה), translated "night," plus the contraction of the preposition בְּ ("in") and the definite article הַ· ("the") producing בַּ [cf. G.15.1(4), p. 29]. בַ lacks a dagesh lene because the preceding word ends in a vowel. The full translation of the word is "in the night."

(3) שִׁמְךָ, masculine singular construct noun, from the absolute שֵׁם, "name," plus second masculine singular pronominal suffix. The writing of שֵׁם with pronominal endings follows the same pattern as בֵּן, "son" [cf. G.28.3(1), p. 73]. Translation: "your name."

(4) יְהוָה, the covenant name for Israel's God, pronounced *Ădōnāy* (אֲדֹנָי), and translated "LORD" (all capital letters) (cf. *G*.16.6, p. 32). יְהוָה is used here as a vocative, a means of addressing a person or thing. Translation: "O LORD."

Translation:

זָכַרְתִּי בַלַּיְלָה שִׁמְךָ יְהוָה "I remember your name in the night, O LORD."

4. וְלֹא־הָלְכוּ בְּתוֹרָתִי (Jer. 44:10)

(1) וְלֹא־, the vav conjunction וְ ("and"), plus the negative particle לֹא ("not"). A maqqef joins וְלֹא to the following word (cf. *G*.4, p. 12).

(2) הָלְכוּ, Qal perfect, third common plural, from the verb הָלַךְ, "he walked," translated "they walked." United by maqqef, the verb and the negative particle are translated as a unit: "they did not walk." The meteg in the initial syllable indicates that the syllable is open and that therefore the sheva under ל is a vocal sheva [cf. *G*.9.2(3), p. 18].

(3) בְּתוֹרָתִי, the preposition בְּ ("in") prefixed to the noun תּוֹרָה, "law," in its construct form (תּוֹרַת), plus the first common singular pronominal suffix, "my." The preposition בְּ lacks a dagesh lene because the preceding word ends in a vowel. Pronominal suffixes on nouns indicate that the nouns are in the construct state. The literal meaning of תּוֹרָתִי is "the law of me." The translation of בְּתוֹרָתִי is "in my law." Translation:

וְלֹא־הָלְכוּ בְּתוֹרָתִי "And they did not walk in my law."

Suggestions for Further Testing

1. Write the Qal perfect inflection of כָּתַב, "he wrote."

3 ms	כתב	3 cp	כתב
3 fs	כתב		
2 ms	כתב	2 mp	כתב
2 fs	כתב	2 fp	כתב
1 cp	כתב	1 cp	כתב

2. Locate and translate the following forms.

Example: שָׁכַבְתִּי Qal Perfect, 1 cs, from שָׁכַב, "he lay down," translated "I lay down."

(1) מָשַׁלְתִּי

(2) שָׁכַבְנוּ

(3) שָׁכַבְתָּ

(4) שְׁמַרְתֶּם

(5) מָלְכוּ

(6) אָהַבְתְּ

(7) פָּקְדָה

(8) מְשַׁלְתֶּן

3. Translate the following:

(1) וְאֵלֶּה הַמְּלָכִים אֲשֶׁר מָלְכוּ   (Gen. 36:31)

(2) וְשָׁמַר יְהוָה אֱלֹהֶיךָ הַבְּרִית   (Deut. 7:12)

(3) אִישׁ הָאֱלֹהִים אֲשֶׁר שָׁלַחְתָּ   (Judg. 13:8)

(4) וְאַתָּה אֶת־עַבְדְּךָ יָדַעְתָּ   (1 Chr. 17:18)

(5) וְהוּא לֹא יָדַע   (Hos. 7:9)

(6) כִּי לֹא יָדְעוּ מַה־הוּא   (Exod. 16:15)

(7) וְהִיא לֹא יָדְעָה   (Hos. 2:10)

(8) הָלַךְ יִשְׂרָאֵל בַּמִּדְבָּר   (Josh. 14:10)

LESSON XIII

Answer Key
(Cf. *G*, pp. 101ff.)

XIII.1 Fill in the blanks with the correct pronouns.

(1) מַה־הַדָּבָר הָרָע הַזֶּה ___What___ is ___this___ evil thing? (Neh. 13:17)

(2) אַיֵּה כְבוֹדִי (a) Where is ___my___ glory (honor)? (Mal. 1:6)

(3) וּמִי כָמוֹךָ בְּיִשְׂרָאֵל And ___who___ is like ___you___ in Israel? (1 Sam. 26:15)

(4) הֲלֹא יְהוָה אֱלֹהֵיכֶם עִמָּכֶם (b) Is not the LORD ___your___ God with ___you___ ? (1 Chr. 22:18)

(5) הֲלֹא כָל־הָאָרֶץ לְפָנֶיךָ (b) Is not all the land before ___you___ ? (Gen. 13:9)

(6) מִי אַתָּה בְּנִי (a) ___Who___ are ___you___ , ___my___ son? (Gen. 27:18)

(7) מִי־אַתָּה (c) ___Who___ are ___you___ ? (Gen. 27:32)

(8) לְמִי־אַתָּה (d) ___To whom___ are ___you___ ? (Gen. 32:18; Eng. 32:17)

(9) מַה־שְּׁמֶךָ (e) ___What___ is ___your___ name? (Gen. 32:28)

(10) מִי הָאֲנָשִׁים הָאֵלֶּה עִמָּךְ ___Who___ are ___these___ men with ___you___ ? (Num. 22:9)

(11) מַה־זֶּה בְיָדֶךָ (f) ___What___ is ___this___ in ___your___ hand? (Exod. 4:2)

(12) הֲזֶה אֲחִיכֶם הַקָּטֹן Is ___this___ ___your___ youngest brother? (Gen. 43:29)

(13) אַחַי מֵאַיִן אַתֶּם ___My___ brothers, where are ___you___ from? (Gen. 29:4)

(14) וְאַיֵּה נְבִיאֵיכֶם And where are ___your___ prophets? (Jer. 37:19)

(15) אֲחֹתִי הִוא (g) ___She___ is ___my___ sister. (Gen. 26:9)

61

XIII.2 Match the following:

(1) (D) מַה־שֶּׁם־בְּנוֹ‎(h)   (A) Where is Sarah your wife? (Gen. 18:9)

(2) (G) הֲלֹא הוּא אָבִיךָ‎(b)   (B) Where is your God? (Ps. 42:4; Eng. 42:3)

(3) (J) מִי זֶה מֶלֶךְ הַכָּבוֹד   (C) the LORD God of your ancestors
                                              (Deut. 1:21)

(4) (A) אַיֵּה שָׂרָה אִשְׁתֶּךָ‎(i)   (D) What is his son's name? (Prov. 30:4)

(5) (K) אַיֵּה אֱלֹהֵיהֶם   (E) Do they not belong to us? (Gen. 34:23)

(6) (B) אַיֵּה אֱלֹהֶיךָ   (F) in the days of your ancestors (Joel 1:2)

(7) (C) יְהוָה אֱלֹהֵי אֲבֹתֶיךָ   (G) Is he not your father? (Deut. 32:6)

(8) (L) יְהוָה אֱלֹהֵי אֲבוֹתָיו   (H) Was not this my word? (Jon. 4:2)

(9) (F) בִּימֵי אֲבֹתֵיכֶם   (I) you and your ancestors (Jer. 44:3)

(10) (H) הֲלוֹא־זֶה דְבָרִי‎(b)   (J) Who is this king of glory? (Ps. 24:8)

(11) (I) אַתֶּם וַאֲבֹתֵיכֶם   (K) Where is their God? (Joel 2:17)

(12) (E) הֲלוֹא לָנוּ הֵם‎(b)   (L) the LORD God of his ancestors
                                              (2 Chr. 30:19)

XIII.3 Match the following:(j)

(1) (O) שְׁנֵיהֶם יַחְדָּו   (A) in one day (Isa. 10:17)

(2) (K) בֵּין שְׁנֵיהֶם   (B) on the fifth day (Num. 7:36)

(3) (F) שְׁנֵיהֶם לְבַדָּם   (C) on the sixth day (Exod. 16:5)

(4) (I) בֵּין שְׁנֵינוּ   (D) on the tenth day (Num. 7:66)

(5) (N) בַּיּוֹם הַשְּׁמִינִי   (E) on the second day (Num. 7:18)

(6) (A) בְּיוֹם אֶחָד   (F) the two of them alone (1 Kgs. 11:29)

(7) (C) בַּיּוֹם הַשִּׁשִּׁי   (G) on the ninth day (Num. 7:60)

(8) (E) בַּיּוֹם הַשֵּׁנִי   (H) on the third day (Gen. 22:4)

(9) (B) בַּיּוֹם הַחֲמִישִׁי   (I) between the two of us (Gen. 31:37)

(10) (D) בַּיּוֹם הָעֲשִׂירִי   (J) on.the seventh day (Exod. 16:27)

(11) (M) בַּיּוֹם הָרִאשׁוֹן   (K) between the two of them (Exod. 22:10;
                                              Eng. 22:11)

(12) (H) בַּיּוֹם הַשְּׁלִישִׁי   (L) on the fourth day (Num. 7:30)

(13) (J) בַּיּוֹם הַשְּׁבִיעִי   (M) on the first day (Exod. 12:15)

(14) (L) בַּיּוֹם הָרְבִיעִי   (N) on the eighth day (Exod. 22:29;
                                              Eng. 22:30)

(15) (G) בַּיּוֹם הַתְּשִׁיעִי   (O) the two of them together (Gen. 22:6)

XIII.4 Answer the following questions by translating the Hebrew phrases.
Example:

On which day did God rest?

בַּיּוֹם הַשְּׁבִיעִי (Gen. 2:2)

Answer: "on the seventh day"

(1) What was the total length of David's reign?

אַרְבָּעִים שָׁנָה (2 Sam. 5:4)

Answer: "forty years"

(2) How long did David reign in Hebron?

שֶׁבַע שָׁנִים וְשִׁשָּׁה חֳדָשִׁים (2 Sam. 5:5)

Answer: "seven years and six months"

(3) How long did David reign in Jerusalem?

שְׁלֹשִׁים וְשָׁלֹשׁ שָׁנָה (2 Sam. 5:5)

Answer: "thirty and three years"

(4) How long did it rain?

אַרְבָּעִים יוֹם וְאַרְבָּעִים לַיְלָה (Gen. 7:12)

Answer: forty days and forty nights"

(5) How long did Adam live?

תְּשַׁע מֵאוֹת שָׁנָה וּשְׁלֹשִׁים שָׁנָה (Gen. 5:5)

Answer: "nine hundred years and thirty years"

(6) How long did Methuselah live?

תֵּשַׁע וְשִׁשִּׁים שָׁנָה וּתְשַׁע מֵאוֹת שָׁנָה (Gen. 5:27)

Answer: "nine and sixty years and nine hundred years"

(7) How long did Abraham live?

מְאַת שָׁנָה וְשִׁבְעִים שָׁנָה וְחָמֵשׁ שָׁנִים (Gen. 25:7)

Answer: "one hundred years and seventy years and five years"

(8) How long did Sarah live?

מֵאָה שָׁנָה וְעֶשְׂרִים שָׁנָה וְשֶׁבַע שָׁנִים (Gen. 23:1)

Answer: "one hundred years and twenty years and seven years"

(9) How long did the Israelites remain in Egypt?

שְׁלֹשִׁים שָׁנָה וְאַרְבַּע מֵאוֹת שָׁנָה (Exod. 12:40)

Answer: "thirty years and four hundred years"

(10) How many faithful Israelites had not bowed the knee to Baal?

שִׁבְעַת אֲלָפִים (1 Kgs. 19:18)

Answer: "seven thousand"

(11)   How many men participated in the exodus from Egypt?

שֵׁשׁ־מֵאוֹת אֶלֶף (Exod. 12:37)

Answer: "six hundred thousand"

(12)   How many sons and daughters were born to Job?

שִׁבְעָה בָנִים וְשָׁלוֹשׁ בָּנוֹת (Job 1:2)

Answer: "seven sons and three daughters"

(13)   How many sheep did Job own?

אַרְבָּעָה עָשָׂר אֶלֶף (Job 42:12)

Answer: "fourteen thousand"

(14)   How many camels did Job own?

שֵׁשֶׁת אֲלָפִים (Job 42:12)

Answer: "six thousand"

(15)   When was Passover celebrated?

בְּאַרְבָּעָה עָשָׂר לַחֹדֶשׁ הָרִאשׁוֹן (2 Chr. 35:1)

Answer: "on the fourteenth of the first month"

(16)   How old was Abram when he left Haran?

חָמֵשׁ שָׁנִים וְשִׁבְעִים שָׁנָה (Gen. 12:4)

Answer: "five years and seventy years"

(17)   How many trained warriors did Abram have in his household?

שְׁמֹנָה עָשָׂר וּשְׁלֹשׁ מֵאוֹת (Gen. 14:14)

Answer: "eighteen and three hundred"

(18)   How many sons were born to Jacob?

שְׁנֵים עָשָׂר (Gen. 35:22)

Answer: "twelve"

XIII.5   Each of the following entries contains a Qal perfect form of a Hebrew verb. Complete the translation of the verb forms by filling in the blanks. In the space marked (a) give the person, gender, and number of the form, and in (b) give its root (Qal perfect 3 ms).

Example:

וּקְרָאתֶם בְּשֵׁם אֱלֹהֵיכֶם And you shall ___call___   (a)   2 mp

on the name of your gods. (1 Kgs. 18:24)   (b)   קָרָא

(1)   וּמִמִּצְרַיִם קָרָאתִי לִבְנִי And from Egypt I ___called___   (a)   1 cs

my son. (Hos. 11:1)   (b)   קָרָא

(2) עַל־כֵּן קָרְאָה שְׁמוֹ יְהוּדָה Therefore she ___called___ his name Judah. (Gen. 29:35)

    (a) 3 fs
    (b) קָרָא

(3) אֵיךְ כָּתַבְתָּ אֵת־כָּל־הַדְּבָרִים הָאֵלֶּה How did you ___write___ all these words? (Jer. 36:17)

    (a) 2 ms
    (b) כָּתַב

(4) לָמָּה לֹא־הָלַכְתָּ עִמִּי Why did you not ___walk___ with me? (2 Sam. 19:26)

    (a) 2 ms
    (b) הָלַךְ

(5) לָמָה אָמַרְתָּ (g)אֲחֹתִי הִוא Why did you ___say___, "She is my sister"? (Gen. 12:19)

    (a) 2 ms
    (b) אָמַר

(6) אֵיךְ נָפַלְתָּ מִשָּׁמַיִם How you have ___fallen___ from heaven! (Isa. 14:12)

    (a) 2 ms
    (b) נָפַל

(7) לֹא יָדַעְתִּי אֵי מִזֶּה הֵמָּה I do not ___know___ where they are from. (1 Sam. 25:11)

    (a) 1 cs
    (b) יָדַע

(8) מַה־(h)יָּדַעְתָּ What do you ___know___? (Job 15:9)

    (a) 2 ms
    (b) יָדַע

(9) וְאָמְרוּ־לִי מַה־(h)שְּׁמוֹ And they shall ___say___ to me, "What is his name?" (Exod. 3:13)

    (a) 3 cp
    (b) אָמַר

(10) הֲלֹא יְדַעְתֶּם מָה־אֵלֶּה Do you not ___know___ what these are? (Ezek. 17:12)

    (a) 2 mp
    (b) יָדַע

(11) לֹא יָדַעְנוּ (l)מֶה־הָיָה לוֹ We do not ___know___ what has become of him. (Exod. 32:1)

    (a) 1 cp
    (b) יָדַע

(12) וּשְׁנֵיהֶם עָמְדוּ עַל־הַיַּרְדֵּן And the two of them ___stood___ beside the Jordan. (2 Kgs. 2:7)

    (a) 3 cp
    (b) עָמַד

Footnotes

(a) כְּבוֹדִי occurs without dagesh lene in its BeGaD KeFaT letters because these are all preceded by vowels. The initial כ is preceded by a word ending in ה, and since final ה (without mappiq) does not close its syllable, כ behaves as if preceded by ṣere. However, if there is a strong disjunctive accent on a word ending in either ה, א, or a vowel, a BeGaD KeFaT letter at the beginning of the following word retains its dagesh lene. A good example is found in exercise *H*.XIII.1(6), p. 61. In מִי אַתָּה בְּנִי, one might have expected בְּנִי to appear without a dagesh lene in the initial בְּ, except for the fact that a strong disjunctive accent appears on אַתָּה, making a separation between it and the following word. Unfortunately, students must determine accentuation by examining the text of a printed Hebrew Bible. In the present exercises the vocalized text is reproduced, but without the accompanying accent signs.

(b) הֲלֹא, the combination of interrogative הֲ and the negative particle לֹא assumes an affirmative response.

(c) אָתָּה is the pausal form (with 'atnaḥ, אָתָּה) for אַתָּה.

(d) אַתָּה is the pausal form for אַתָּה. The accent is one of the weaker disjunctives, however, and while it causes the initial syllable to be stressed, being accented does not cause the vowel to be lengthened.

(e) The dagesh forte in שְׁמֶךָ is called a "conjunctive," or "euphonic" dagesh forte [cf. *G.*34.2(2)(a), p. 95; 45, p. 147]. The conjunctive dagesh forte is very common after words such as זֶה and מָה (מַה־שְּׁמֶךָ). שְׁמֶךָ is also the pausal form (with 'atnaḥ, שְׁמֶךָ).

(f) בְּיָדֶךָ is the pausal form of יָדְךָ (with 'atnaḥ) plus the preposition בְּ, "in," minus dagesh lene because the preceding open syllable ends in הָ (without mappiq).

(g) אֲחֹתִי is normally accented on the final syllable. However, since the accented הוּא follows it, אֲחֹתִי is forced to be written אֲחֹתִי. The shift in accent was done for euphonic reasons: to avoid juxtaposing two tone syllables in adjoining words. There are many occurrences of this type of accentuation change in the Hebrew Bible.

(h) This is another example of the conjunctive dagesh forte [cf. footnote (e) above].

(i) אִשְׁתֶּךָ is the pausal form (with 'atnaḥ, אִשְׁתֶּךָ) for אִשְׁתְּךָ.

(j) This exercise provides students an opportunity to review the pointing of the definite article, before both gutturals and non-gutturals (cf. *G.*14, pp. 24ff.).

(k) Numerals from 1-10 are followed by plural nouns. Those beginning with 11 and above are followed by nouns in their singular form.

Examples: (1) עֶשֶׂר שָׁנִים 10 years (Gen. 5:14)

(2) עֶשְׂרִים שָׁנָה 20 years (Gen. 31:38)

(3) שְׁלֹשָׁה אֲנָשִׁים 3 men (Gen. 18:2)

(4) שְׁלֹשִׁים אִישׁ 30 men (Judg. 14:19)

(l) The pointing of the interrogative מָה is normally מֶה when it stands before words beginning with ה or ע [cf. *G.*34.2(2)(c), p. 96].

Suggestions for Further Testing

1. Translate the following:

   (1)   כִּי־גָדֹל עַד־שָׁמַיִם חַסְדֶּךָ   (Ps. 57:11; Eng. 57:10)

   (2)   כִּי־עִם־יְהוָה הַחֶסֶד   (Ps. 130:7)

   (3)   כִּי־גָדוֹל כְּבֹד יְהוָה   (Ps. 138:5)

   (4)   זֶה עֶשְׂרִים שָׁנָה אָנֹכִי עִמָּךְ   (Gen. 31:38)

   (5)   זֶה אַרְבָּעִים שָׁנָה יְהוָה אֱלֹהֶיךָ עִמָּךְ   (Deut. 2:7)

   (6)   כִּי רַבִּים אֲשֶׁר אִתָּנוּ מֵאֲשֶׁר אוֹתָם   (2 Kgs. 6:16)

   (7)   וְשָׁמַר יְהוָה אֱלֹהֶיךָ לְךָ הַבְּרִית   (Deut. 7:12)

   (8)   וְאָהַבְתָּ לְרֵעֲךָ כָּמוֹךָ   (Lev. 19:18)

   (9)   לָמָה אָמַרְתָּ אֲחֹתִי הִוא   (Gen. 12:19)

   (10)   וְגַם לֶחֶם וָיַיִן יֶשׁ־לִי   (Judg. 19:19)

2. Match the following:

   (1) ( )   וְשָׁם אֶבֶן גְּדֹלָה   (A) This is none other than the house of God. (Gen. 28:17)

   (2) ( )   וְשָׁם אִתָּנוּ נַעַר עִבְרִי   (B) You are more righteous than I. (1 Sam. 24:17)

   (3) ( )   וְזֶה פִּרְיָהּ   (C) Who is the wise man? (Jer. 9:11)

   (4) ( )   כָּל־נֶפֶשׁ שִׁבְעָה   (D) And a Hebrew lad was there with us. (Gen. 41:12)

   (5) ( )   אֵין זֶה כִּי אִם־בֵּית אֱלֹהִים   (E) all that was good in the eyes of Israel (2 Sam. 3:19)

   (6) ( )   אִישׁ אֲשֶׁר רוּחַ אֱלֹהִים בּוֹ   (F) O LORD, the God of Israel, you are righteous. (Ezra. 9:15)

   (7) ( )   כָּל־אֲשֶׁר טוֹב בְּעֵינֵי יִשְׂרָאֵל   (G) Am I not a Benjaminite? (1 Sam. 9:21)

   (8) ( )   צַדִּיק אַתָּה מִמֶּנִּי   (H) Where are your mercies, O Lord? (Ps. 89:50; Eng. 89:49)

   (9) ( )   יְהוָה אֱלֹהֵי יִשְׂרָאֵל צַדִּיק אַתָּה   (I) All the living beings were seven. (Gen. 46:25)

   (10) ( )   הֲלֹא בֶן־יְמִינִי אָנֹכִי   (J) And a great stone was there. (1 Sam. 6:14)

   (11) ( )   מִי־הָאִישׁ הֶחָכָם   (K) a man in whom there is the spirit of God (Gen. 41:38)

   (12) ( )   אַיֵּה חֲסָדֶיךָ אֲדֹנָי   (L) And this is its fruit. (Num. 13:27)

3. Complete the translation by supplying the correct pronouns.

(1) מַה־הוּא

_____ is _____? (Exod. 16:5)

(2) מִי־אֵלֶּה

_____ are _____? (Gen. 48:8)

(3) מַה־שְּׁמוֹ וּמַה־שֶּׁם־בְּנוֹ

_____ is _____ name, and _____ is _____ son's name? (Prov. 30:4)

(4) וּמָה־הָאָרֶץ הֲיֵשׁ־בָּהּ עֵץ אִם־אַיִן

And _____ of the land? Are there trees in _____ or not (none)? (Num. 13:20)

(5) אֵת אֲשֶׁר־טוֹב בְּעֵינֶיךָ

that which is good in _____ eyes (2 Sam. 19:38)

(6) כְּכֹל אֲשֶׁר בִּלְבָבִי

according to all that is in _____ heart (2 Kgs. 10:30)

(7) וְשָׁפַטְתִּי בֵּין אִישׁ וּבֵין רֵעֵהוּ

And _____ will judge between a man and (between) _____ neighbor (Exod. 18:16)

(8) שְׁנֵים־עָשָׂר אֲנַחְנוּ אַחִים בְּנֵי אָבִינוּ

_____ are twelve brothers, the sons of _____ father. (Gen. 42:32)

(9) הוּא וְשֵׁשׁ־מֵאוֹת אִישׁ אֲשֶׁר אִתּוֹ

_____ and six hundred men _____ (were) with _____ (1 Sam. 30:9)

(10) אֲשֶׁר הִיא טוֹבָה לָךְ מִשִּׁבְעָה בָּנִים

_____ is better to _____ than seven sons. (Ruth 4:15)

(11) הֲלֹא־הוּא אָבִיךָ

Is _____ not _____ father? (Deut. 32:6)

(12) וְעִמּוֹ אַרְבַּע מֵאוֹת אִישׁ

and with _____ four hundred men (Gen. 33:1)

68

LESSON XIV

Answer Key
(Cf. *G*, pp. 121ff.)

XIV.1 Write the full perfect inflection of the verb מָשַׁל, "he ruled," in each of the
following stems, indicating the person, gender, and number of each form (cf.
G.37, pp. 113ff.).

	(1) Qal Perfect		(2) Nifᶜal Perfect	
3 ms	מָשַׁל	he ruled	נִמְשַׁל	he was ruled
3 fs	מָשְׁלָה	she ruled	נִמְשְׁלָה	she was ruled
2 ms	מָשַׁלְתָּ	you ruled	נִמְשַׁלְתָּ	you were ruled
2 fs	מָשַׁלְתְּ	you ruled	נִמְשַׁלְתְּ	you were ruled
1 cs	מָשַׁלְתִּי	I ruled	נִמְשַׁלְתִּי	I was ruled
3 cp	מָשְׁלוּ	they ruled	נִמְשְׁלוּ	they were ruled
2 mp	מְשַׁלְתֶּם	you ruled	נִמְשַׁלְתֶּם	you were ruled
2 fp	מְשַׁלְתֶּן	you ruled	נִמְשַׁלְתֶּן	you were ruled
1 cp	מָשַׁלְנוּ	we ruled	נִמְשַׁלְנוּ	we were ruled

	(3) Piᶜel Perfect		(4) Hifᶜil Perfect	
3 ms	מִשֵּׁל	he ruled (with force)	הִמְשִׁיל	he caused to rule
3 fs	מִשְּׁלָה	she ruled (with force)	הִמְשִׁילָה	she caused to rule
2 ms	מִשַּׁלְתָּ	you ruled (with force)	הִמְשַׁלְתָּ	you caused to rule
2 fs	מִשַּׁלְתְּ	you ruled (with force)	הִמְשַׁלְתְּ	you caused to rule
1 cs	מִשַּׁלְתִּי	I ruled (with force)	הִמְשַׁלְתִּי	I caused to rule
3 cp	מִשְּׁלוּ	they ruled (with force)	הִמְשִׁילוּ	they caused to rule
2 mp	מִשַּׁלְתֶּם	you ruled (with force)	הִמְשַׁלְתֶּם	you caused to rule
2 fp	מִשַּׁלְתֶּן	you ruled (with force)	הִמְשַׁלְתֶּן	you caused to rule
1 cp	מִשַּׁלְנוּ	we ruled (with force)	הִמְשַׁלְנוּ	we caused to rule

XIV.2 Indicate the three root consonants in each of the following perfects.

Example: קָטַל   הִקְטִיל

(1)	מָשַׁל	הִמְשִׁילוּ	(10)	[לחם]	נִלְחַם
(2)	נָתַן	נָתְנָה	(11)	קָטַל	הָקְטַלְתֶּן
(3)	שָׁמַר	שְׁמַרְתְּ	(12)	רדף	רֻדְּפוּ
(4)	גָּדַל	גָּדְלָה	(13)	נפל	נָפְלוּ
(5)	[דבר](a)	דִּבַּרְנוּ	(14)	זכר	הִזְכַּרְתִּי
(6)	קדשׁ	הִתְקַדְּשָׁה	(15)	כשׁל	הִכְשַׁלְתָּ
(7)	כשׁל	הִכְשַׁלְתֶּם	(16)	קדשׁ	קִדַּשָׁנוּ
(8)	שׁבר	נִשְׁבְּרוּ	(17)	פקד	הִתְפָּקְדוּ
(9)	מָשַׁל	הִמְשַׁלְתִּי	(18)	[ברך](a)	הִבְרַכְתֶּם

XIV.3 Indicate the stem to which each of the following perfects belongs.

Example: מְשַׁלְתֶּם   Qal

(1)	בִּקֵּשׁ	Pi'el	(10)	נִלְכְּדָה	Nif'al
(2)	הִבְדַּלְתִּי	Hif'il	(11)	לֻמַּדְתָּ	Pi'el
(3)	דִּבְּרוּ	Pi'el	(12)	הָשְׁבַּרְתִּי	Hof'al
(4)	שָׁמַעְתִּי	Qal	(13)	הִכְשַׁלְתֶּם	Hif'il
(5)	הִשְׁמִיד	Hif'il	(14)	נִמְכַּרְנוּ	Nif'al
(6)	לֻקַּח	Pu'al	(15)	סֻפַּר	Pu'al
(7)	נִכְרַת	Nif'al	(16)	נִסְתְּרָה	Nif'al
(8)	הִכְבַּדְתִּי	Hif'il	(17)	הִסְתִּיר	Hif'il
(9)	קִדַּשְׁתִּי	Pi'el	(18)	הִבְדִּיל	Hif'il

XIV.4 Vocabulary Review: Match the following words so that opposites are paired. For example, the opposite of זָכָר, "male," is נְקֵבָה, "female," therefore the letter E (E) is placed in the block opposite זָכָר.

(1)	(E)	זָכָר	(10)	(P)	אֵשׁ	(A)	נָתַן	(J)	הִיא
(2)	(O)	מִלְחָמָה	(11)	(A)	לָקַח	(B)	אִשָּׁה	(K)	לַיְלָה
(3)	(L)	בֹּקֶר	(12)	(M)	אָח	(C)	רָחֹק	(L)	עֶרֶב
(4)	(N)	מֶלֶךְ	(13)	(H)	גָּדוֹל	(D)	רוּחַ	(M)	אָחוֹת
(5)	(Q)	אֶרֶץ	(14)	(J)	הוּא	(E)	נְקֵבָה	(N)	עֶבֶד
(6)	(R)	אוֹר	(15)	(C)	קָרֵב	(F)	רַע	(O)	שָׁלוֹם
(7)	(K)	יוֹם	(16)	(I)	בָּנוֹת	(G)	אָב	(P)	מַיִם
(8)	(B)	אִישׁ	(17)	(D)	בָּשָׂר	(H)	קָטֹן	(Q)	שָׁמַיִם
(9)	(F)	טוֹב	(18)	(G)	אֵם	(I)	בָּנִים	(R)	חֹשֶׁךְ

XIV.5 Each of the following entries contains a perfect form of a Hebrew verb. Supply the proper translation of the verb form by filling in the blank. In the space marked (a) give its stem, in (b) its person, gender, and number (abbreviated), and in (c) its root.

Example:

וְנִכְרַת מֵעַמָּיו

He shall be __cut off__ from his people.

(Exod. 30:33)

(a) ___Nif'al___

(b) ___3 ms___

(c) ___כָּרַת___

(1) מִי־בִקֵּשׁ זֹאת מִיֶּדְכֶם

Who has __sought__ this from your hand? (Isa. 1:12)

(a) ___Pi'el___

(b) ___3 ms___

(c) ___[בקשׁ](a)___

(2) לֶחֶם לֹא אָכַלְתִּי

I have not __eaten__ bread. (Deut. 9:9)

(a) ___Qal___

(b) ___1 cs___

(c) ___אָכַל___

(3) כִּי מִמֶּנָּה (b)לֻקָּחְתָּ

For from it you were __taken__ . (Gen. 3:19)

(a) ___Pu'al___

(b) ___2 ms___

(c) ___לָקַח___

(4) הֲלֹא כָתַבְתִּי לָךְ

Have I not __written__ to (for) you? (Prov. 22:20)

(a) ___Qal___

(b) ___1 cs___

(c) ___כָּתַב___

(5) וְאָנֹכִי עָמַדְתִּי בָהָר

And I __stood__ on the mountain. (Deut. 10:10)

(a) ___Qal___

(b) ___1 cs___

(c) ___עָמַד___

(6) לֹא־שָׁלַחְתִּי אֶת־הַנְּבִאִים

I did not __send__ the prophets. (Jer. 23:21)

(a) ___Qal___

(b) ___1 cs___

(c) ___שָׁלַח___

(7) כִּי־(c)מָצָאתָ חֵן בְּעֵינָי

For you have __found__ favor in my eyes.

(Exod. 33:17)

(a) ___Qal___

(b) ___2 ms___

(c) ___מָצָא___

(8) נִמְצְאוּ דְבָרֶיךָ

Your words were __found__ . (Jer. 15:16)

(a) ___Nif'al___

(b) ___3 cp___

(c) ___מָצָא___

71

(9) וְהִנֵּה נָפְלוּ אֲבוֹתֵינוּ בְּחָרֶב (d)

And behold, our ancestors have __fallen__ by
the sword. (2 Chr. 29:9)

(a) ___Qal___
(b) ___3 cp___
(c) נָפַל

(10) פָּקַד יְהוָה אֶת־עַמּוֹ

The LORD had __visited__ his people. (Ruth 1:6)

(a) ___Qal___
(b) ___3 ms___
(c) פָּקַד

(11) שָׁלַחְתִּי אֲלֵיכֶם אֵת הַמִּצְוָה הַזֹּאת

I have __sent__ to you this commandment.
(Mal. 2:4)

(a) ___Pi‘el___
(b) ___1 cs___
(c) שָׁלַח

(12) דִּבַּרְנוּ אֵלֶיךָ בְּמִצְרַיִם

We __spoke__ to you in Egypt. (Exod. 14:12)

(a) ___Pi‘el___
(b) ___1 cp___
(c) [דבר](a)

XIV.6 Fill in the blanks with the correct pronouns.

(1) הִבְדַּלְתִּי אֶתְכֶם מִן־הָעַמִּים ___I___ have separated ___you___
from the peoples. (Lev. 20:24)

(2) מָצָאתִי דָוִד עַבְדִּי (c) ___I___ have found David ___my___ servant.
(Ps. 89:21; Eng. 89:20)

(3) וּבִקְשׁוּ אֶת־יְהוָה אֱלֹהֵיהֶם (e) And ___they___ shall seek the LORD
___their___ God. (Hos. 3:5)

(4) לֹא אֶת־אֲבֹתֵינוּ כָּרַת יְהוָה אֶת־הַבְּרִית הַזֹּאת כִּי אִתָּנוּ Not with
___our___ ancestors did the LORD make (cut) ___this___ covenant, but
with ___us___ . (Deut. 5:3)

(5) וְהִכְרַתִּי אֹתָהּ מִקֶּרֶב עַמָּהּ (e) And ___I___ will cut ___her___ off
from the midst of ___her___ people. (Lev. 17:10)

(6) וְהִכְרַתִּי סוּסֶיךָ מִקִּרְבֶּךָ (e)(f) And ___I___ will cut off ___your___
horses from the midst of ___you___ . (Mic. 5:9; Eng. 5:10)

(7) אֵיךְ כָּתַבְתָּ אֶת־כָּל־הַדְּבָרִים הָאֵלֶּה מִפִּיו How did ___you___ write
all ___these___ words from ___his___ mouth? (Jer. 36:17)

(8) וְאֶת־אִשְׁתּוֹ לָקָחְתָּ And ___his___ wife ___you___ have taken.
(2 Sam. 12:9)

(9) וְנָפַלְתָּ אַתָּה וִיהוּדָה עִמָּךְ (e)(g) And ___you___ shall fall, and Judah with
___you___ . (2 Chr. 25:19)

(10) וַעֲבַדְתֶּם אֹתָנוּ (h) And ___they___ shall serve ___us___ . (1 Sam. 17:9)

72

(11) וְשָׁכַבְתִּי עִם־אֲבֹתַי (e) And ___I___ will lie down with ___my___ ancestors. (Gen. 47:30)

(12) וְשִׁלַּחְתִּי־אֵשׁ בְּעָרָיו (e) And ___I___ will send fire upon ___his___ cities. (Hos. 8:14)

(13) דִּבַּרְנוּ אֵלֶיךָ בְמִצְרַיִם ___We___ spoke to ___you___ in Egypt. (Exod. 14:12)

(14) דִּבְּרוּ אֶחָיו אִתּוֹ ___His___ brothers spoke with ___him___. (Gen. 45:15)

Footnotes

(a) A bracketed verb root indicates one that rarely, if ever, occurs in the Qal stem (cf. *G*, "Vocabulary, " pp. 374ff.).

(b) לְקַחְתָּ is pausal (with 'atnaḥ, לְקַחְתָּ) for לְקַחְתְּ.

(c) The Lamed 'Alef מָצָא is a weak verb (cf. *G*, pp. 275ff.). When א occurs at the end of a word or a syllable within a word, as in מָצָאת, it becomes quiescent (ceases to function as a consonant). Because quiescent א cannot close its syllable, the preceding vowel must be long. Thus, pataḥ has been lengthened to qameṣ. Note also that the ת loses its dagesh lene because it follows an open syllable.

(d) בֶּחָרֶב is pausal (with 'atnaḥ, בֶּחָרֶב) for בַּחֶרֶב. Note the additional change in the pointing of the definite article. Before חֶ (חֶרֶב) the definite article is הַ (הַחֶרֶב); however, before the pausal long vowel חָ (חָרֶב), the definite article occurs as הֶ (הֶחָרֶב) [cf. *G*.14.3(2)(c), p. 25]. The preposition בְּ is also added and הֶחָרֶב becomes בֶּחָרֶב [cf. *G*.15.1(4), p. 29].

(e) A perfect that is prefixed with vav conjunction will ordinarily be translated in the future tense [cf. *G*.31.1(4), p. 86]. Note that these forms are accented on the final syllable.

(f) מִקִּרְבֶּךָ is the pausal (with 'atnaḥ, מִקִּרְבֶּךָ) for מִקִּרְבְּךָ, with prefixed מִן, "from," and second masculine singular pronominal suffix: "from your midst."

(g) עִמָּךְ is pausal (with silluq, עִמָּךְ) for עִמְּךָ.

(h) The volatilization of the long vowel in the nearest open syllable before the תֶּם ending caused ḥatef-pataḥ to be placed under the initial guttural in עֲבַדְתֶּם (gutturals prefer compound shevas). For the pointing of vav conjunction before compound shevas, see *G*.16.4, p. 31.

Suggestions for Further Testing

1. The following quotations from the Hebrew Bible contain examples of perfect forms representing a variety of stems. Locate the verb in each of the quotations, using the form suggested here.

   Example: נָפְלוּ Qal perfect, 3 cp, from נָפַל, "he fell." Trans. "They fell."

   (1)   וְלֹא שָׁמַעְנוּ בְּקֹלוֹ   (Dan. 9:14)

   (2)   וְנִכְרַת הָאִישׁ הַהוּא מִקֶּרֶב עַמּוֹ   (Lev. 17:4)

   (3)   מִיּוֹם דִּבַּרְתִּי אֵלֶיךָ   (Jer. 36:2)

   (4)   אַתָּה יָדַעְתָּ אֶת־הָעָם   (Exod. 32:22)

   (5)   יְדַעְתֶּם אֶת־הָאִישׁ   (2 Kgs. 9:11)

   (6)   כִּי עַתָּה שְׁלַחְתִּי אֵלֶיךָ   (Dan. 10:11)

   (7)   כִּי שִׁלַּחְנוּ אֶת־יִשְׂרָאֵל   (Exod. 14:5)

   (8)   אַתָּה הִמְלַכְתָּ אֶת־עַבְדֶּךָ   (1 Kgs. 3:7)

   (9)   וּמָלַךְ יְהוָה עֲלֵיהֶם   (Mic. 4:7)

   (10)   אֲשֶׁר שָׁמַעְתִּי בְּאַרְצִי   (1 Kgs. 10:6)

   (11)   וְלֹא־שְׁמַעְתֶּם בְּקֹלוֹ   (Deut. 9:23)

   (12)   וְנִכְרְתָה הַנֶּפֶשׁ הַהוּא מִיִּשְׂרָאֵל   (Gen. 17:14)

2. Translate the sentences and clauses given in #1.

LESSON XV

Answer Key
(Cf. *G*, pp. 132ff.)

XV.1 Write the Qal imperfect of כָּתַב, "he wrote." Translate each of the forms.

(1) 3 ms יִכְתֹּב he will write   (6) 3 mp יִכְתְּבוּ(a) they will write

(2) 3 fs תִּכְתֹּב she will write   (7) 3 fp תִּכְתֹּבְנָה they will write

(3) 2 ms תִּכְתֹּב you will write   (8) 2 mp תִּכְתְּבוּ(a) you will write

(4) 2 fs תִּכְתְּבִי(a) you will write   (9) 2 fp תִּכְתֹּבְנָה you will write

(5) 1 cs אֶכְתֹּב I will write   (10) 1 cp נִכְתֹּב we will write

XV.2 Match the following:

(1) (I)   יִכְבְּדוּ בָנָיו(a)   (A) In order that you may learn. (Deut. 14:23)

(2) (L)   לְמַעַן תִּזְכְּרוּ(a)   (B) I shall keep your flock. (Gen. 30:31)

(3) (G)   אֲנִי אֶמְלֹךְ   (C) They shall lie down together. (Isa. 43:17)

(4) (O)   שָׁאוּל יִמְלֹךְ עָלֵינוּ   (D) The LORD will rule over you. (Judg. 8:23)

(5) (A)   לְמַעַן תִּלְמַד   (E) And you shall keep my commandments. (Lev. 26:3)

(6) (C)   יַחְדָּו יִשְׁכָּבוּ(a)   (F) These things I remember. (Ps. 42:5; Eng. 42:4)

(7) (B)   צֹאנְךָ אֶשְׁמֹר   (G) I shall reign. (1 Kgs. 1:5)

(8) (E)   וְאֶת־מִצְוֺתַי(b) תִּשְׁמֹרוּ(a)   (H) And you shall keep his commandments. (Deut. 13:5)

(9) (H)   וְאֶת־מִצְוֺתָיו(c) תִּשְׁמֹרוּ   (I) His children are honored. (Job 14:21)

(10) (J)   אֶשְׁפֹּט אֶתְכֶם   (J) I shall judge you. (Ezek. 11:11)

(11) (F)   אֵלֶּה אֶזְכְּרָה(d)   (K) In order that they may learn. (Deut. 31:12)

(12) (D)   יְהוָה יִמְשֹׁל בָּכֶם   (L) In order that you may remember. (Num. 15:40)

(13) (M)   אֶזְכְּרָה(d) אֱלֹהִים   (M) I will remember God. (Ps. 77:4; Eng. 77:3)

(14) (K)　　　　לְמַעַן (a)יִלְמְדוּ　　　(N) Perhaps the LORD will hear.
　　　　　　　　　　　　　　　　　　　　　(Isa. 37:4)

(15) (N)　　　　אוּלַי (e)יִשְׁמַע יְהוָה　　(O) Saul shall reign over us.
　　　　　　　　　　　　　　　　　　　　　(1 Sam. 11:12)

XV.3 Fill in the blanks with the correct pronouns.

(1)　פֶּן־(e)תִּשְׁכַּח אֶת־יְהוָה אֱלֹהֶיךָ　Lest ___you___ forget the LORD ___your___
　　　God. (Deut. 8:11)

(2)　כִּי־תִשְׁמֹר אֶת־כָּל־הַמִּצְוָה הַזֹּאת　For ___you___ shall keep all
　　　___this___ commandment. (Deut. 19:9)

(3)　אִם־(a)יִשְׁמְרוּ בָנֶיךָ בְּרִיתִי　If ___your___ sons keep ___my___ covenant.
　　　(Ps. 132:12)

(4)　(c)נִשְׁלְחָה אֲנָשִׁים לְפָנֵינוּ　Let ___us___ send men before ___us___ .
　　　(Deut. 1:22)

(5)　וְלֹא (e)אֶשְׁמַע אֲלֵיהֶם　And ___I___ will not listen to ___them___ .
　　　(Jer. 11:11)

(6)　לֹא־אֶמְשֹׁל אֲנִי בָּכֶם　___I___ will not rule over ___you___ .
　　　(Judg. 8:23)

(7)　(c)נִכְרְתָה בְרִית אֲנִי (f)וְאַתָּה　Let ___us___ make (cut) a covenant,
　　　___I___ and ___you___ . (Gen. 31:44)

(8)　וְאַתָּה אֶת־בְּרִיתִי תִשְׁמֹר　But ___you___ shall keep ___my___
　　　covenant. (Gen. 17:9)

(9)　(g)הֲיִכְרֹת בְּרִית (h)עִמָּךְ　Will ___he___ make (cut) a covenant with
　　　___you___ ? (Job. 40:28; Eng. 41:4)

(10)　(c)וְנִכְרְתָה בְרִית (h)עִמָּךְ　And let ___us___ make a covenant with
　　　___you___ . (Gen. 26:28)

(11)　(a)וְיִכְרְתוּ אִתְּךָ בְּרִית　And ___they___ shall make a covenant with
　　　___you___ . (2 Sam. 3:21)

(12)　כִּי־שְׁלֹמֹה בְנֶךָ יִמְלֹךְ אַחֲרַי　For Solomon ___your___ son shall reign
　　　after ___me___ . (1 Kgs. 1:13)

76

(13) אֶשְׁמְרָה דְרָכַי[d] _____ I _____ will guard _____ my _____ ways. (Ps. 39:2; Eng. 39:1)

(14) אֶשְׁמְרָה תוֹרָתְךָ תָמִיד[d] _____ I _____ will keep _____ your _____ law continually. (Ps. 119:44)

(15) וְאֵיךְ נִגְנֹב מִבֵּית אֲדֹנֶיךָ כֶּסֶף אוֹ זָהָב For how shall _____ we _____ steal silver or gold from the house of _____ your _____ master (lord)? (Gen. 44:8)

XV.4 Each of the following entries contains a Qal imperfect form of a Hebrew verb. Give its correct translation by filling in the blank. In the space marked (a) give its person, gender, and number, and in (b) its root (i.e., its Qal perfect 3 ms form).

(1) לֹא תִגְנֹב You shall not _____ steal _____. (Exod. 20:15)   (a) 2 ms   (b) גָּנַב

(2) לֹא תִּגְנֹבוּ[i] You shall not _____ steal _____. (Lev. 19:11)   (a) 2 mp   (b) גָּנַב

(3) וְחַטֹּאתֶיךָ לֹא אֶזְכֹּר And your sins I will not _____ remember _____. (Isa. 43:25)   (a) 1 cs   (b) זָכַר

(4) לְמַעַן תִּזְכְּרִי[a] In order that you may _____ remember _____. (Ezek. 16:63)   (a) 2 fs   (b) זָכַר

(5) אַל־תִּזְכְּרוּ[a] רִאשֹׁנוֹת _____ Remember _____ not the former things. (Isa. 43:18)   (a) 2 mp   (b) זָכַר

(6) וְאַתָּה תִּמְלֹךְ עַל־יִשְׂרָאֵל And you shall _____ reign _____ over Israel. (1 Sam. 23:17)   (a) 2 ms   (b) מָלַךְ

(7) כִּי אֶשְׁבֹּר אֶת־עֹל מֶלֶךְ בָּבֶל For I will _____ break _____ the yoke of the king of Babylon. (Jer. 28:4)   (a) 1 cs   (b) שָׁבַר

(8) וְהוּא יִשְׁפֹּט־תֵּבֵל בְּצֶדֶק And he will _____ judge _____ the world with righteousness. (Ps. 9:9; Eng. 9:8)   (a) 3 ms   (b) שָׁפַט

(9) הֲתִשְׁפֹּט אֹתָם בֶּן־אָדָם[g] Will you _____ judge _____ them, son of man? (Ezek. 20:4)   (a) 2 ms   (b) שָׁפַט

(10) וּמִצְוֹתַי לֹא יִשְׁמֹרוּ[j] And they do not _____ keep _____ my commandments. (Ps. 89:32; Eng. 89:31)   (a) 3 mp   (b) שָׁמַר

(11) וְיִזְכֹּר אֶת־יְמֵי הַחֹשֶׁךְ But let him __remember__   (a)   __3 ms__

the days of darkness. (Eccl. 11:8)   (b)   זָכַר

(12) וּמִצְרַיִם לֹא ^(a)תִזְכְּרִי־עֹוד And you shall __remember__ (a)   __2 fs__

Egypt no more. (Ezek. 23:27)   (b)   זָכַר

(13) אֶפְקֹד אֶתְכֶם I will __visit__ you. (Jer. 29:10)   (a)   __1 cs__

                                                                 (b)   פָּקַד

(14) לְמַעַן אֶלְמַד חֻקֶּיךָ In order that I may __learn__   (a)   __1 cs__

your statutes. (Ps. 119:71)   (b)   לָמַד

(15) כָּכָה אֶשְׁבֹּר אֶת־הָעָם הַזֶּה וְאֶת־הָעִיר הַזֹּאת (a)   __1 cs__

So will I __break__ this people and this city.   (b)   שָׁבַר

(Jer. 19:11)

Footnotes

(a) When two shevas occur under adjacent consonants within a word, the first will be silent and the second vocal. The first will end its syllable and the second will begin the new syllable. Note the effect this has on BeGaD KeFaT letters.

(b) מִצְוֹתַי, "my commandments," has three full vowels, thus three syllables (מִצְ/וֹ/תַי). The first is closed (מִצְ), the second is open (וֹ), and the third is open (תַי). In the middle syllable וֹ functions as a consonant (a syllable begins with a consonant) and is followed by ḥolem. It would be transliterated as vō.

(c) תִשְׁמֹרוּ is pausal (with minor disjunctive accent) for תִּשְׁמְרוּ.

(d) אַזְכְּרָה has the cohortative ending הָ (cf. G.41.2, p. 132). A cohortative involves first person imperfect forms, either singular or plural, and is used to express the speaker's desire, intention, self-encouragement, or strong determination to perform a certain action.

(e) A Lamed Guttural verb (cf. G.70, pp. 263ff.) occurs with an "a" class vowel before the final guttural. In Qal imperfect forms of the Lamed Guttural verb, the ḥolem is usually replaced with pataḥ (cf. G, Verb Chart 1, p. 400, and Verb Chart 5, p. 408).

(f) וָאַתָּה is pausal (with 'atnaḥ, וָאַתָּה) for וְאַתָּה. The vav conjunction is pointed with qameṣ instead of the usual sheva because the accented syllable has moved to the front of the word (cf. G.16.5, pp. 31f.).

(g) הֲתִשְׁפֹּט is prefixed with interrogative ה (cf. *G*.34.1, pp. 94f.). Interrogative ה usually serves to introduce a simple yes-or-no question.

(h) עִמָּךְ is pausal (usually with ʾatnaḥ, עִמָּךְ [cf. Gen. 32:13]) for עִמְּךָ.

(i) תִּגְנֹבוּ is pausal (with ʾatnaḥ, תִּגְנֹבוּ) for תִּגְנְבוּ.

(j) יִשְׁמֹרוּ is pausal (with silluq, יִשְׁמֹרוּ) for יִשְׁמְרוּ.

Suggestions for Further Testing

1. Match the following:

(1) ( )   וְאֶת־הָרָשָׁע יִשְׁפֹּט   (A) Forever I will keep my steadfast love for him. (Ps. 89:29; Eng. 89:28)

(2) ( )   וּמִלְחָמָה אֶשְׁבּוֹר מִן־הָאָרֶץ   (B) And I will make an everlasting covenant with them. (Isa. 61:8)

(3) ( )   לְעוֹלָם אֶשְׁמָר־לוֹ חַסְדִּי   (C) And you shall break it. (Lev. 11:33)

(4) ( )   לֹא יִזְכְּרוּ־בוּ   (D) And a strong king shall rule over them. (Isa. 19:4)

(5) ( )   פֶּן־תִּכְרֹת בְּרִית   (E) Lest you seek after their gods. (Deut. 12:30)

(6) ( )   וְאֹתוֹ תִשְׁבֹּרוּ   (F) And I will remember the land. (Lev. 26:42)

(7) ( )   פֶּן־תִּדְרֹשׁ לֵאלֹהֵיהֶם   (G) And the wicked he will judge. (Eccl. 3:17)

(8) ( )   וּבְרִית עוֹלָם אֶכְרוֹת לָהֶם   (H) the king who shall rule over them (1 Sam. 8:9)

(9) ( )   וּמֶלֶךְ עַז יִמְשָׁל־בָּם   (I) They shall not remember it. (Jer. 31:16)

(10) ( )   אֶת־בְּרִיתִי אַבְרָהָם אֶזְכֹּר   (J) Lest you make a covenant. (Exod. 34:12)

(11) ( )   הַמֶּלֶךְ אֲשֶׁר יִמְלֹךְ עֲלֵיהֶם   (K) And I will abolish (break) war from the land. (Hos. 2:20; Eng. 2:18)

(12) ( )   וְהָאָרֶץ אֶזְכֹּר   (L) My covenant (with) Abraham I will remember. (Lev. 26:42)

2. Circle the word that does not belong to the category indicated.

(1)	verbs of movement	עָלָה	הָלַךְ	שָׁכַח	בּוֹא
(2)	verbs of making	בָּנָה	בָּרָא	עָשָׂה	אָכַל
(3)	verbs of acquisition	נָפַל	לָקַח	גָּנַב	מָצָא
(4)	verbs of authority	שָׁפַט	מָלַךְ	עָבַד	מָשַׁל
(5)	verbs of mental activity	זָכַר	שָׁכַח	יָדַע	כָּרַת
(6)	metals	נְחֹשֶׁת	צֶלֶם	כֶּסֶף	בַּרְזֶל
(7)	visible in the sky	עָנָן	תְּהוֹם	כּוֹכָב	אוֹר
(8)	architectural structures	בְּהֵמָה	הֵיכָל	חוֹמָה	בַּיִת
(9)	symbols of violence	יֶלֶד	חֶרֶב	דָּם	מִלְחָמָה
(10)	segments of time	מַלְכוּת	שָׁנָה	חֹדֶשׁ	יוֹם

3. Locate the following verbs using the form suggested in the example (cf. Exercise XV.1 above).

Example: יִשְׁפֹּט Qal imperfect 3 ms, from שָׁפַט, "he judged." Translated: "he will judge"

(1) אֶשְׁבּוֹר

(2) אֶשְׁמֹר

(3) יִזְכְּרוּ

(4) תִּכְרֹת

(5) תִּשְׁבְּרוּ

(6) תִּדְרֹשׁ

(7) אֶכְרוֹת

(8) יִמְשֹׁל

(9) אֶזְכֹּר

(10) יִמְלֹךְ

(11) נִמְשֹׁל

(12) תִּשְׁמֹרְנָה

LESSON XVI

Answer Key
(Cf. *G*, pp. 148ff.)

XVI.1 Write the following inflections of the imperfect:

	Qal	Nifʻal	Piʻel	Puʻal	Hitpaʻel	Hifʻil	Hofʻal
3 ms	יִמְשֹׁל	יִקָּבֵר	יְדַבֵּר	יְכֻתַּב	יִתְהַלֵּךְ	יַסְתִּיר	יֻשְׁלַח
3 fs	תִּמְשֹׁל	תִּקָּבֵר	תְּדַבֵּר	תְּכֻתַּב	תִּתְהַלֵּךְ	תַּסְתִּיר	תֻּשְׁלַח
2 ms	תִּמְשֹׁל	תִּקָּבֵר	תְּדַבֵּר	תְּכֻתַּב	תִּתְהַלֵּךְ	תַּסְתִּיר	תֻּשְׁלַח
2 fs	תִּמְשְׁלִי	תִּקָּבְרִי	תְּדַבְּרִי	תְּכֻתְּבִי	תִּתְהַלְּכִי	תַּסְתִּירִי	תֻּשְׁלְחִי
1 cs	אֶמְשֹׁל	אֶקָּבֵר	אֲדַבֵּר	אֲכֻתַּב	אֶתְהַלֵּךְ	אַסְתִּיר	אֻשְׁלַח
3 mp	יִמְשְׁלוּ	יִקָּבְרוּ	יְדַבְּרוּ	יְכֻתְּבוּ	יִתְהַלְּכוּ	יַסְתִּירוּ	יֻשְׁלְחוּ
3 fp	תִּמְשֹׁלְנָה	תִּקָּבַרְנָה	תְּדַבֵּרְנָה	תְּכֻתַּבְנָה	תִּתְהַלֵּכְנָה	תַּסְתֵּרְנָה	תֻּשְׁלַחְנָה
2 mp	תִּמְשְׁלוּ	תִּקָּבְרוּ	תְּדַבְּרוּ	תְּכֻתְּבוּ	תִּתְהַלְּכוּ	תַּסְתִּירוּ	תֻּשְׁלְחוּ
2 fp	תִּמְשֹׁלְנָה	תִּקָּבַרְנָה	תְּדַבֵּרְנָה	תְּכֻתַּבְנָה	תִּתְהַלֵּכְנָה	תַּסְתֵּרְנָה	תֻּשְׁלַחְנָה
1 cp	נִמְשֹׁל	נִקָּבֵר	נְדַבֵּר	נְכֻתַּב	נִתְהַלֵּךְ	נַסְתִּיר	נֻשְׁלַח

XVI.2 Each of the following examples contains an imperfect form of a Hebrew verb. Complete the translation by supplying the meaning of the verb form. In the space marked (a) give its stem, in (b) its person, gender, and number, and in (c) its root.

Example:

וַיִּגְנֹב(a) אַבְשָׁלוֹם אֶת־לֵב אַנְשֵׁי יִשְׂרָאֵל

Absalom ___stole___ the heart of the people of Israel. (2 Sam. 15:6)

(a)   Piʻel
(b)   3 ms
(c)   גָּנַב

(1) וַיִּכְתֹּב(a) בַּסֵּפֶר

And he ___wrote___ in the book. (1 Sam. 10:25)

(a)   Qal
(b)   3 ms
(c)   כָּתַב

(2) אֶת־פָּנֶיךָ יְהוָה אֲבַקֵּשׁ

Your face, O LORD, I will ___seek___ . (Ps. 27:8)

(a)   Piʻel
(b)   1 cs
(c)   [בקשׁ]

(3) וַיִּכְרְתוּ(a) בְרִית בִּבְאֵר(b) שָׁבַע

And they ___made (cut)___ a covenant at Beer-sheba. (Gen. 21:32)

(a)   Qal
(b)   3 mp
(c)   כָּרַת

(4)	וּרְשָׁעִים מֵאֶרֶץ יִכָּרֵתוּ(c)	(a)	Nifʻal
	But the wicked will be __cut off__ from the land.	(b)	3 mp
	(Prov. 2:22)	(c)	כָּרַת
(5)	וָאֶזְכֹּר אֶת־בְּרִיתִי(a)	(a)	Qal
	And I __remembered__ my covenant. (Exod. 6:5)	(b)	1 cs
		(c)	זָכַר
(6)	וַיִּזְכֹּר בְּרִיתוֹ(a)	(a)	Qal
	And he __remembered__ his covenant. (Ps. 106:45)	(b)	3 ms
		(c)	זָכַר
(7)	וְלֹא יִזָּכְרוּ עוֹד	(a)	Nifʻal
	And they shall not be __remembered__ again. (Zech. 13:2)	(b)	3 mp
		(c)	זָכַר
(8)	בֵּן יְכַבֵּד אָב וְעֶבֶד אֲדֹנָיו	(a)	Piʻel
	A son __honors__ (his) father and a servant	(b)	3 ms
	his master. (Mal. 1:6)	(c)	כָּבֵד
(9)	וְאֶת־בְּנֵיהֶם יְלַמֵּדוּן(d)	(a)	Piʻel
	And they shall __teach__ their children (sons).	(b)	3 mp
	(Deut. 4:10)	(c)	לָמַד
(10)	יְהוָה יִלָּחֵם לָכֶם(e)	(a)	Nifʻal
	The LORD shall __fight__ for you. (Exod. 14:14)	(b)	3 ms
		(c)	[לחם]
(11)	וָאֲמַלֵּא אֹתוֹ רוּחַ אֱלֹהִים(a)	(a)	Piʻel
	And I have __filled__ him (with) the Spirit of God.	(b)	1 cs
	(Exod. 31:3)	(c)	מָלֵא
(12)	אַסְתִּירָה פָנַי מֵהֶם(f)	(a)	Hifʻil
	I will __hide__ my face from them. (Deut. 32:20)	(b)	1 cs
		(c)	סָתַר
(13)	וְשָׁם תִּקָּבֵר	(a)	Nifʻal
	And there you shall be __buried__. (Jer. 20:6)	(b)	2 ms
		(c)	קָבַר
(14)	פֶּן־נִשְׂרֹף(g) אוֹתָךְ(h) וְאֶת־בֵּית אָבִיךְ בָּאֵשׁ	(a)	Qal
	Lest we __burn__ you and your father's house	(b)	1 cp
	with fire. (Judg. 14:15)	(c)	שָׂרַף

(15) יְדַבֶּר־נָא ^(j)אֲדֹנִי הַמֶּלֶךְ ⁽ⁱ⁾

    Let my lord the king ___speak___ . (2 Sam. 14:18)

    (a) ___Pi'el___

    (b) ___3 ms___

    (c) ___[דבר]___

XVI.3 Fill in the blanks with the correct pronouns.

(1) וַתֹּאמֶר מִי־אַתְּ בִּתִּי ^(a) And ___she___ said, " ___Who___ are ___you___ , ___my___ daughter?" (Ruth 3:16)

(2) וַיֹּאמֶר לִי מִי־אָתָּה ^(a) And ___he___ said to ___me___ , " ___Who___ are ___you___ ?" (2 Sam. 1:8)

(3) מַה־נֹּאמַר לַאדֹנִי ^(k)מַה־נְּדַבֵּר ^(k) ___What___ shall ___we___ say to ___my___ lord? ___What___ shall ___we___ speak? (Gen. 44:16)

(4) וְשָׁם אֲדַבֵּר ^(b)אוֹתָךְ And there ___I___ will speak with ___you___ . (Ezek. 3:22)

(5) וְלֹא־אֲדַבֵּר עוֹד בִּשְׁמוֹ ___I___ will speak no more in ___his___ name. (Jer. 20:9)

(6) וַיִּשְׂרְפוּ אוֹתָהּ וְאֶת־אָבִיהָ בָּאֵשׁ ^(a) And ___they___ burned ___her___ and ___her___ father with fire. (Judg. 15:6)

(7) בֵּיתֵךְ נִשְׂרֹף בָּאֵשׁ ___Your___ house ___we___ will burn with fire. (Judg. 12:1)

(8) אַל־תַּסְתֵּר מִמֶּנִּי מִצְוֹתֶיךָ ^(m) Do not hide ___your___ commandments from ___me___ . (Ps. 119:19)

(9) וְאַתָּה לֹא תִמָּלֵט מִיָּדוֹ But ___you___ shall not escape (be delivered) from ___his___ hand. (Jer. 34:3)

(10) וּמִפָּנֶיךָ אֶסָּתֵר And from ___your___ face ___I___ shall be hidden. (Gen. 4:14)

(11) וְלֹא־תִלָּחֲמוּ עִם־אֲחֵיכֶם ⁽ⁿ⁾ And ___you___ shall not fight against ___your___ brothers. (2 Chr. 11:4)

(12) יְהַלְלוּ שְׁמוֹ ^(o) Let ___them___ praise ___his___ name. (Ps. 149:3)

XVI.4 Complete the translation of the following entries by filling in the blanks.

(1) וַיִּשְׁכַּב דָּוִד עִם־אֲבֹתָיו ^(a) Then David lay down with ___his___ ___ancestors___ . (1 Kgs. 2:10)

(2) בְּיָדְךָ אַפְקִיד רוּחִי Into ___your___ ___hand___ I commit ___my___ ___spirit___ . (Ps. 31:6; Eng. 31:5)

83

(3) וַיִּשְׁמֹר מִצְוֹתָיו [(a)] But he ___kept___ his ___commandments___ . (2 Kgs. 18:6)

(4) הֲלוֹא אֲבַקֵּשׁ אֶת־דָּמוֹ מִיֶּדְכֶם [(p)] Shall I not ___seek___ his ___blood___ from your ___hand___ ? (2 Sam. 4:11)

(5) עַתָּה יִזְכֹּר עֲוֹנָם Now he will ___remember___ their ___iniquity___ . (Jer. 14:10)

(6) וַיְשַׁבֵּר אֹתָם [(a)] And he ___broke___ ___them___ . (Exod. 32:19)

(7) יִשָּׁפְטוּ גוֹיִם עַל־פָּנֶיךָ [(q)] Let the ___nations___ be ___judged___ before you. (Ps. 9:20; Eng. 9:19)

(8) וַעֲבָדַי יִשְׁכְּנוּ־[(r)]שָׁמָּה And my ___servants___ shall ___dwell___ there. (Isa. 65:9)

(9) וְלֹא־יִזָּכְרוּ עוֹד And ___they___ shall be ___remembered___ no more. (Zech. 13:2)

(10) יִזָּכֵר עֲוֹן אֲבֹתָיו [(s)] May the iniquity of his ___ancestors___ be ___remembered___ . (Ps. 109:14)

(11) וַיִּכְתֹּב בְּשֵׁם הַמֶּלֶךְ [(a)] And he ___wrote___ in the ___name___ of the ___king___ . (Est. 8:10)

(12) וְלֹא־יִזָּכֵר שֵׁם־יִשְׂרָאֵל עוֹד [(t)] Let the ___name___ of Israel be ___remembered___ no more. (Ps. 83:5; Eng. 83:4)

Footnotes

(a) וַיִּגְנֹב is an imperfect verb form that is prefixed with a vav consecutive (cf. *G*.43, pp. 145ff.). The vav consecutive occurs only with imperfects and indicates that the translation is to be in the past tense and always in the indicative mode. Vav consecutive is usually written ־וַ (vav, plus pataḥ, plus dagesh forte in the following consonant). Before א (the preformative for first common singular imperfect forms) it is written וָ (since gutturals cannot be doubled) [e.g., *H*.XVI.2(5), (11), pp. 81f.]. Before non-gutturals supported by vocal sheva, the dagesh forte sometimes drops out, leaving וַ unchanged [cf. *H*.XVII.2(1), (3), (6), pp. 81f.].

(b) שָׁבַע is pausal (with 'atnaḥ, שָׁבַע) for שֶׁבַע.

(c) יִכָּרֵתוּ is pausal (with 'atnaḥ, יִכָּרֵתוּ) for יִכָּרְתוּ.

(d) לָמַד, "he learned," expresses a causative meaning in the Piʿel [cf. *G*.36.2(2), p. 109]. יְלַמֵּדוּן is pausal (with silluq, יְלַמֵּדוּן) for יְלַמְּדוּן. The fact that a nun has been added to the end of this Piʿel imperfect third masculine plural form in no way changes its meaning [cf. *G*.39.3(4), p. 128].

(e) The root verb here is [לחם], set off in brackets to indicate that no Qal forms occur in the Hebrew Bible. יִלָּחֵם is the Nifʻal stem, but translated with a simple active sense, "he will fight," similar to that normally found in the Qal stem [cf. *G*.36.1(3), p. 109].

(f) אַסְתִּירָה, a Hifʻil imperfect first common singular, has a הָ suffix, indicating that it is a cohortative (cf. *G*.41.2, p. 132).

(g) Words like פֶּן ("lest"), אִם ("if"), and אוּלַי ("perhaps") introduce verbs that in modern usage would be assigned to the subjunctive mode, i.e., verbs used for subjective, doubtful, hypothetical, or grammatically subordinate statements or questions (cf. *G*.40.3, pp. 130f.).

(h) אוֹתָךְ is אֵת, the sign of the direct object, plus ךְ, the second feminine singular pronominal suffix [cf. *G*.27.2(1), p. 71].

(i) יְדַבֶּר־נָה is the jussive use of the imperfect (cf. *G*.41.1, p. 131).

(j) The word אָדוֹן is used over 300 times in reference to an earthly "lord" (king, master, husband, etc.), and about 30 times in reference to a divine "Lord." The singular form of the noun together with the first person pronominal suffix (אֲדֹנִי) refers to an earthly lord. The plural form (plural of majesty?) with the added first person pronominal suffix (אֲדֹנָי) generally refers to the divine Lord. אֲדֹנָי as a title for God appears 449 times in the Hebrew Bible. [Note: אָדוֹן is not to be confused with יְהוָה, which is only pronounced as אֲדֹנָי, and is translated in most English versions with all capital letters, "LORD."]

(k) The conjunctive dagesh forte is sometimes placed in the initial consonant of a word in order to link it with such words as מַה and זֶה (cf. *G*.45, p. 147).

(l) אוֹתָךְ is pausal (with silluq) for אוֹתָךְ, which consists of the preposition אֵת, "with," plus the second masculine singular pronominal suffix, "with you" [cf. *G*.27.1(3)(a), p. 69].

(m) A negative command or a prohibition is not expressed by the imperative form of the verb. Instead, for this purpose, Hebrew uses either לֹא with the imperfect or אַל ("not") with the jussive (cf. *G*.55, pp. 173f.). The jussive is also an imperfect used in a special way (cf. *G*.41.1, p. 131).

(n) לֹא with an imperfect expresses a prohibition in stronger terms than אַל with the jussive [cf. (m) above].

(o) יְהַלְלוּ is the jussive use of the imperfect.

(p) הֲלֹא introduces a question that presupposes an affirmative answer.

(q) יִשְׁפְּטוּ is the jussive use of the imperfect.

(r) שָׁמָּה is שָׁם, "there," plus the הָ suffix, known as "He-directive" (cf. *G*.44, pp. 146f.). The "He-directive" suffix is never accented. It expresses direction or motion toward a person, place, or thing.

(s) יִזְכֹּר is the jussive use of the imperfect.

(t) לֹא, when used with an imperfect, expresses a strong prohibition (cf. *G*.55, p. 173).

Suggestions for Further Testing

1. Translate the following entries.

(1)	וַיִּקְבְּרוּ אֹתוֹ	(Gen. 35:29)
(2)	וְהִסְתַּרְתִּי פָנַי מֵהֶם	(Deut. 31:17)
(3)	שִׁכַּנְתִּי שְׁמִי שָׁם	(Jer. 7:12)
(4)	דִּבְּרוּ בִּשְׁמֶךָ	(Dan. 9:6)
(5)	הַנָּבִיא דִּבֶּר אֵלֶיךָ	(2 Kgs. 5:13)
(6)	חַסְדֵי יְהוָה אַזְכִּיר	(Isa. 63:7)
(7)	וְלֹא אֲדַבֵּר עוֹד בִּשְׁמוֹ	(Jer. 20:9)
(8)	כִּי יְדַבֵּר שָׁלוֹם אֶל־עַמּוֹ	(Ps. 85:9; Eng. 85:8)
(9)	כִּי בֵיתִי בֵּת־תְּפִלָּה יִקָּרֵא	(Isa. 56:7)
(10)	וְלֹא בְכֶסֶף תִּגָּאֵלוּ	(Isa. 52:3)

2. Locate the following verb forms, which are drawn from exercise #1.

(1)	וַיִּקְבְּרוּ	(6)	אַזְכִּיר
(2)	וְהִסְתַּרְתִּי	(7)	אֲדַבֵּר
(3)	שִׁכַּנְתִּי	(8)	יְדַבֵּר
(4)	דִּבְּרוּ	(9)	יִקָּרֵא
(5)	דִּבֶּר	(10)	תִּגָּאֵלוּ

86

LESSON XVII

Answer Key
(Cf. *G*, pp. 160ff.)

XVII.1 Match the following:

(1)	(L)	וַיִּשְׂרְפָה בָאֵשׁ(a)	(A)	They seek him with all the heart. (Ps. 119:2)
(2)	(G)	שָׁמָּה תִקְבְּרֵנִי(b)	(B)	They did not kill them. (Josh. 9:26)
(3)	(D)	עַל־הָאָרֶץ (c)תִּשְׁפְּכֶנּוּ	(C)	And they clothed them. (2 Chr. 28:15)
(4)	(A)	בְּכָל־לֵב יִדְרְשׁוּהוּ	(D)	You shall pour it out upon the earth. (Deut. 12:16)
(5)	(I)	וְלֹא הֲרַגְתִּיךָ	(E)	I will honor him. (Ps. 91:15)
(6)	(O)	וְלֹא הֲרַגְתָּנִי	(F)	And he clothed them. (Gen. 3:21)
(7)	(B)	וְלֹא הֲרָגוּם	(G)	There you shall bury me. (Gen. 50:5)
(8)	(C)	וַיַּלְבִּשׁוּם(a)	(H)	You shall sacrifice (offer) it. (Lev. 19:5)
(9)	(F)	וַיַּלְבִּשֵׁם(a)	(I)	I did not kill you. (1 Sam. 24:12; Eng. 24:11)
(10)	(H)	תִּזְבָּחֵהוּ(d)	(J)	You shall honor (glorify) me. (Ps. 50:15)
(11)	(N)	אֲכַבֶּדְךָ	(K)	They shall glorify you. (Isa. 25:3)
(12)	(J)	תְּכַבְּדֵנִי	(L)	And he burned it with fire. (1 Kgs. 9:16)
(13)	(E)	אֲכַבְּדֵהוּ	(M)	And they clothed him. (Zech. 3:5)
(14)	(K)	יְכַבְּדוּךָ	(N)	I will honor you. (Num. 22:17)
(15)	(M)	וַיַּלְבִּשֻׁהוּ(a)	(O)	You did not kill me. (1 Sam. 24:19; Eng. 24:18)

XVII.2 Fill in the blanks with the correct pronouns in the following phrases and sentences.

(1) יְהוָה יִשְׁמָרְךָ מִכָּל־רָע The LORD will keep ___you___ from all evil. (Ps. 121:7)

(2) מָה־אֱנוֹשׁ כִּי־(c)תִזְכְּרֶנּוּ What is man that you remember ___him___? (Ps. 8:5; Eng. 8:4)

(3) אַךְ טוֹב וָחֶסֶד יִרְדְּפוּנִי   Surely goodness and mercy shall pursue
    __me__ . (Ps. 23:6)

(4) וַיְשַׁלְּחֵהוּ יְהוָה אֱלֹהִים מִגַּן־עֵדֶן (a)   And the LORD God sent __him__
    out of the garden of Eden. (Gen. 3:23)

(5) תְּבַקְשֵׁם וְלֹא תִמְצָאֵם   You shall seek __them__ but you shall not find
    __them__ . (Isa. 41:12)

(6) וְכָל־עֲבָדָיו אֲהֵבוּךָ   And all __his__ servants love __you__ .
    (1 Sam. 18:22)

(7) יִרְאַת יְהוָה אֲלַמֶּדְכֶם   The fear of the LORD I will teach __you__ .
    (Ps. 34:12; Eng. 34:11)

(8) יְהוָה אֱלֹהֵי הַשָּׁמַיִם אֲשֶׁר לְקָחַנִי מִבֵּית אָבִי   the LORD, the God of the
    heavens, who took __me__ from the house of __my__ father
    (Gen. 24:7)

(9) וַיִּשְׁלָחֵנִי אֱלֹהִים לִפְנֵיכֶם (a)   And God sent __me__ before __you__ .
    (Gen. 45:7)

(10) וַאֲנִי לֹא שְׁלַחְתִּיו   But __I__ did not send __him__ . (Jer. 29:31)

(11) וַאֲנִי לֹא־שְׁלַחְתִּים   But __I__ did not send __them__ . (Jer. 14:15)

(12) וַיִּרְדְּפֵם יִשְׂרָאֵל (a)   And Israel pursued __them__ . (1 Kgs. 20:20)

XVII.3 Supply the correct translation of the verb forms by filling in the blanks. In the space marked (a) give the stem of the verb, in (b) its form (perfect, imperfect), in (c) its person, gender, and number, and in (d) its root.

   Example:

   וּנְבַקְשֶׁנּוּ עִמָּךְ (c)   Let us __seek__ him with you. (Song of Sol. 6:1)
       (a) __Pi'el__   (b) __imperfect__   (c) __1 cp__   (d) [בקש]

(1) וְלֹא בִקְּשֻׁהוּ בְּכָל־זֹאת (d)   Yet they do not __seek__ him, for all this.
    (Hos. 7:10)
       (a) __Pi'el__   (b) __perfect__   (c) __3 cp__   (d) [בקש]

(2) יְהַלְלוּהוּ שָׁמַיִם וָאָרֶץ (e)   Let heavens and earth __praise__ him. (Ps. 69:35;
    Eng. 69:34)
       (a) __Pi'el__   (b) __imperfect__   (c) __3 mp__   (d) הָלַל

(3) אִם־תְּבַקְשֶׁנָּה כַכָּסֶף (c)   If you __seek__ it like silver. (Prov. 2:4)
       (a) __Pi'el__   (b) __imperfect__   (c) __2 ms__   (d) [בקש]

(4) עַל־כֵּן אֶזְכָּרְךָ מֵאֶרֶץ יַרְדֵּן Therefore I __remember__ you from the land of the Jordan. (Ps. 42:7; Eng. 42:6)

    (a) __Qal__ (b) __imperfect__ (c) __1 cs__ (d) זָכַר

(5) יַבְדִּילַנִי יְהֹוָה מֵעַל עַמּוֹ The LORD will __separate__ me from his people. (Isa. 56:3)

    (a) __Hifʻil__ (b) __imperfect__ (c) __3 ms__ (d) בָּדַל

(6) וָאֲשַׁבְּרֵם לְעֵינֵיכֶם(a) And I __broke__ them before your eyes. (Deut. 9:17)

    (a) __Piʻel__ (b) __imperfect__ (c) __1 cs__ (d) שָׁבַר

(7) וּמִתּוֹרָתְךָ תְלַמְּדֶנּוּ(c) And out of your law you __teach__ him. (Ps. 94:12)

    (a) __Piʻel__ (b) __imperfect__ (c) __2 ms__ (d) לָמַד

(8) שֶׁבַע בַּיּוֹם הִלַּלְתִּיךָ I __praise__ you seven times in the day. (Ps. 119:164)

    (a) __Piʻel__ (b) __perfect__ (c) __1 cs__ (d) הָלַל

(9) בְּצֵל כְּנָפֶיךָ תַּסְתִּירֵנִי You will __hide__ me in the shadow of your wings. (Ps. 17:8)

    (a) __Hifʻil__ (b) __imperfect__ (c) __2 ms__ (d) סָתַר

(10) אַל־נָא תִקְבְּרֵנִי בְּמִצְרָיִם(f) Do not __bury__ me in Egypt. (Gen. 47:29)

    (a) __Qal__ (b) __imperfect__ (c) __2 ms__ (d) קָבַר

(11) וַיִּקְבְּרֻהוּ בְּבֵיתוֹ בָרָמָה(a) And they __buried__ him in his house at Ramah. (1 Sam. 25:1)

    (a) __Qal__ (b) __imperfect__ (c) __3 mp__ (d) קָבַר

(12) אֲנִי יְדַעְתִּיךָ בַּמִּדְבָּר I __knew__ you in the wilderness. (Hos. 13:5)

    (a) __Qal__ (b) __perfect__ (c) __1 cs__ (d) יָדַע

Footnotes

(a) וַיִּשְׂרְפָהּ is a Qal imperfect verb form prefixed with a vav consecutive (See *H*.XVI.fn.(a), p. 84; cf. *G*.43, pp. 145ff.). הָ is a third feminine singular pronominal suffix which functions as the direct object of the verb [cf. *G*.27.1(1), p. 68].

(b) שָׁמָּה is שָׁם, "there," plus the "He-directive" ending הָ (cf. *G*.44, pp. 146f.).

(c) תִּשְׁפְּכֵנוּ has an example of a variant class of pronominal suffixes that are sometimes used with verbs ending in consonants (cf. *G*.47.3, p. 159).

(d) When a pronominal suffix is added to a verb form ending in šureq, the šureq is sometimes written defectively, i.e., as a qibbuṣ (תְּזֻבְּחֵהוּ). Such a change is most common when the suffix is the third masculine singular [cf. *G*.47.1(1), p. 157]. When standing as the defective writing of šureq, qibbuṣ functions as a long vowel. (Note: Look for other examples of this change in the exercises for this lesson.)

(e) An imperfect second or third person form may be used as a jussive, expressing the speaker's desire, wish, or command directed toward another person (or persons) or a thing. It is the most common way of saying, "Let such and such a thing take place" (cf. *G*.41.1, p. 131).

(f) אַל with the jussive is used to express a negative wish or a prohibition (cf. *G*.55, pp. 173f.). It constitutes a milder form of the prohibition than לֹא with an imperfect, especially when אַל is followed by the particle of entreaty נָא, almost as if the speaker were saying, "Please do not."

Suggestions for Further Testing

1. Each of the following sentences contains a verb form that is either perfect or imperfect. It may belong to either one of the seven stems (Qal, Nifʿal, Piʿel, etc.). In the space marked (a) give the stem; in (b) give the form (perfect, imperfect); in (c) indicate person, gender, and number (abbreviated); and in (d) give the three consonants of the root.
   Example:

   וָאֶשְׁלָחֲךָ אֶל־פַּרְעֹה And I will send you to Pharaoh. (Exod. 3:10)

   (a) ___Qal___ (b) ___Imperfect___ (c) ___1 cs___ (d) ___שלה___

   (1) וְאֵלֶּה הַמְּלָכִים אֲשֶׁר מָלְכוּ בְּאֶרֶץ אֱדוֹם And these are the kings who reigned in the land of Edom. (Gen. 36:31)

   (a) _____ (b) _____ (c) _____ (d) _____

   (2) וִיבַקְשׁוּ שִׁמְךָ יְהוָה And let them seek your name, O LORD.
   (Ps. 83:17; Eng. 83:16)

   (a) _____ (b) _____ (c) _____ (d) _____

   (3) וַתַּלְבֵּשׁ אֶת־יַעֲקֹב בְּנָהּ הַקָּטָן And she clothed (dressed) Jacob, her younger son. (Gen. 27:15)

   (a) _____ (b) _____ (c) _____ (d) _____

(4) וַיִּמָּלֵא בֵית־הַבַּעַל And the house of Baal was filled. (2 Kgs. 10:21)

(a) _____ (b) _____ (c) _____ (d) _____

(5) וְלֹא־נְתָנוֹ אֱלֹהִים בְּיָדוֹ And God did not give him into his hand. (1 Sam. 23:14)

(a) _____ (b) _____ (c) _____ (d) _____

(6) לֹא שְׁלָחֲךָ יְהוָה אֱלֹהֵינוּ The LORD our God has not sent you. (Jer. 43:2)

(a) _____ (b) _____ (c) _____ (d) _____

(7) וְעַתָּה אֲדֹנָי יְהוִה שְׁלָחַנִי And now the Lord GOD has sent me. (Isa. 48:16)

(a) _____ (b) _____ (c) _____ (d) _____

(8) וַיִּשְׁלָחֲךָ יְהוָה בְּדֶרֶךְ And the LORD sent you on a journey (way). (1 Sam. 15:18)

(a) _____ (b) _____ (c) _____ (d) _____

(9) נִשְׁלְחָה אֲנָשִׁים לְפָנֵינוּ Let us send men before us. (Deut. 1:22)

(a) _____ (b) _____ (c) _____ (d) _____

(10) וַנְּשַׁלֵּחֲךָ בְּשָׁלוֹם And we sent you (away) in peace. (Gen. 26:29)

(a) _____ (b) _____ (c) _____ (d) _____

2. Match the following. [Note: In the translation of pronouns, (s) indicates a singular and (p) a plural pronoun.]

(1) ( ) וַיִּשְׁלְחֵם   (A) You (s) shall send us. (Josh. 1:16)

(2) ( ) וַיְשַׁלְּחוּם   (B) And I will send you (s) (away). (1 Sam. 9:19)

(3) ( ) וַתְּשַׁלְּחוּנִי   (C) You (p) sent me. (Gen. 45:8)

(4) ( ) וְשִׁלַּחְתִּיךָ   (D) I sent them. (Jer. 14:14)

(5) ( ) תְּשַׁלְּחֵנִי   (E) He has sent me. (Isa. 48:16)

(6) ( ) תְּשַׁלְּחֵנוּ   (F) And he sent you (s). (1 Sam. 15:18)

(7) ( ) וְשִׁלַּח אֹתוֹ   (G) And they sent them (away). (1 Sam. 6:6)

(8) ( ) וַיְשַׁלְּחֶךָ   (H) And I will send them. (Josh. 18:4)

(9) ( ) וְאֶשְׁלְחֵם   (I) And he sent them (away). (Josh. 22:6)

(10) ( ) שְׁלַחְתִּים   (J) And he sent him (away). (Gen. 28:6)

(11) ( ) שְׁלָחָנִי   (K) And you (p) have sent me (away). (Gen. 26:27)

(12) ( ) שְׁלַחְתֶּם אֹתִי   (L) You (s) shall send me (away). (1 Kgs. 11:22)

3.   Translate the following:

(1)   כִּי יִפְקְדֵם יְהוָה אֱלֹהֵיהֶם   (Zeph. 2:7)

(2)   יְהוָה צְבָאוֹת שְׁלָחַנִי אֲלֵיכֶם   (Zech. 6:15)

(3)   אֱלֹהַי בְּךָ בָטַחְתִּי   (Ps. 25:2)

(4)   וּבֵרַכְתִּי אֹתָהּ   (Gen. 17:16)

(5)   וְשִׁלַּחְתִּיךָ וְהָלַכְתָּ לְשָׁלוֹם   (1 Sam. 20:13)

(6)   לֹא שְׁלַחְתִּים וְלֹא דִבַּרְתִּי אֲלֵיהֶם   (Jer. 14:14)

(7)   הֲלֹא שְׁלַחְתִּיךָ   (Judg. 6:14)

(8)   וַיִּשְׂרְפוּ אֶת־בֵּית הָאֱלֹהִים   (2 Chr. 36:19)

(9)   זֶה־יָדַעְתִּי כִּי־אֱלֹהִים לִי   (Ps. 56:10; Eng. 56:9)

(10)   כִּי מָלֵא כְבוֹד־יְהוָה אֶת־בֵּית הָאֱלֹהִים   (2 Chr. 5:14)

LESSON XVIII

Answer Key
(Cf. *G*, pp. 174ff.)

XVIII.1 Locate fully the following imperatives:

Example: דַּבֵּר Piʻel impv., 2 ms from [דבר], "he spoke." Trans. "Speak!"

(1) קִרְאוּ Qal impv., 2 mp from קָרָא, "he called." Trans. "Call, proclaim!"

(2) כִּתְבוּ Qal impv., 2 mp from כָּתַב, "he wrote." Trans. "Write!"

(3) הִשָּׁמֶר(a) Nifʻal impv., 2 ms from שָׁמַר, "he kept." Trans. "Keep, guard yourself!"

(4) הַלְלוּ(b) Piʻel impv., 2 mp from הָלַל, "he praised." Trans. "Praise!"

(5) שִׁמְעִי Qal impv., 2 fs from שָׁמַע, "he heard." Trans. "Hear!"

(6) לַמֵּדְנָה(c) Piʻel impv., 2 fp from לָמַד, "he learned." Trans. "Teach!"

(7) מְשֹׁל Qal impv., 2 ms from מָשַׁל, "he ruled." Trans. "Rule!"

(8) פַּלְּטוּ Piʻel impv., 2 mp from פָּלַט, "he escaped, delivered." Trans. "Deliver, liberate!"

(9) הִתְפַּלְלוּ Hitpaʻel impv., 2 mp from [פלל], "he prayed." Trans. "Pray!"

(10) הַסְתֵּר Hifʻil impv., 2 ms from [סתר], "he concealed, hid." Trans. "Hide!"

XVIII.2 Fill in the imperative form that appears in the Hebrew Bible in each of the following sentences or clauses. Be prepared to translate each sentence or clause and to locate the imperative form found in it.

(1) מֵחֲטָאַי(d) פָנֶיךָ __הַסְתֵּר__ (Ps. 51:11; Eng. 51:9)

"Hide your face from my sins." Hifʻil impv., 2 ms, from [סתר], "he concealed, hid." Trans. "Hide!"

(2) הָרִים אֶת־רִיב יְהוָה __שִׁמְעוּ__ (Mic. 6:2)

"Hear, O mountains, the controversy of the LORD." Qal Impv. 2 mp, from שָׁמַע, "he heard." Trans. "Hear!"

(3) אֶל־בְּנֵי יִשְׂרָאֵל __דַּבֵּר__ (Lev. 18:2)

"Speak to the people of Israel." Piʻel impv., 2 ms, from [דבר], "he spoke." Trans. "Speak!"

(4) אֱלֹהַיִךְ צִיּוֹן __הַלְלִי__ (Ps. 147:12)

"Praise your God, O Zion." Piʻel impv., 2 fs, from הָלַל, "he praised." Trans. "Praise!"

93

(5)   הִתְקַדְּשׁוּ   אַתֶּם וַאֲחֵיכֶם   (1 Chr. 15:12)

"Sanctify yourselves and your brothers." Hitpaʻel impv., 2 mp, from קָדַשׁ, "he was holy." Trans. "Sanctify yourselves!"

(6)   זִכְרוּ   תּוֹרַת מֹשֶׁה עַבְדִּי   (Mal. 3:22)

"Remember the law of Moses, my servant." Qal impv., 2 mp, from זָכַר, "he remembered." Trans. "Remember!"

(7)   כִּתְבוּ   לָכֶם אֶת־הַשִּׁירָה הַזֹּאת   (Deut. 31:19)

"Write for yourselves this song." Qal impv., 2 mp, from כָּתַב, "he wrote." Trans. "Write!"

(8)   וּמִשְׁפָּטֶיךָ   לַמְּדֵנִי   (Ps. 119:108)

"Teach me your judgments." Piʻel impv., 2 ms (plus 1 cs pronominal suffix), from לָמַד, "he learned." Trans. "Teach me!"

(9)   וַיֹּאמֶר הִשָּׁבְעָה(e) לִי   (Gen. 47:31)

"And he said, 'Swear to me.'" Nifʻal impv., 2 ms, from [שבע], "he swore." Trans. "Swear!"

XVIII.3   Write the imperatives for the following verbs in the stems indicated:

Examples: Qal imperative of שָׁמַר, "he kept"

2 ms שְׁמֹר   2 mp שִׁמְרוּ   2 fs שִׁמְרִי   2 fp שְׁמֹרְנָה

(1) Qal imperative of שָׁפַט, "he judged"

2 ms שְׁפֹט   2 mp שִׁפְטוּ   2 fs שִׁפְטִי   2 fp שְׁפֹטְנָה

(2) Nifʻal imperative of שָׁמַר, "he kept"

2 ms הִשָּׁמֵר   2 mp הִשָּׁמְרוּ   2 fs הִשָּׁמְרִי   2 fp הִשָּׁמַרְנָה

(3) Piʻel imperative of לָמַד, "he learned" (Piʻel, "taught")

2 ms לַמֵּד   2 mp לַמְּדוּ   2 fs לַמְּדִי   2 fp לַמֵּדְנָה

(4) Hitpaʻel imperative of [פלל], "he prayed"

2 ms הִתְפַּלֵּל   2 mp הִתְפַּלְלוּ   2 fs הִתְפַּלְלִי   2 fp הִתְפַּלֵּלְנָה

(5) Hifʻil imperative of [שלך], "he threw, cast"

2 ms הַשְׁלֵךְ   2 mp הַשְׁלִיכוּ   2 fs הַשְׁלִיכִי   2 fp הַשְׁלֵכְנָה

XVIII.4   Fill in the blanks with the correct imperatives based on the imperfect forms found in parentheses. Check the scripture references for the accuracy of your work, but only after the blanks have been filled in.

(1) הַסְתֵּר (תַּסְתֵּר) (Ps. 51:11)   (4) בַּקֵּשׁ (תְּבַקֵּשׁ) (Ps. 34:15)

(2) הִתְקַדְּשׁוּ (תִּתְקַדְּשׁוּ) (1 Chr. 15:12)   (5) זִכְרוּ (תִּזְכְּרוּ) (Mal. 3:22)

(3) הַלְלוּ (תְּהַלְלוּ) (Ps. 113:1)   (6) הִלָּחֵם (תִּלָּחֵם) (1 Sam. 18:17)

94

(7) _____ קִרְבוּ (תִּקְרְבוּ) (Isa. 48:16)   (9) הַשְׁלִיכוּ (תַּשְׁלִיכוּ) (Gen. 37:22)

(8) _____ שִׁכְבִי (תִּשְׁכְּבִי) (2 Sam. 13:11)   (10) הִשָּׁבְעוּ (תִּשָּׁבְעוּ) (Josh. 2:12)

XVIII.5 Match the following imperatives with the proper translation:

(1)	(K)	עָבְדֵהוּ	(1 Chr. 28:9)	(A)	send me
(2)	(E)	לַמְּדֵנִי	(Ps. 119:108)	(B)	seek me
(3)	(H)	לַמְּדָהּ	(Deut. 31:19)	(C)	judge me
(4)	(A)	שְׁלָחֵנִי	(Isa. 6:8)	(D)	cause me to hear
(5)	(D)	הַשְׁמִיעֵנִי	(Ps. 143:8)	(E)	teach me
(6)	(J)	הַלְלוּהוּ	(Ps. 150:1)	(F)	remember me
(7)	(B)	בַּקְשׁוּנִי	(Isa. 45:19)	(G)	write them
(8)	(G)	כָּתְבֵם	(Prov. 3:3)	(H)	teach it (f)
(9)	(C)	שָׁפְטֵנִי	(Ps. 43:1)	(I)	help me
(10)	(L)	רְפָאֵנִי	(Jer. 17:14)	(J)	praise him
(11)	(F)	זָכְרֵנִי	(Jer. 15:15)	(K)	serve him
(12)	(I)	עָזְרֵנִי	(Ps. 109:26)	(L)	heal me

XVIII.6 Fill in the blanks with the correct pronouns.

(1) שִׁכְבִי עִמִּי אֲחוֹתִי Lie with ___me___ , ___my___ sister. (2 Sam. 13:11)

(2) מְשָׁל־בָּנוּ גַם־אַתָּה גַם־בִּנֶךָ (f) Rule over ___us___ , both ___you___ and ___your___ son. (Judg. 8:22)

(3) שָׁמְרֵם בְּתוֹךְ לְבָבֶךָ (g) Keep ___them___ within ___your___ heart. (Prov. 4:21)

(4) כָּתְבֵם עַל־לוּחַ לִבֶּךָ (h) Write ___them___ on the tablet of ___your___ heart. (Prov. 3:3)

(5) וּמַלְּטִי אֶת־נַפְשֵׁךְ וְאֶת־נֶפֶשׁ בְּנֵךְ שְׁלֹמֹה (i) Save ___your___ life and the life of ___your___ son Solomon. (1 Kgs. 1:12)

(6) וּקְבֹר אֶת־אָבִיךָ כַּאֲשֶׁר הִשְׁבִּיעֶךָ (j) And bury ___your___ father, as he caused ___you___ to swear. (Gen. 50:6)

(7) קִבְרוּ אֹתִי אֶל־אֲבֹתָי Bury ___me___ with ___my___ ancestors. (Gen. 49:29)

95

(8) זִבְחוּ לֵאלֹהֵיכֶם בָּאָרֶץ Sacrifice to ___your___ God in the land. (Exod. 8:21)

(9) כַּבְּדֵנִי נָא נֶגֶד זִקְנֵי־עַמִּי Honor ___me___ now before the elders of ___my___ people. (1 Sam. 15:30)

(10) רִדְפוּ אַחֲרֵי אֹיְבֵיכֶם Pursue after ___your___ enemies. (Josh. 10:19)

(11) וְעִבְדוּ אֹתוֹ וְעַמּוֹ Serve ___him___ and ___his___ people. (Jer. 27:12)

(12) וְעַתָּה בְנִי שְׁמַע בְּקֹלִי And now, ___my___ son, hear ___my___ voice. (Gen. 27:8)

(13) שְׁמַע־נָא(k) וְאָנֹכִי אֲדַבֵּר Hear now, and ___I___ will speak. (Job. 42:4)

(14) שִׁמְעָה(e) עַמִּי וַאֲדַבֵּרָה(l) Hear, O ___my___ people, and ___I___ will speak. (Ps. 50:7)

(15) שִׁמְעוּ־נָא(m) דְבָרָי Hear now ___my___ words. (Num. 12:6)

(16) וְעִבְדֻהוּ(n) לְבַדּוֹ And serve ___him___ only. (1 Sam. 7:3)

XVII.7 Verb review

(1) Write the Qal perfect forms for מָשַׁל. (Cf. *G*.30.5, p. 85)

(2) Write the Qal imperfect forms for מָשַׁל. (Cf. *G*.39.3, p. 128)

(3) Write the Qal imperative forms for מָשַׁל. [Cf. *G*48.1(1), p. 165]

(4) Write the Pi‛el perfect forms for [דבר]. (Cf. *G*.37, Table 2, p. 114)

(5) Write the Pi‛el imperfect forms for [דבר]. (Cf. *G*.42.2, p. 140)

(6) Write the Pi‛el imperative form for [דבר]. [Cf. *G*.50.1 (1), p. 169]

	Qal Perf.		Qal Imp.	Qal Impv.		Pi‛el Perf.		Pi‛el Imp.	Pi‛el Impv.
3 ms	מָשַׁל	3 ms	יִמְשֹׁל		3 ms	דִּבֶּר	3 ms	יְדַבֵּר	
3 fs	מָשְׁלָה	3 fs	תִּמְשֹׁל		3 fs	דִּבְּרָה	3 fs	תְּדַבֵּר	
2 ms	מָשַׁלְתָּ	2 ms	תִּמְשֹׁל	מְשֹׁל	2 ms	דִּבַּרְתָּ	2 ms	תְּדַבֵּר	דַּבֵּר
2 fs	מָשַׁלְתְּ	2 fs	תִּמְשְׁלִי	מִשְׁלִי	2 fs	דִּבַּרְתְּ	2 fs	תְּדַבְּרִי	דַּבְּרִי
1 cs	מָשַׁלְתִּי	1 cs	אֶמְשֹׁל		1 cs	דִּבַּרְתִּי	1 cs	אֲדַבֵּר	
3 cp	מָשְׁלוּ	3 mp	יִמְשְׁלוּ		3 cp	דִּבְּרוּ	3 mp	יְדַבְּרוּ	
		3 fp	תִּמְשֹׁלְנָה				3 fp	תְּדַבֵּרְנָה	
2 mp	מְשַׁלְתֶּם	2 mp	תִּמְשְׁלוּ	מִשְׁלוּ	2 mp	דִּבַּרְתֶּם	2 mp	תְּדַבְּרוּ	דַּבְּרוּ
2 fp	מְשַׁלְתֶּן	2 fp	תִּמְשֹׁלְנָה	מְשֹׁלְנָה	2 fp	דִּבַּרְתֶּן	2 fp	תְּדַבֵּרְנָה	דַּבֵּרְנָה
1 cp	מָשַׁלְנוּ	1 cp	נִמְשֹׁל		1 cp	דִּבַּרְנוּ	1 cp	נְדַבֵּר	

Footnotes

(a) Some Nifʻal verbs are essentially reflexive [cf. *G*.36.1(2), p. 109]. For example, הִשָּׁמֶר is translated "Guard yourself!" "Take heed to yourself!"

(b) Dagesh forte often drops out of consonants pointed with a vocal sheva (הַלְלוּ) [cf. *G*.50.1(3), p. 169]; however, XVIII.1(8) and (9), p. 93, of the present exercise, are exceptions to this rule.

(c) Some verbs occur in the Piʻel with a causative sense [cf. *G*.36.2(2), p. 109]. לָמַד, "he learned," is such a verb. In the Piʻel stem, it means "he teaches."

(d) מֵחֲטָאַי is pausal (with ʾatnah, מֵחֲטָאָי) for מֵחֲטָאַי ("from my sins").

(e) Some second masculine singular forms of imperatives occur with a ה֔ suffix, which seems to have little or no impact on their meaning (cf. *G*.53, pp. 172f.). הִשָּׁבְעָה, "Swear!" always follows this pattern.

(f) Words joined by maqqef are pronounced as one speech unit, with the primary accent falling on the last word in the unit (cf. *G*.4, p. 12). Words losing their accent often undergo internal vowel changes. מְשֹׁל, "Rule!" for example, has the vowel in its final syllable shortened from holem to qames–hatuf, thus resulting in the present form מְשָׁל־בָּנוּ (unaccented closed syllables require short vowels).

(g) לְבָבְךָ is pausal (with silluq, לְבָבֶךָ) for לְבָבְךָ. (לֵבַב and לֵב are alternate forms of the same word.)

(h) לְבֶךָ is pausal (with silluq, לְבֶּךָ) for לִבְּךָ.

(i) Students should note the second feminine singular form of the imperative and the second feminine singular pronominal suffixes in this sentence (words addressed to Bathsheba).

(j) הִשְׁבִּיעֵךְ is pausal (with silluq, הִשְׁבִּיעֵךְ) for הִשְׁבִּיעֵךְ. (Note the compound sheva under the guttural ע. Without the pronominal suffix, the form is הִשְׁבִּיעַ, Hifʻil perfect, third masculine singular.)

(k) Lamed Guttural verb forms take "a" class vowels in final syllables ending in a guttural (cf. *G*.70, pp. 263ff.).

(l) The ה֔ cohortative ending on this first person imperfect form expresses the speaker's (God's) determination to speak (cf. *G*.41.2, p. 132).

(m) דְּבָרַי is pausal (with ʾatnah, דְּבָרָי) for דְבָרַי (וּ at the end of the preceding word accounts for the loss of dagesh lene in ד).

(n) When the third masculine singular pronominal suffix is added to a verb form ending in šureq, šureq will often be written defectively, i.e., as a qibbuṣ [See H.XVII.fn.(d), p. 90; cf. G.47.1(1),p. 157]. The qibbuṣ is still considered to be a long vowel.

Suggestions for Further Testing

1. Vocabulary Review: Circle the word that does not fit the category indicated.

(1) verbs of speaking	עָנָה	[דבר]	שָׁמַע	אָמַר
(2) verbs of physical activity	עָמַד	נָשָׂא	הָלַךְ	לָמַד
(3) verbs of cultic activity	[כפר]	[שלך]	[פלל]	זָבַח
(4) verbs of oppression	רָדַף	הָרַג	אָהַב	[לחם]
(5) verbs of liberation	גָּאַל	מָלֵא	[ישע]	שָׁפַט
(6) verbs of emotional response	לָבַשׁ	שָׂמַח	יָרֵא	הָלַל
(7) verbs of physical posture	קוּם	יָשַׁב	עָזַב	שָׁכַב
(8) verbs of destruction	בָּרָא	שָׁבַר	שָׂרַף	כָּרַת
(9) verbs of being (life, death)	הָיָה	לָקַח	חָיָה	מוּת
(10) verbs of inquiry	[בקש]	עָבַד	שָׁאַל	דָּרַשׁ

2. Match the following:

(1) ( )	שָׁפְטֵנִי	(A) Help me! (Ps. 109:26)
(2) ( )	הוֹשִׁיעֵנִי	(B) Seek me! (Isa. 45:19)
(3) ( )	הוֹשִׁיעֵנוּ	(C) Judge me! (Ps. 35:24)
(4) ( )	עָבְדֵהוּ	(D) Remember me! (Judg. 16:28)
(5) ( )	רְפָאֵנִי	(E) Bless me! (Gen. 27:34)
(6) ( )	עָזְרֵנִי	(F) Save me! (Ps. 3:8; Eng. 3:7)
(7) ( )	זָכְרֵנִי	(G) Heal me! (Jer. 17:14)
(8) ( )	לָמְדָהּ	(H) Praise him! (Ps. 150:1)
(9) ( )	בַּקְשׁוּנִי	(I) Write them! (Prov. 3:3)
(10) ( )	הַלְלוּהוּ	(J) Save us! (Ps. 106:47)
(11) ( )	בָּרְכֵנִי	(K) Teach it (fem.)! (Deut. 31:19)
(12) ( )	כָּתְבֵם	(L) Serve him! (1 Chr. 28:9)

3. Translate the following:

(1)   בְּטַח אֶל־יְהוָה בְּכָל־לִבֶּךָ   (Prov. 3:5)

(2)   אַל־תִּשְׁפְּכוּ־דָם   (Gen. 37:22)

(3)   שְׁלַח אוֹרְךָ וַאֲמִתְּךָ   (Ps. 43:3)

(4)   יְהוָה זָכְרֵנִי וּפָקְדֵנִי   (Jer. 15:15)

(5)   אִמְרוּ בַגּוֹיִם יְהוָה מָלָךְ   (Ps. 96:10)

(6)   שִׁלְחָה נָא לִי אֶחָד מִן־הַנְּעָרִים   (2 Kgs. 4:22)

(7)   שִׁמְעוּ בְּקוֹל יְהוָה אֱלֹהֵיכֶם   (Jer. 26:13)

(8)   הַשְׁמִיעֵנִי בַבֹּקֶר חַסְדֶּךָ   (Ps. 143:8)

(9)   הַשְׁמִיעוּהָ בִיהוּדָה   (Jer. 5:20)

(10)   חֶסֶד וּמִשְׁפָּט שְׁמֹר   (Hos. 12:7)

(11)   וְאָזְנָיו הַכְבֵּד   (Isa. 6:10)

(12)   וְגַם אֶת־אַחֶיךָ הַקְרֵב אִתָּךְ   (Num. 18:2)

LESSON XIX

Answer Key
(Cf, *G*, pp. 186ff.)

XIX.1 Write the Qal infinitives for the following verbs:

	Verb	Infinitive Construct	Infinitive Absolute
(1)	שָׁפַט	שְׁפֹט	שָׁפוֹט
(2)	לָמַד	לְמֹד	לָמוֹד
(3)	קָרַב	קְרֹב	קָרוֹב
(4)	שָׁכַב	שְׁכַב	שָׁכוֹב
(5)	מָשַׁל	מְשֹׁל	מָשׁוֹל
(6)	פָּקַד	פְּקֹד	פָּקוֹד
(7)	קָטַל	קְטֹל	קָטוֹל

XIX.2 Each of the following entries contains an infinitive construct. Complete the translation by giving the meaning of the infinitive. In the space marked (a) give the stem of the infinitive and in (b) give its root. If it has a pronominal suffix, give the person, gender, and number of the suffix in (c), and indicate whether it is used as subject or object in (d).

כְּהַזְכִּירוֹ אֶת־אֲרוֹן הָאֱלֹהִים when he __mentioned__(a) the ark of God
(1 Sam. 4:18)

(a) Hif'il (b) זָכַר (c) 3 ms (d) subject

(1) לִשְׁכַּב אֶת־בַּת־יַעֲקֹב(b) to __lie__ with the daughter of Jacob
(Gen. 34:7)

(a) Qal (b) שָׁכַב

(2) לִשְׁמֹר אֶת־דֶּרֶךְ עֵץ הַחַיִּים to __keep__ the way of the tree of life
(Gen. 3:24)

(a) Qal (b) שָׁמַר

(3) בְּכָתְבוֹ אֶת־הַדְּבָרִים הָאֵלֶּה when he __wrote__ these words (Jer. 45:1)

(a) Qal (b) כָּתַב (c) 3 ms (d) subject

(4) לִשְׁפֹּט אֶת־הָעָם to __judge__ the people (Exod. 18:13)

(a) Qal (b) שָׁפַט

(5) לְלַמְּדָם מִלְחָמָה to __teach__ them war (Judg. 3:2)

(a) Pi'el (b) לָמַד (c) 3 mp (d) object

(6) לְהִלָּחֵם עִם־יִשְׂרָאֵל (c) to __fight__ with Israel (Josh. 11:5)

                               (a) __Nif'al__ (b) [לחם]

(7) לְקָבְרָהּ to __bury__ her (2 Kgs. 9:35)

          (a) __Qal__ (b) קָבַר (c) __3 fs__ (d) __object__

(8) לְשָׂרְפוֹ בָאֵשׁ to __burn__ it with fire (Judg. 9:52)

          (a) __Qal__ (b) שָׂרַף (c) __3 ms__ (d) __object__

(9) בְּשָׁפְכְּךָ אֶת־חֲמָתְךָ עַל־יְרוּשָׁלַ͏ִם when you __pour out__ your wrath upon Jerusalem (Ezek. 9:8)

          (a) __Qal__ (b) שָׁפַךְ (c) __2 ms__ (d) __subject__

(10) לִדְרוֹשׁ אֶת־תּוֹרַת יְהוָה to __seek__ the law of the LORD (Ezr. 7:10)

                               (a) __Qal__ (b) דָּרַשׁ

(11) וַיְבַקֵּשׁ לַהֲרֹג אֶת־מֹשֶׁה And he sought to __kill__ Moses. (Exod. 2:15)

                               (a) __Qal__ (b) [בקשׁ]

(12) וּבֶגֶד לִלְבֹּשׁ and clothing to __wear__ (Gen. 28:20)

                               (a) __Qal__ (b) לָבֵשׁ

XIX.3 Fill in the blanks with the correct pronouns.

(1) יְהוָה יִשְׁמַע בְּקָרְאִי אֵלָיו The LORD hears when __I__ call to __him__. (Ps. 4:4; Eng. 4:3)

(2) וַיָּקָם הַמֶּלֶךְ (d) לִקְרָאתָהּ And the king rose to meet __her__. (1 Kgs. 2:19)

(3) וְאֵלֶּה יָצְאוּ מִן־הָעִיר (d) לִקְרָאתָם And these went forth from the city to meet __them__. (Josh. 8:22)

(4) בְּבָרְחוֹ מִפְּנֵי אַבְשָׁלוֹם בְּנוֹ when __he__ fled from Absalom __his__ son (Ps. 3:1; Eng. title)

(5) כִּי אִתְּכֶם אָנִי (e) לְהוֹשִׁיעַ אֶתְכֶם For __I__ am with __you__ to deliver __you__. (Jer. 42:11)

(6) עַד שׁוּבִי בְשָׁלוֹם until __I__ return in peace (2 Chr. 18:26)

(7) עִמּוֹ זְרוֹעַ בָּשָׂר וְעִמָּנוּ יְהוָה אֱלֹהֵינוּ לְעָזְרֵנוּ וּלְהִלָּחֵם מִלְחֲמֹתֵנוּ With __him__ is an arm of flesh; but with __us__ is the LORD __our__ God, to help __us__ and to fight __our__ battles. (2 Chr. 32:8)

(8) וַיֹּאמְרוּ לוֹ אֶחָיו (f)הֲמָלֹךְ תִּמְלֹךְ עָלֵינוּ And ___his___ brothers said to ___him___, "Shall ___you___ indeed reign over ___us___?" (Gen. 37:8)

(9) הִנֵּה יָצָא לְהִלָּחֵם אִתָּךְ Behold, ___he___ has come forth to fight with ___you___. (2 Kgs. 19:9)

(10) לֹא יִקְרַב (g)לְהַקְרִיב לֶחֶם אֱלֹהָיו ___He___ shall not draw near to offer the bread of ___his___ God. (Lev. 21:17)

(11) וַיִּשְׁמַע יְהוָה (h)אֶת־קוֹל דִּבְרֵיכֶם בְּדַבֶּרְכֶם אֵלָי And the LORD heard ___your___ words when ___you___ spoke to ___me___. (Deut. 5:28)

(12) וּכְשָׁמְעוֹ אֶת־דִּבְרֵי רִבְקָה אֲחֹתוֹ and when ___he___ heard the words of Rebekah ___his___ sister (Gen. 24:30)

XIX.4 Translate the following:

(1) לִשְׁמֹר אֶת־מִצְוֹת יְהוָה (Deut. 4:2)
to keep the commandments of the LORD

(2) לְבַקֵּשׁ אֶת־יְהוָה צְבָאוֹת בִּירוּשָׁלַם (Zech. 8:22)
to seek the LORD of hosts in Jerusalem

(3) לְהַבְדִּיל בֵּין הַיּוֹם וּבֵין הַלָּיְלָה (Gen. 1:14)
to separate between the day and between the night

(4) לִשְׁפֹּט אֶת־עַמְּךָ (1 Kgs. 3:9)
to judge your people

(5) לְהַלֵּל אֶת־יְהוָה (Ezr. 3:10)
to praise the LORD

(6) לְמַלֵּא אֶת־דְּבַר יְהוָה (i) (1 Kgs. 2:27)
to fulfill the word of the LORD

(7) לִקְבֹּר אֶת־אָבִיו (Gen. 50:7)
to bury his father

(8) לִדְרֹשׁ אֶת־יְהוָה (Gen. 25:22)
to seek the LORD

(9) לִרְדֹּף אַחֲרֵיהֶם (Josh. 8:16)
to pursue after them

(10) לִרְדָּפְךָ וּלְבַקֵּשׁ אֶת־נַפְשֶׁךָ (1 Sam. 25:29)
to pursue you and to seek your life (soul)

(11) לְדַבֵּר בִּשְׁמֶךָ (Exod. 5:23)

to speak in your name

(12) לְדַבֵּר דָּבָר בִּשְׁמִי (Deut. 18:20)

to speak a word in my name

XIX.5 Match the following verbs so that those expressing similar actions or states of being are paired:

(1) (E)	בּוֹא	(A)	דָּרַשׁ	
(2) (I)	שָׁתָה	(B)	שָׁכַן	
(3) (G)	עָלָה	(C)	בִּין	
(4) (J)	רָבָה	(D)	בָּרָא	
(5) (C)	יָדַע	(E)	הָלַךְ	
(6) (A)	[בקשׁ]	(F)	[ישׁע]	
(7) (B)	יָשַׁב	(G)	קוּם	
(8) (D)	עָשָׂה	(H)	מָשַׁל	
(9) (H)	מָלַךְ	(I)	אָכַל	
(10) (F)	[נצל]	(J)	גָּדַל	

XIX.6 In each of the following examples an infinitive absolute stands before a finite verb of the same root and serves to intensify the action of the finite verb. Try to think of other ways the sentences might be translated in order to express the intensification. Consult at least two modern translations to see how they have rendered these sentences. In the space marked (a) give the stem of the infinitive absolute, and in (b) give its root.

(1) אִם־מָשׁוֹל תִּמְשֹׁל בָּנוּ⁽ʲ⁾

Will you indeed rule over us? (Gen. 37:8)

(a) Qal

(b) מָשַׁל

(2) הַבְדֵּל יַבְדִּילַנִי יְהוָה מֵעַל עַמּוֹ

The LORD will surely separate me from his people. (Isa. 56:3)

(a) Hifʿil

(b) בָּדַל

(3) זָכֹר אֶזְכְּרֶנּוּ עוֹד

I still remember him. (Jer. 31:20)

(a) Qal

(b) זָכַר

(4) אִם־לָמֹד יִלְמְדוּ אֶת־דַּרְכֵי עַמִּי

if they will diligently learn the ways of my people (Jer. 12:16)

(a) Qal

(b) לָמַד

(5) וְאָנֹכִי הַסְתֵּר אַסְתִּיר פָּנַי בַּיּוֹם הַהוּא	(a)	Hif'il
And I will surely hide my face in that day. (Deut. 31:18)	(b)	[סתר]
(6) כִּי־קָבוֹר תִּקְבְּרֶנּוּ בַּיּוֹם הַהוּא	(a)	Qal
You shall certainly bury him on that (same) day. (Deut. 21:23)	(b)	קָבַר
(7) דָּרֹשׁ דָּרַשׁ מֹשֶׁה	(a)	Qal
Moses searched diligently. (Lev. 10:16)	(b)	דָּרַשׁ
(8) כִּי־כַבֵּד אֲכַבֶּדְךָ מְאֹד	(a)	Pi'el
For I will surely honor you greatly. (Num. 22:17)	(b)	כָּבַד
(9) יָדַעְתִּי כִּי־דַבֵּר יְדַבֵּר הוּא	(a)	Pi'el
I know that he can speak well. (Exod. 4:14)	(b)	[דבר]
(10) אִם־שָׁמוֹעַ תִּשְׁמְעוּ בְּקֹלִי(k)	(a)	Qal
if you truly harken to my voice (Exod. 19:5)	(b)	שָׁמַע

Footnotes

(a) "Mentioned" is a more idiomatic translation than "he caused to remember." A literal causative rendering is seldom needed for Hif'il forms.

(b) אֶת, a preposition meaning "with," is easily confused with אֵת, the sign of the direct object [cf. G.5, p. 12; (3)(a), p. 69].

(c) The final mem (ם) of this form is part of the verb root (לחם), and not to be confused with the third masculine plural pronominal suffix (cf. G.46.3, p. 155).

(d) לִקְרָאתָה is Qal infinitive construct, plus preposition לְ, plus third feminine singular pronominal suffix, from קָרָא, "he met, encountered," (not to be confused with קָרָא, "he called, read aloud"), translated "to meet her." This infinitive construct form occurs 121 times and always with the prefixed preposition לְ. The second occurrence of the form in this exercise has the third masculine plural pronominal suffix, translated "to meet them." (Cf. G.56.1(3)(o), p. 181.]

(e) לְהוֹשִׁיעַ is a Hif'il infinitive construct, plus לְ, from [ישע], a doubly weak verb (Pe Vav/Pe Yod; 'Ayin Guttural) which occurs only in the Hif'il stem and is translated "to save." [Cf. G.56.1(3)(g), p. 180.]

(f) The infinitive absolute may take a prefixed interrogative ה (cf. *G*.34.1, pp. 94f.).

(g) "To draw near" and "to offer" are from the same verb root (קָרַב). The Hifʻil means "to cause to come near," and thus "to offer (upon an altar)."

(h) The literal translation of אֶת־קוֹל דִּבְרֵיכֶם is "the voice (sound) of your words." A noun is definite when it has a pronominal suffix (cf. *G*.28, p. 71).

(i) "To fill" can also mean "to fulfill."

(j) אִם can be used to introduce a question, in which case it is somewhat similar to interrogative ה. A question introduced by אִם alone presupposes a negative response: "Certainly not!" אִם־לֹא, on the other hand, implies a positive answer: "Certainly!"

(k) The verb root שָׁמַע means both "he listened" and "he obeyed." The two actions are complementary.

Suggestions for Further Testing

1. Translate the following:

(1)	וַיְמָאֵן לֶאֱכוֹל	(1 Sam. 13:9)
(2)	לְהַכְרִית מִמֶּנָּה אָדָם וּבְהֵמָה	(Ezek. 14:19)
(3)	לְשַׁכֵּן אֶת־שְׁמִי שָׁם	(Neh. 1:9)
(4)	כִּי בָרֵךְ יְבָרֶכְךָ יְהוָה בָּאָרֶץ	(Deut. 15:4)
(5)	וּלְמַעַן סַפֵּר שְׁמִי בְּכָל־הָאָרֶץ	(Exod. 9:16)
(6)	יַעַן דַּבֶּרְכֶם אֶת־הַדָּבָר הַזֶּה	(Jer. 5:14)
(7)	לְהַמְלִיךְ אֶת־דָּוִיד עַל־כָּל־יִשְׂרָאֵל	(1 Chr. 12:39)
(8)	לִשְׂרֹף אֶת־בְּנֵיכֶם בָּאֵשׁ	(Jer. 19:5)
(9)	לְסַפֵּר בְּצִיּוֹן שֵׁם יְהוָה	Ps. 102:22; Eng. 102:21)
(10)	לִקְרָאתִי בַּדֶּרֶךְ	(Num. 22:34)
(11)	וַיִּשְׁלַח לִקְרָאתָם	2 Sam. 10:5)
(12)	בְּעָזְבָם אֶת־יְהוָה אֱלֹהֵי אֲבוֹתָם	(2 Chr. 28:6)
(13)	וּבָאֵשׁ שָׂרוֹף יִשָּׂרְפוּ	(2 Sam. 23:7)

(14)   דִּרְשׁוּ יְהוָה בְּהִמָּצְאוֹ   (Isa. 55:6)

(15)   קְרָאֻהוּ בִּהְיוֹתוֹ קָרוֹב   (Isa. 55:6)

2. Locate the following infinitives, together with all prefixes and suffixes. Note that the infinitives are drawn from the exercises in the preceding section.

Example: בְּדַבְּרָם   Pi'el inf. const., plus preposition בְּ, plus 3 mp pronominal suffix, from [דבר], "he spoke." Trans. "When they spoke."

(1) לֶאֱכֹל	(6) דַּבֶּרְכֶם	(11) לִקְרָאתָם
(2) לְהַכְרִית	(7) לְהַמְלִיךְ	(12) בְּעָזְבָם
(3) לְשַׁכֵּן	(8) לִשְׂרֹף	(13) שָׂרוֹף
(4) בָּרֵךְ	(9) לִסְפֹּר	(14) בְּהִמָּצְאוֹ
(5) סָפֹר	(10) לִקְרָאתִי	(15) בִּהְיוֹתוֹ

3. Match the following:

(1) ( )   יִרְדֹּף אֶחָד אֶלֶף   (A) to teach you to do (Deut. 6:1)

(2) ( )   פָּקֹד יִפְקֹד אֶתְכֶם   (B) to teach them (the skills of) war (Judg. 3:2)

(3) ( )   יְהוָה שְׁלָחֲךָ לִקְרָאתִי   (C) when we remember Zion (Ps. 137:1)

(4) ( )   שַׁלֵּחַ תְּשַׁלְּחֵנִי   (D) to hear the wisdom of Solomon (1 Kgs. 5:14)

(5) ( )   אִם בָּרֵךְ תְּבָרֲכֵנִי   (E) If you truly bless me. (1 Chr. 4:10)

(6) ( )   לְלַמֵּד אֶתְכֶם לַעֲשׂוֹת   (F) There is power with God to help. (2 Chr. 25:8)

(7) ( )   שָׁמוֹר תִּשְׁמְרוּן אֶת־מִצְוֹת   (G) You shall surely send me away. (1 Kgs. 11:22)

(8) ( )   אִם־שָׁמוֹעַ תִּשְׁמְעוּן בְּקוֹל יְהוָה   (H) One shall pursue a thousand. (Deut. 32:30)

(9) ( )   לְלַמְּדָם מִלְחָמָה   (I) You shall diligently keep the commandments. (Deut. 6:17)

(10) ( )   לִשְׁמֹעַ אֵת חָכְמַת שְׁלֹמֹה   (J) He will surely visit you. (Gen. 50:24)

(11) ( )   בְּזָכְרֵנוּ אֶת־צִיּוֹן   (K) If you diligently obey the voice of the LORD. (Zech. 6:15)

(12) ( )   יֶשׁ־כֹּחַ בֵּאלֹהִים לַעֲזוֹר   (L) The LORD sent you to meet me. (1 Sam. 25:32)

LESSON XX

Answer Key
(Cf. *G*, pp. 203ff.)

XX.1 Write the synopsis for the verb כָּתַב[(a)]. (Cf. *G*,61, p. 203)

	Qal	Nifʻal	Piʻel	Puʻal	Hitpaʻel	Hifʻil	Hofʻal
Perf. 3 ms	כָּתַב	נִכְתַּב	כִּתֵּב	כֻּתַּב	הִתְכַּתֵּב	הִכְתִּיב	הָכְתַּב
Impf. 3 ms	יִכְתֹּב	יִכָּתֵב	יְכַתֵּב	יְכֻתַּב	יִתְכַּתֵּב	יַכְתִּיב	יָכְתַּב
Impv. 2 ms	כְּתֹב	הִכָּתֵב	כַּתֵּב		הִתְכַּתֵּב	הַכְתֵּב	
Inf. const.	כְּתֹב	הִכָּתֵב	כַּתֵּב	(כֻּתַּב)	הִתְכַּתֵּב	הַכְתִּיב	(הָכְתַּב)
Inf. Abs.	כָּתוֹב	הִכָּתֹב נִכְתֹּב	כַּתֵּב כַּתֹּב	כֻּתֹּב	הִתְכַּתֵּב	הַכְתֵּב	הָכְתֵּב
Part. Act. ms	כֹּתֵב		מְכַתֵּב		מִתְכַּתֵּב	מַכְתִּיב	
Part. Act. fs	כֹּתְבָה כֹּתֶבֶת		מְכַתֶּבֶת		מִתְכַּתֶּבֶת	מַכְתִּיבָה	
Part. Pass. ms	כָּתוּב	נִכְתָּב	מְכֻתָּב				מָכְתָּב
Part. Pass. fs	כְּתוּבָה	נִכְתֶּבֶת	מְכֻתָּבָה				מָכְתֶּבֶת

XX.2 Fill in the blanks with the correct pronouns.

(1) וְאַתָּה [(b)]מוֹשֵׁל בַּכֹּל ___You___ rule over all. (1 Chr. 29:12)

(2) וּזְרֹעוֹ [(c)]מָשְׁלָה לוֹ ___His___ arm rules for ___him___ . (Isa. 40:10)

(3) אַל־יָנוּם שֹׁמְרֶךָ The one keeping ___you___ will not slumber. (Ps. 121:3)

(4) [(d)]לְאֹהֲבָיו [(d)]וּלְשֹׁמְרֵי מִצְוֹתָיו to those who love ___him___ and keep ___his___ commandments (Dan. 9:4)

(5) וְלֹא אִתְּכֶם לְבַדְּכֶם אָנֹכִי כֹּרֵת אֶת־הַבְּרִית הַזֹּאת And not with ___you___ alone am ___I___ making (cutting) ___this___ covenant. (Deut. 29:13; Eng. 29:14)

(6) הִנֵּה בְנִי מְבַקֵּשׁ אֶת־נַפְשִׁי Behold, ___my___ son is seeking ___my___ life. (2 Sam. 16:11)

(7) כָּל־מְבַקְשֶׁיהָ all who seek ___it/her___ (Jer. 2:24)

(8) אֶת־חֲטָאַי אֲנִי מַזְכִּיר הַיּוֹם   <u>My</u> sins <u>I</u> remember today. (Gen. 41:9)

(9) הֲלוֹא דָוִד ^(e)מִסְתַּתֵּר עִמָּנוּ Is not David hiding among <u>us</u>? (1 Sam. 23:19)

(10) וְהַשֹּׂרֵף אֹתָם יְכַבֵּס בְּגָדָיו And the one burning <u>them</u> shall wash <u>his</u> garments. (Lev. 16:28)

(11) הִיא שֹׁפְטָה אֶת־יִשְׂרָאֵל בָּעֵת הַהִיא <u>She</u> was judging Israel at <u>that</u> time. (Judg. 4:4)

(12) ^(f)לָמָּה זֶּה אֲדֹנִי רֹדֵף אַחֲרֵי עַבְדּוֹ Why is <u>my</u> lord pursuing after <u>his</u> servant? (1 Sam. 26:18)

XX.3 Underscore the correct form of the participle in each of the following sentences and phrases. Check the scripture references for accuracy, but only after completing the assignment.

(1) וְחַנָּה הִיא (מְדַבֵּר / ^(g)<u>מְדַבֶּרֶת</u>) עַל־לִבָּהּ

And Hannah was speaking in her heart. (1 Sam. 1:13)

(2) הָאִישׁ (<u>הַשֹּׁכֵב</u> / הַשֹּׁכֶבֶת) עִמָּהּ

the man who lay with her (Deut. 22:29)

(3) הֲלֹא־הִיא (כָּתוּב / <u>כְּתוּבָה</u>) עַל־סֵפֶר הַיָּשָׁר

Is this not written in the Book of Jashar? (Josh. 10:13)

(4) ^(h)(בָּרוּךְ / <u>בְּרוּכָה</u>) אַתְּ לַיהוָה בִּתִּי

May you be blessed by the LORD, my daughter. (Ruth 3:10)

(5) (בְּרוּכִים / <u>בְּרוּכוֹת</u>) אַתֶּם לַיהוָה

May you be blessed by the LORD. (1 Sam. 23:21)

(6) זִבְחֵי אֱלֹהִים רוּחַ (נִשְׁבָּר / <u>נִשְׁבָּרָה</u>)

The sacrifices of God are a broken spirit. (Ps. 51:19; Eng. 51:17)

(7) עִיר (שֹׁפֵךְ / <u>שֹׁפֶכֶת</u>) דָּם בְּתוֹכָהּ

a city shedding blood in her midst (Ezek. 22:3)

(8) ⁽ⁱ⁾וְיָדַיִם (שֹׁפְכִים / <u>שֹׁפְכוֹת</u>) דָּם־נָקִי

and hands shedding innocent blood (Prov. 6:17)

(9) (<u>וּבָרוּךְ</u> / וּבְרוּכָה) אַתָּה בַּשָּׂדֶה

And blessed shall you be in the field. (Deut. 28:3)

108

(10) וְהִנֵּה [הָעִיר] שָׂרוּף / שְׂרוּפָה) בָּאֵשׁ (

Behold, [the city] was burned with fire. (1 Sam. 30:3)

(11) וָאֶשְׁמַע אֶת־הָאִישׁ) לָבוּשׁ / לְבוּשָׁה) הַבַּדִּים (

And I heard the man clothed in linen. (Dan. 12:7)

(12) כָּל־הָעִיר) עָזוּב / עֲזוּבָה(j) (

Every city is forsaken. (Jer. 4:29)

(13)) עֲזוּבִים / (k)עֲזֻבוֹת) עָרֵי עֲרֹעֵר (

The cities of Aroer are forsaken. (Isa. 17:2)

(14) אַחֲרֵי מִי אַתָּה) רֹדֵף / רֹדְפָה (

After whom are you pursuing? (1 Sam. 24:15; Eng. 24:14)

(15) מָה אֲדֹנִי) מְדַבֵּר / מְדַבֶּרֶת) אֶל־עַבְדּוֹ (

What is my lord saying to his servant? (Josh. 5:14)

(16) חָמֵשׁ עָרִים בְּאֶרֶץ מִצְרַיִם) מְדַבְּרִים / מְדַבְּרוֹת) שְׂפַת כְּנַעַן (

five cities in the land of Egypt which speak the language of Canaan
(Isa. 19:18)

(17) וַיֹּאמֶר מָה־אַתָּה) רֹאֶה / רֹאָה) עָמוֹס (

And he said, "What do you see, Amos?" (Amos 8:2)

(18) הֵם) הַמְדַבְּרִים(l) / הַמְדַבְּרוֹת) אֶל־פַּרְעֹה מֶלֶךְ־מִצְרַיִם (

It was they who spoke to Pharaoh king of Egypt. (Exod. 6:27)

XX.4 Each of the following entries contains a participial form. In the space marked
(a) give its stem, in (b) its voice (active or passive), in (c) its gender and
number, and in (d) its root.

Example:

מִסְתַּתֵּר(e) אָכֵן אַתָּה אֵל Truly, you are a God who hides yourself.
(Isa. 45:15)

(a) __Hitpaᶜel__ (b) __active__ (c) __ms__ (d) __[סתר]__

(1) וּשְׁמוּאֵל שֹׁכֵב בְּהֵיכַל יהוה And Samuel was lying down in the temple
of the LORD. (1 Sam. 3:3)

(a) __Qal__ (b) __active__ (c) __ms__ (d) __שָׁכַב__

(2) וּשְׁלֹמֹה הָיָה(m) מוֹשֵׁל בְּכָל־הַמַּמְלָכוֹת Solomon ruled over all the
kingdoms. (1 Kgs. 5:1; Eng. 4:21)

(a) __Qal__ (b) __active__ (c) __ms__ (d) __מָשַׁל__

109

(3) שׁוֹמֵר יִשְׂרָאֵל he who keeps Israel (Ps. 121:4)

    (a) __Qal__ (b) __active__ (c) __ms__ (d) שָׁמַר

(4) [n]הֲשֹׁמְרִים הֵם אֶת־דֶּרֶךְ יְהוָה Are they keeping the way of the LORD? (Judg. 2:22)

    (a) __Qal__ (b) __active__ (c) __mp__ (d) שָׁמַר

(5) כַּאֲשֶׁר כָּתוּב בְּתוֹרַת מֹשֶׁה as it is written in the law of Moses (Dan. 9:13)

    (a) __Qal__ (b) __passive__ (c) __ms__ (d) כָּתַב

(6) כִּי אֹתָהּ אַתֶּם מְבַקְשִׁים For that is what you seek (what you desire). (Exod. 10:11)

    (a) __Pi‘el__ (b) __active__ (c) __mp__ (d) [בקשׁ]

(7) בְּיַד מְבַקְשֵׁי נַפְשָׁם into the hand of those who seek their life (Jer. 46:26)

    (a) __Pi‘el__ (b) __active__ (c) __mp__ (d) [בקשׁ]

(8) קָרוֹב יְהוָה לְנִשְׁבְּרֵי־לֵב The LORD is near to the broken-hearted. (Ps. 34:19; Eng. 34:18)

    (a) __Nif‘al__ (b) __passive__ (c) __mp__ (d) שָׁבַר

(9) מַשְׁבִּית מִלְחָמוֹת עַד־קְצֵה הָאָרֶץ who makes wars to cease to the end of the earth (Ps. 46:10; Eng. 46:9)

    (a) __Hif‘il__ (b) __active__ (c) __ms__ (d) שָׁבַת

(10) מְלַמֵּד יָדַי לַמִּלְחָמָה who teaches (trains) my hands for war (2 Sam. 22:35)

    (a) __Pi‘el__ (b) __active__ (c) __ms__ (d) לָמַד

(11) הַנִּסְתָּרֹת לַיהוָה אֱלֹהֵינוּ The hidden things belong to the LORD our God. (Deut. 29:28; Eng. 29:29)

    (a) __Nif‘al__ (b) __passive__ (c) __fp__ (d) [סתר]

(12) הַמַּסְתִּיר פָּנָיו מִבֵּית יַעֲקֹב who is hiding his face from the house of Jacob (Isa. 8:17)

    (a) __Hif‘il__ (b) __active__ (c) __ms__ (d) [סתר]

(13) כִּי יְהוָה שֹׁפְטֵנוּ For the LORD is our judge. (Isa. 33:22)

    (a) __Qal__ (b) __active__ (c) __ms__ (d) שָׁפַט

(14) [o]יְהַלְלוּ יְהוָה דֹּרְשָׁיו Those who seek him shall praise the LORD. (Ps. 22:27; Eng. 22:26)

    (a) __Qal__ (b) __active__ (c) __mp__ (d) דָּרַשׁ

(15)   רַבִּים רֹדְפָי   Many are my pursuers (persecutors). (Ps. 119:157)

      (a) ___ Qal ___ (b) ___ active ___ (c) ___ mp ___ (d) רָדַף ___

Footnotes

(a) כָּתַב, "he wrote," is made up of three BeGaD KeFaT consonants. Caution is needed in determining when dagesh lenes are to be included in the synopsis forms. A BeGaD KeFaT consonant takes a dagesh lene whenever it is not immediately preceded by a vowel (full vowel or vocal sheva). (Cf. *G*.39.4, p. 128f.)

(b) A participle depicts continuous action taking place in either the past, present, or future, i.e., from the standpoint of the writer or the participants in the story. The reader must use the clues furnished by the context to determine which time was intended. Most of the participles chosen for this exercise describe actions taking place in the present, although that used in exercise XX.2(11) (שֹׁפְטָה) is to be translated in the past, as indicated by the phrase "at that time."

(c) מֹשְׁלָה would ordinarily be accented on the final syllable. But since the following word (לוֹ) is pausal (with silluq, לוֹ), the accent on מֹשְׁלָה recedes one syllable. This is a change that frequently occurs in other similar situations.

(d) Two masculine plural construct participial forms appear side by side: "the ones loving (him)" and "the ones keeping."

(e) When the prefix of the Hitpaʿel is placed before a verb whose initial consonant is a sibilant (ס, צ, שׁ, or שׂ), the ת of the prefix changes position with the sibilant in order to facilitate pronunciation. The participle מִתְסַתֵּר becomes מִסְתַּתֵּר. The meaning remains the same, "one hiding himself." [Cf. *G*.36.4(3), p. 111.]

(f) An alternate translation would be: "Why is this (that) my lord is pursuing after his servant?"

(g) Participles agree in gender and number with the nouns and pronouns that are described by them or that serve as subjects of the participles.

(h) בָּרוּךְ is a Qal passive participle, masculine singular, from [בּרךְ]. [בּרךְ] occurs a total of 71 times in its various forms. בָּרוּךְ often functions as if it were a jussive, expressing a wish, desire, or invocation.

(i) Nouns designating parts of the body that exist in pairs (eyes, ears, hands, etc.) are usually feminine [cf. *G*.18.2(5), p. 37], thus requiring feminine participles.

(j) ע is pointed with a compound sheva rather than a simple sheva, since it is a guttural.

(k) עֲזֻבוֹת contains a defective šureq (וּ), both here and in its only other occurrence in the book of Isaiah (10:14). The qibbuṣ still remains a long vowel that stands in an open, unaccented syllable.

(l) Since participles can describe continuous action, the use of the participle in Exodus 6:27 suggests that Moses and Aaron spoke to Pharaoh on numerous occasions (cf. *G*.60.2, p. 200).

(m) Forms of the verb "to be" (הָיָה) may be followed by either active or passive participles. This construction describes a continuous or progressive action or state of being in either the past, present, or future. The combination of a form of הָיָה plus the participle is more likely to occur in late Biblical Hebrew.

(n) Participles that stand at the beginning of a question may have the prefixed interrogative ה (cf. *G*.34.1, pp. 94f.).

(o) An alternate translation based on the interpretation of the initial verb as a jussive: "Let those praise the LORD who are his seekers."

Suggestions for Further Testing

1. (Vocabulary Review) Match the following so that words with opposite meanings are paired.

(1) ( ) אָרַר	(11) ( ) [דבר]	(A) מָשַׁל	(K) לָקַח
(2) ( ) שָׂנֵא	(12) ( ) יָרֵא	(B) יָשַׁב	(L) חָיָה
(3) ( ) מוּת	(13) ( ) שָׁאַל	(C) יָרַד	(M) קוּם
(4) ( ) גָּלָה	(14) ( ) הָלַךְ	(D) שָׁמַע	(N) [ברך]
(5) ( ) עָבַד	(15) ( ) שָׁבַר	(E) עָנָה	(O) רוֹעֶה
(6) ( ) נָתַן	(16) ( ) עָזַר	(F) רָפָא	(P) סָתַר
(7) ( ) עָמַד	(17) ( ) אָכַל	(G) שׁוּב	(Q) פֶּשַׁע
(8) ( ) עָלָה	(18) ( ) [אמן]	(H) עָזַב	(R) אָהַב
(9) ( ) זָכַר	(19) ( ) צֹאן	(I) מִלְחָמָה	(S) שָׂמַח
(10) ( ) שָׁכַב	(20) ( ) שָׁלוֹם	(J) שָׁתָה	(T) שָׁכַח

2. Underscore the correct participial form in each of the following sentences and phrases.

(1)   וּמָה־יְהוָה (דּוֹרֵשׁ / דֹּרְשָׁה) מִמְּךָ (Mic. 6:8)

(2)   קוֹל אֱלֹהִים (מְדַבֵּר / מְדַבְּרִים) מִתּוֹךְ־הָאֵשׁ (Deut. 4:33)

112

(Judg. 11:34) וְהִנֵּה בִתּוֹ (יוֹצֵא / יֹצֵאת / לִקְרָאתוֹ) (3)

(Judg. 4:22) אֶת־הָאִישׁ אֲשֶׁר־אַתָּה (מְבַקֵּשׁ / מְבַקֶּשֶׁת / מְבַקֵּשׁ) (4)

(Gen. 3:8) יְהוָה אֱלֹהִים (מִתְהַלֵּךְ / מְתַהֲלֵךְ / מִתְהַלְּכִים) בַּגָּן (5)

(Gen. 45:26) כִּי־הוּא (מֹשְׁלָה / מֹשֵׁל) בְּכָל־אֶרֶץ מִצְרָיִם (6)

(Exod. 4:19) כָּל־הָאֲנָשִׁים (הַמְבַקֵּשׁ / הַמְבַקְשִׁים) אֶת־נַפְשֶׁךָ (7)

(Isa. 40:10) וּזְרֹעוֹ (מֹשְׁלָה / מֹשֵׁל) לוֹ (8)

(Mal. 3:1) הָאָדוֹן אֲשֶׁר־אַתֶּם (מְבַקֵּשׁ / מְבַקְשִׁים) (9)

(Judg. 2:22) (הֲשֹׁמֵר / הֲשֹׁמְרִים) הֵם אֶת־דֶּרֶךְ יְהוָה (10)

3. Fill in the blanks with the correct pronouns. (Note the participial forms.)

(1) אֲנַחְנוּ שֹׁלְחִים אֹתְךָ אֵלָיו

_____ are sending _____ to _____. (Jer. 42:6)

(2) אָנֹכִי שֹׁלֵחַ אוֹתְךָ אֲלֵיהֶם

_____ am sending _____ to _____. (Jer. 25:15)

(3) וְקִדַּשְׁתּוֹ כִּי־אֶת־לֶחֶם אֱלֹהֶיךָ הוּא מַקְרִיב

_____ shall sanctify _____ for _____ is offering (bringing near) the bread (food) of _____ God. (Lev. 21:8)

(4) הִנְנִי מִתְפַּלֵּל אֶל־יְהוָה אֱלֹהֵיכֶם כְּדִבְרֵיכֶם

Behold, _____ am praying to the LORD _____ God according to _____ words. (Jer. 42:4)

(5) אֶת־אָבִיהָ הִיא מְחַלֶּלֶת בָּאֵשׁ תִּשָּׂרֵף

_____ is profaning _____ father; _____ shall be burned with fire. (Lev. 21:9)

(6) הַמְכַבֵּד דָּוִד אֶת־אָבִיךָ בְּעֵינֶיךָ

Is David honoring _____ father in _____ eyes? (2 Sam. 10:3)

(7) כָּל־עַמָּהּ מְבַקְשִׁים לֶחֶם

All _____ people are seeking bread. (Lam. 1:11)

(8) גֹּאֲלֵנוּ יְהוָה צְבָאוֹת שְׁמוֹ

_____ redeemer, the LORD of hosts is _____ name. (Isa. 47:4)

(9) עוֹד הֵם מְדַבְּרִים וַאֲנִי אֶשְׁמַע

While _____ are yet speaking, _____ will hear. (Isa. 65:24)

(10) יְהוָה צוּרִי וְגֹאֲלִי

O LORD, _____ rock and _____ redeemer. (Ps. 19:15; Eng. 19:14)

LESSON XXI

Answer Key
(Cf. *G*, pp. 216ff.)

XXI.1 In the following clauses and sentences, identify (a) the verb sequence, (b) the verb stems, and (c) the verb roots.

Example:

^(a)קַח־לְךָ מְגִלַּת־סֵפֶר Take a scroll and write on it. (Jer. 36:2)

^(f)וְכָתַבְתָּ אֵלֶיהָ

   (a) __Imperative__ + __Perfect__ sequence (b) __Qal__ , __Qal__

         (c) __כָּתַב__ __לָקַח__ , _____

(1) ^(b)שַׁלַּח אֶת־עַמִּי ^(c)וְיַעַבְדֻנִי Send my people out, that they may serve me. (Exod. 7:26; Eng. 8:1)

   (a) __Imperative__ + __Imperfect__ sequence (b) __Pi‘el__ , __Qal__

         (c) __עָבַד__ __שָׁלַח__ , _____

(2) ^(a)בְּנֵה־לְךָ בַיִת בִּירוּשָׁלַָם Build yourself a house in Jerusalem, and dwell there. (1 Kgs. 2:36)

^(f)וְיָשַׁבְתָּ שָׁם

   (a) __Imperative__ + __Perfect__ sequence (b) __Qal__ , __Qal__

         (c) __יָשַׁב__ __בָּנָה__ , _____

(3) ^(a)הִנָּבֵא בֶן־אָדָם ^(f)וְאָמַרְתָּ Prophesy, son of man, and say to the wind (breath). (Ezek. 37:9)

אֶל־הָרוּחַ

   (a) __Imperative__ + __Perfect__ sequence (b) __Nif‘al__ , __Qal__

         (c) __אָמַר__ __[נבא]__ , _____

(4) ^(d)וְלֹא יִקָּרֵא עוֹד שִׁמְךָ No longer shall your name be called Abram, but your name shall be Abraham (Gen. 17:5)

אַבְרָם וְהָיָה שִׁמְךָ אַבְרָהָם

   (a) __Imperfect__ + __Perfect__ sequence (b) __Nif‘al__ , __Qal__

         (c) __הָיָה__ __קָרָא__ , _____

(5) ^(e)כִּי תִשְׁמֹר אֶת־מִצְוֹת יְהוָה if you keep the commandments of the LORD your God, and walk in his ways (Deut. 28:9)

אֱלֹהֶיךָ ^(f)וְהָלַכְתָּ בִּדְרָכָיו

   (a) __Imperfect__ + __Perfect__ sequence (b) __Qal__ , __Qal__

         (c) __הָלַךְ__ __שָׁמַר__ , _____

114

(6)   נִבְנֶה־^(h)לָּנוּ עִיר^(g)   Let us build for ourselves a city,
וְנַעֲשֶׂה־^(h)לָּנוּ שֵׁם   and let us make for ourselves a name.
(Gen. 11:4)

(a) <u>Imperfect</u> + <u>Imperfect</u> sequence (b) <u>Qal</u> , <u>Qal</u>
(c) <u>עָשָׂה</u> , <u>בָּנָה</u>

(7)   יִקְרָאֵנִי וְאֶעֱנֵהוּ⁽ⁱ⁾   He will call to me, and I will answer
him. (Ps. 91:15)

(a) <u>Imperfect</u> + <u>Imperfect</u> sequence (b) <u>Qal</u> , <u>Qal</u>
(c) <u>עָנָה</u> , <u>קָרָא</u>

(8)   קְרַב עַד־הֵנָּה וַאֲדַבְּרָה^(b)   Come near, that I may speak to you.
אֵלֶיךָ   (2 Sam. 20:16)

(a) <u>Imperative</u> + <u>Imperfect</u> sequence (b) <u>Qal</u> , <u>Pi'el</u>
(c) <u>[דבר]</u> , <u>קָרַב</u>

(9)   פְּקַח־נָא אֶת־עֵינָיו וְיִרְאֶה^(b)   Open his eyes, that he may see.
(2 Kgs. 6:17)

(a) <u>Imperative</u> + <u>Imperfect</u> sequence (b) <u>Qal</u> , <u>Qal</u>
(c) <u>רָאָה</u> , <u>פָּקַח</u>

(10)   תְּנוּ־לָנוּ מַיִם וְנִשְׁתֶּה^(b)   Give^(j) to us water, that we may drink.
(Exod. 17:2)

(a) <u>Imperative</u> + <u>Imperfect</u> sequence (b) <u>Qal</u> , <u>Qal</u>
(c) <u>שָׁתָה</u> , <u>נָתַן</u>

(11)   שִׂנְאוּ־רָע וְאֶהֱבוּ טוֹב^(k)   Hate evil and love good.
(Amos 5:15)

(a) <u>Imperative</u> + <u>Imperative</u> sequence (b) <u>Qal</u> , <u>Qal</u>
(c) <u>שָׂנֵא</u> , <u>אָהֵב</u>

(12) שִׁמְרוּ מִשְׁפָּט וַעֲשׂוּ צְדָקָה^(l)   Keep justice, and do righteousness.
(Isa. 56:1)

(a) <u>Imperative</u> + <u>Imperative</u> sequence (b) <u>Qal</u> , <u>Qal</u>
(c) <u>שָׁמַר</u> , <u>עָשָׂה</u>

XXI.2 Translate the following clauses and sentences, and locate fully all verb forms, following the guidelines given in *G*.XIV.38, pp. 117ff.

(1) זָכַרְתִּי (m) בַלַּיְלָה שִׁמְךָ (n) וָאֶשְׁמְרָה תּוֹרָתֶךָ (Ps. 119:55)

"I remember your name in the night, and I keep your law."

(a) זָכַרְתִּי Qal perfect, 1 cs, from זָכַר, "he remembered." Trans. "I remember."

(b) וָאֶשְׁמְרָה Qal imperfect, 1 cs, plus vav consecutive [cf. *G*.43, pp. 145f.; 63.1(2), p. 211], plus cohortative ה (cf. *G*.41.2, p. 132), from שָׁמַר, "he kept." Trans. "And I keep."

(2) וַיֹּאמֶר (o) צֵא (f) וְעָמַדְתָּ בָהָר לִפְנֵי יְהוָה (1 Kgs. 19:11)

"And he said, 'Go out and stand on the mountain before the LORD.'"

(a) וַיֹּאמֶר Qal imperfect, 3 ms, plus vav consecutive, from אָמַר, "he said." Trans. "And he said."

(b) צֵא Qal imperative, 2 ms, from יָצָא, "he went out." Trans. "Go out!"

(c) וְעָמַדְתָּ Qal perfect, 1 cs, plus vav conjunction, from עָמַד, "he stood." Trans. "Stand!"

(3) כִּי־יִצְעַק אֵלַי (f) וְשָׁמַעְתִּי (Exod. 22:26; Eng. 22:27)

"If he cries out to me, I will listen."

(a) יִצְעַק Qal imperfect, 3 ms, from צָעַק, "he cried out." Trans. "He will cry out."

(b) וְשָׁמַעְתִּי Qal perfect, 1 cs, plus vav consecutive, from שָׁמַע, "he listened." Trans. "I will listen, hear."

(4) וַיִּזְכֹּר אֱלֹהִים אֶת־בְּרִיתוֹ אֶת־אַבְרָהָם (Exod. 2:24)

"And God remembered his covenant with Abraham."

וַיִּזְכֹּר Qal imperfect, 3 ms, plus vav consecutive, from זָכַר, "he remembered." Trans. "And he (God) remembered."

XXI.3 Match each of these weak verbs with its proper classification, according to the traditional classification system.[p]

(1) (J) מָדַד	(6) (B) שָׁמַע	(A) Pe Nun	(F) ʿAyin Vav
(2) (H) עָזַב	(7) (I) בִּין	(B) Lamed Guttural	(G) Lamed He
(3) (G) פָּנָה	(8) (C) מָצָא	(C) Lamed ʾAlef	(H) Pe Guttural
(4) (F) קוּם	(9) (K) יָלַד	(D) ʿAyin Guttural	(I) ʿAyin Yod
(5) (A) נָתַן	(10) (D) זָעַק	(E) Pe ʾAlef	(J) Double ʿAyin
	(11) (E) אָבַד		(K) Pe Vav/Pe Yod

XXI.4 Copy the infinitives in the following examples and give (a) the stem, and (b) the root of each.

Example:

לֶחֶם ⁽q⁾לֶאֱכֹל וּבֶגֶד לִלְבֹּשׁ

bread to eat, and clothes to wear
(Gen. 28:20)

	Inf.		לֶאֱכֹל
(a) Qal	(b)	אָכַל
	Inf.		לִלְבֹּשׁ
(a) Qal	(b)	לָבַשׁ

(1) ⁽r⁾הָלוֹךְ וְדִבַּרְתָּ אֶל־דָּוִד

Go and say to David. (2 Sam. 24:12)

	Inf.		הָלוֹךְ
(a) Qal	(b)	הָלַךְ

(2) לְהַבְדִּיל בֵּין הַיּוֹם וּבֵין הַלָּיְלָה

to separate between the day and between the night (Gen. 1:14)

	Inf.		לְהַבְדִּיל
(a) Hifʻil	(b)	[בדל]

(3) ⁽s⁾וַיִּשְׁאַל דָּוִד בַּיהוָה לֵאמֹר

And David inquired (asked) of the LORD, saying: (1 Sam. 23:2)

	Inf.		לֵאמֹר
(a) Qal	(b)	אָמַר

(4) אֲשֶׁר עֵינַיִם לָהֶם ⁽t⁾לִרְאוֹת וְלֹא רָאוּ אָזְנַיִם לָהֶם לִשְׁמֹעַ וְלֹא שָׁמֵעוּ

who have eyes to see, but see not; who have ears to hear, but hear not (Ezek. 12:2)

	Inf.		לִרְאוֹת
(a) Qal	(b)	רָאָה
	Inf.		לִשְׁמֹעַ
(a) Qal	(b)	שָׁמַע

(5) לֹא ⁽u⁾אֵדַע ⁽v⁾צֵאת וָבֹא

I do not know (how) to go out or to come in. (1 Kgs. 3:7)

	Inf.		צֵאת
(a) Qal	(b)	יָצָא
	Inf.		וָבֹא
(a) Qal	(b)	בּוֹא

(6) וְלִמְשֹׁל בַּיּוֹם וּבַלָּיְלָה

to rule over the day and over the night (Gen. 1:18)

	Inf.		וְלִמְשֹׁל
(a) Qal	(b)	מָשַׁל

(7) לִדְרוֹשׁ אֶת־תּוֹרַת יְהוָה וְלַעֲשֹׂת וּלְלַמֵּד בְּיִשְׂרָאֵל חֹק ⁽w⁾וּמִשְׁפָּט

to seek the law of the LORD, and to do (it); and to teach statutes and ordinances in Israel (Ezra 7:10)

	Inf.		לִדְרוֹשׁ
(a) Qal	(b)	דָּרַשׁ
	Inf.		וְלַעֲשֹׂת
(a) Qal	(b)	עָשָׂה
	Inf.		לְלַמֵּד
(a) Piʻel	(b)	לָמַד

117

(8) וַיַּנִּחֵהוּ^(x) בְּגַן־עֵדֶן לְעָבְדָהּ וּלְשָׁמְרָהּ

And he placed him in the garden of Eden to tend it and to keep it. (Gen. 2:15)

	Inf.	לְעָבְדָהּ
(a)	Qal (b)	עָבַד
	Inf.	וּלְשָׁמְרָהּ
(a)	Qal (b)	שָׁמַר

(9) לֹא־טוֹב ^(y)הֱיוֹת הָאָדָם ^(z)לְבַדּוֹ

It is not good for the man to be alone. (Gen. 2:18)

	Inf.	הֱיוֹת
(a)	Qal (b)	הָיָה

Footnotes

(a) For the Imperative/Perfect sequence, cf. *G*.63.3(1), pp. 214f.

(b) For the Imperative/Imperfect sequence, cf. *G*.63.3(2), p. 215.

(c) When a pronominal suffix is added to an imperfect ending in šureq, the šureq will often be written defectively, i.e., as a qibbuṣ. Changes of this nature most often occur when the pronominal suffix is third masculine singular, although in this instance it is first common singular [cf. *G*.47.1(1), p. 157].

(d) For the Indicative Imperfect/Perfect sequence, cf. *G*.63.2(2)(a), pp. 212f.

(e) כִּי often introduces a subjunctive clause, i.e., one that expresses a conditional, doubtful, contrary to fact, or hypothetical statement or question. It can mean "if," "lest," "when," "indeed," "that," "since," or "because." For the Subjunctive Imperfect/Perfect sequence, cf. *G*.63.2(2)(d), pp. 213f.

(f) When perfects are prefixed with vav conjunction, the accent shifts to the final syllable in second masculine singular and first common singular forms in all classes of verbs except Lamed He [cf. *G*.63.2(2), p. 212].

(g) A Cohortative Imperfect may be in a coordinate relationship with another (Cohortative) Imperfect.

(h) For the use of the conjunctive dagesh forte, which occurs twice in this example, cf. *G*.45, p. 147.

(i) For the Indicative Imperfect/Imperfect sequence, cf. *G*.63.2(1), p. 212.

(j) The verb תְּנוּ is Qal imperative, second masculine plural, from נָתַן, "he gave." Trans. "You (pl.) give!" [Cf. *G*.48.2(6), p. 166.]

(k) Since טוֹב is a pausal form (carries a heavy accent), the accent on the preceding word is forced back one syllable (away from the final syllable) to avoid having two accented syllables standing side by side in the sentence.

(l) וַעֲשׂוּ is Qal imperative, second masculine plural, plus vav conjunction, from עָשָׂה, "he did, made." Trans. "You (pl.) do!" (Cf. *G*.72.6, p. 290)

(m) A perfect (and its coordinated imperfect) may be translated in the present tense when it represents a verb of perception, attitude, disposition, or mental or physical state of being [cf. *G*.31.1(3), p. 86].

(n) For the cohortative (emphatic) ה on first person imperfects, cf. *G*.41.2, p. 132.

(o) On the form of this imperative, cf. *G*.75.2(2)(b), p. 341.

(p) Cf. *G*.29.6, pp. 81f.

(q) On the form of this infinitive, cf. *G*.56.1(3)(c), p. 180.

(r) The infinitive absolute may be used as a substitute for an imperative [cf. *G*.57.3(4), p. 185].

(s) On the form and function of לֵאמֹר, cf. *G*.56.1(3)(d), p. 180; 56.2(2)(c), p. 182.

(t) On the form of this infinitive, cf. *G*.56.1(3)(j), p. 181.

(u) אֵדַע is a Qal imperfect, first common singular, from יָדַע, "he knows (knew)." Trans. "I know" [cf. *G*.75.2(2)(a), p. 340].

(v) For the form of this infinitive, cf. *G*.75.2(2)(c), p. 341.

(w) The two final nouns in this sentence are singular in form but collective in meaning.

(x) וַיַּנִּחֵהוּ is Hifʻil imperfect, third masculine singular, plus vav consecutive, plus third masculine singular pronominal suffix, from נוּחַ, "to rest." Trans. (with causative force) "he placed him."

(y) For the form of this infinitive, cf. *G*.56.1(3)(k), p. 181; 72.7, p. 291.

(z) On the form and meaning of לְבַדּוֹ, cf. *G*.27.1(3)(b), p. 69.

Suggestions for Further Testing

1. Translate the clauses and sentences, and locate all verb forms.

(1)   הָלוֹךְ וְדִבַּרְתָּ אֶל־דָּוִד   (2 Sam. 24:12)

(2)   כִּי אַתֶּם מְבַקְשִׁים   (Exod. 10:11)

(3)   וַיהוָה הִשְׁלִיךְ עֲלֵיהֶם אֲבָנִים גְּדֹלוֹת   (Josh. 10:11)

(4)   שִׁמְעָה עַמִּי וַאֲדַבֵּרָה   (Ps. 50:7)

(5)   וַיִּתְפַּלֵּל אַבְרָהָם אֶל־הָאֱלֹהִים   (Gen. 20:17)

(6)   וַנִּתְפַּלֵּל אֶל־אֱלֹהֵינוּ   (Neh. 4:3)

(7)   אֱלֹהֵינוּ יִלָּחֶם לָנוּ   (Neh. 4:14)

(8)   כִּי יְהוָה אֱלֹהֶיךָ הוּא הַהֹלֵךְ עִמָּךְ   (Deut. 31:6)

(9)   יִזְכָּר־נָא הַמֶּלֶךְ אֶת־יְהוָה אֱלֹהֶיךָ   (2 Sam. 14:11)

(10)   וְהַשְׁלֵךְ לִפְנֵי־פַרְעֹה   (Exod. 7:9)

LESSON XXII

Answer Key
(Cf. *G*, pp. 229ff.)

XXII.1 Write the synopsis of עָבַד, "he served," in the Qal, Nifʿal, Piʿel, Hifʿil, and Hofʿal stems.

	Qal	Nifʿal	Piʿel	Hifʿil	Hofʿal
Perf. 3 ms	עָבַד	נֶעֱבַד	עִבֵּד	הֶעֱבִיד	הָעֳבַד
Impf. 3 ms	יַעֲבֹד	יֵעָבֵד	יְעַבֵּד	יַעֲבִיד	יָעֳבַד
Impv. 2 ms	עֲבֹד	הֵעָבֵד	עַבֵּד	הַעֲבֵד	X X X
Inf. Const.	עֲבֹד	הֵעָבֵד	עַבֵּד	הַעֲבִיד	הָעֳבַד
Inf. Abs.	עָבוֹד	נַעֲבֹד	עַבֵּד	הַעֲבֵד	הָעֳבֵד
Part. Act. (ms)	עֹבֵד	X X X	מְעַבֵּד	מַעֲבִיד	X X X
Part. Pass. (ms)	עָבוּד	נֶעֱבָד	X X X	X X X	מָעֳבַד

XXII.2 Write the full inflection of the perfect of עָבַד, "he served," in the Qal, Nifʿal, Piʿel, and Hifʿil stems.

	Qal	Nifʿal	Piʿel	Hifʿil
3 ms	עָבַד	נֶעֱבַד	עִבֵּד	הֶעֱבִיד
3 fs	עָבְדָה	נֶעֶבְדָה	עִבְּדָה	הֶעֱבִידָה
2 ms	עָבַדְתָּ	נֶעֱבַדְתָּ	עִבַּדְתָּ	הֶעֱבַדְתָּ
2 fs	עָבַדְתְּ	נֶעֱבַדְתְּ	עִבַּדְתְּ	הֶעֱבַדְתְּ
1 cs	עָבַדְתִּי	נֶעֱבַדְתִּי	עִבַּדְתִּי	הֶעֱבַדְתִּי
3 cp	עָבְדוּ	נֶעֶבְדוּ	עִבְּדוּ	הֶעֱבִידוּ
2 mp	עֲבַדְתֶּם	נֶעֱבַדְתֶּם	עִבַּדְתֶּם	הֶעֱבַדְתֶּם
2 fp	עֲבַדְתֶּן	נֶעֱבַדְתֶּן	עִבַּדְתֶּן	הֶעֱבַדְתֶּן
1 cp	עָבַדְנוּ	נֶעֱבַדְנוּ	עִבַּדְנוּ	הֶעֱבַדְנוּ

121

XXII.3 Each of the following sentences contains a perfect form of a Pe Guttural verb. In the space numbered (a) give the perfect's stem, in (b) its person, gender, and number, and in (c) its root.

Example:

נַחֲלָתֵנוּ נֶהֶפְכָה לְזָרִים		(a)	Nif'al
Our inheritance has been turned over to strangers.		(b)	3 fs
(Lam. 5:2)		(c)	הָפַךְ
(1) אֵיפֹה הָאֲנָשִׁים אֲשֶׁר הֲרַגְתֶּם בְּתָבוֹר		(a)	Qal
Where are the men whom you killed at Tabor? (Judg. 8:18)		(b)	2 mp
		(c)	הָרַג
(2) וַעֲבַדְתֶּם אֶת־יְהוָה בְּכָל־לְבַבְכֶם (a)		(a)	Qal
And you shall serve the LORD with all your heart.		(b)	2 mp
(1 Sam. 12:20)		(c)	עָבַד
(3) וְהוּא הֶעֱבִיר אֶת־בָּנָיו בָּאֵשׁ (b)		(a)	Hif'il
And he caused his sons to pass through the fire.		(b)	3 ms
(2 Chr. 33:6)		(c)	עָבַר
(4) אֵלִי אֵלִי לָמָה עֲזַבְתָּנִי		(a)	Qal
My God, my God, why have you forsaken me? (Ps. 22:2;		(b)	2 ms
Eng. 22:1)		(c)	עָזַב
(5) בָּנַיִךְ עֲזָבוּנִי		(a)	Qal
Your children (sons) have forsaken me. (Jer. 5:7)		(b)	3 mp
		(c)	עָזַב
(6) בְּיוֹם יְשׁוּעָה עֲזַרְתִּיךָ		(a)	Qal
In a day of salvation I have helped you. (Isa. 49:8)		(b)	1 cs
		(c)	עָזַר
(7) וְהֶעֱמִיד הַכֹּהֵן אֶת־הָאִשָּׁה לִפְנֵי יְהוָה (a)		(a)	Hif'il
And the priest shall set the woman (shall cause the woman		(b)	3 ms
to stand) before the LORD. (Num. 5:18)		(c)	עָמַד
(8) בַּמָּה אֲהַבְתָּנוּ		(a)	Qal
In what (wherein) have you loved us? (Mal. 1:2)		(b)	2 ms
		(c)	אָהַב
(9) וְלֹא הֶאֱמִין לָהֶם גְּדַלְיָהוּ		(a)	Hif'il
But Gedaliah did not believe them. (Jer. 40:14)		(b)	3 ms
		(c)	[אמן]

(10) לָמָה זֶּה עֲזַבְתֶּן אֶת־הָאִישׁ   (a)   Qal

Why is it that you have left the man? (Exod. 2:20)   (b)   2 fp

(c)   עָזַב

XXII.4   Each of the following sentences contains an imperfect form of a Pe Guttural verb. In the space numbered (a) give the imperfect's stem, in (b) its person, gender, and number, and in (c) its root.
Example:

וַיַּחֲלֹם יוֹסֵף חֲלוֹם ^(c)   (a)   Qal

And Joseph dreamed a dream. (Gen. 37:5)   (b)   3 ms

(c)   חָלַם

(1) ^(d)הֲיַהֲפֹךְ ^(e)כּוּשִׁי עוֹרוֹ   (a)   Qal

Can the Ethiopian change his skin? (Jer. 13:23)   (b)   3 ms

(c)   הָפַךְ

(2) הַשֶּׁמֶשׁ יֵהָפֵךְ לְחֹשֶׁךְ   (a)   Nif‘al

The sun shall be turned to darkness. (Joel 3:4)   (b)   3 ms

(c)   הָפַךְ

(3) ^(f)וַיַּהֲרֹג יְהוָה כָּל־בְּכוֹר בְּאֶרֶץ מִצְרַיִם   (a)   Qal

And the LORD killed all the firstborn in the land of Egypt.   (b)   3 ms
(Exod. 13:15)   (c)   הָרַג

(4) זִקְנֵיכֶם חֲלֹמוֹת ^(g)יַחֲלֹמוּן   (a)   Qal

Your old men shall dream dreams. (Joel 3:1; Eng. 2:28)   (b)   3 mp

(c)   חָלַם

(5) גַּם־אֲנַחְנוּ נַעֲבֹד אֶת־יְהוָה כִּי־הוּא אֱלֹהֵינוּ   (a)   Qal

We also will serve the LORD, for he is our God.   (b)   1 cp
(Josh. 24:18)   (c)   עָבַד

(6) ^(f)וַיַּעֲבֹד יִשְׂרָאֵל אֶת־יְהוָה כֹּל יְמֵי יְהוֹשֻׁעַ   (a)   Qal

And Israel served the LORD all the days of Joshua.   (b)   3 ms
(Josh. 24:31)   (c)   עָבַד

(7) לֹא תַעַבְדוּ אֶת־מֶלֶךְ בָּבֶל   (a)   Qal

You shall not serve the king of Babylon. (Jer. 27:9)   (b)   2 mp

(c)   עָבַד

(8)	כִּי־תַעֲבֹר בַּמַּיִם אִתְּךָ־אָנִי	(a)	Qal
	When you pass through the waters, I will be with you.	(b)	2 ms
	(Isa. 43:2)	(c)	עָבַר
(9)	אֲנִי אַעֲבִיר כָּל־טוּבִי עַל־פָּנֶיךָ	(a)	Hifʻil
	I will cause all my goodness to pass before you (before	(b)	1 cs
	your face). (Exod. 33:19)	(c)	עָבַר
(10)	תַּעֲרֹךְ לְפָנַי שֻׁלְחָן נֶגֶד צֹרְרָי	(a)	Qal
	You prepare a table before me in the presence of my	(b)	2 ms
	harassers. (Ps. 23:5)	(c)	עָרַךְ
(11)	(f)וַיֶּחֱזַק הָרָעָב בְּאֶרֶץ מִצְרָיִם	(a)	Qal
	For the famine was severe (strong) in the land of Egypt.	(b)	3 ms
	(Gen. 41:56)	(c)	חָזַק
(12)	(f)וַיֶּאֱהַב גַּם־אֶת־רָחֵל (h)מִלֵּאָה	(a)	Qal
	And he loved Rachel more than Leah. (Gen. 29:30)	(b)	3 ms
		(c)	אָהַב

XXII.5 Each of the following sentences contains an imperative form of a Pe Guttural verb. In the space numbered (a) give the imperative's stem, in (b) its person, gender, and number, and in (c) its root.

(1)	הַאֲמִינוּ בִנְבִיאָיו	(a)	Hifʻil
	Believe (in) his prophets. (2 Chr. 20:20)	(b)	2 mp
		(c)	[אמן]
(2)	עֲבֹר אֶת־הַיַּרְדֵּן הַזֶּה	(a)	Qal
	Cross over this Jordan. (Josh. 1:2)	(b)	2 ms
		(c)	עָבַר
(3)	בֶּן־אָדָם עֲמֹד עַל־רַגְלֶיךָ	(a)	Qal
	Son of man, stand upon your feet. (Ezek. 2:1)	(b)	2 ms
		(c)	עָמַד
(4)	(i)עֲלֵה רֹאשׁ הַפִּסְגָּה	(a)	Qal
	Go up to the top of Pisgah. (Deut. 3:27)	(b)	2 ms
		(c)	עָלָה

XXII.6 Each of the following contains an infinitive construct of a Pe Guttural verb. Give the stem (a) and root (b) of each. (The verb יוּכַל, used in 3, 4, 5 below is from יָכֹל, a Pe Vav/Pe Yod verb.)

(1) בַּהֲרֹג אִיזֶבֶל אֵת נְבִיאֵי יְהוָה   (a) _Qal_

when Jezebel killed the prophets of the LORD   (b) _הָרַג_
(1 Kgs. 18:13)

(2) וְאָדָם אַיִן לַעֲבֹד אֶת־הָאֲדָמָה   (a) _Qal_

And there was no man to till the ground. (Gen. 2:5)   (b) _עָבַד_

(3) לֹא־יוּכַל הַנַּעַר לַעֲזֹב אֶת־אָבִיו   (a) _Qal_

The lad is not able to leave his father. (Gen. 44:22)   (b) _עָזַב_

(4) אָמְרוּ (d)הֲיוּכַל אֵל לַעֲרֹךְ שֻׁלְחָן בַּמִּדְבָּר   (a) _Qal_

They said, "Can God spread a table in the wilderness?"   (b) _עָרַק_
(Ps. 78:19)

(5) (j)מִי יוּכַל לַעֲמֹד לִפְנֵי יְהוָה   (a) _Qal_

Who is able to stand before the LORD? (1 Sam. 6:20)   (b) _עָמַד_

(6) וּלְהַעֲמִיד אֶת־יְרוּשָׁלָ͏ִם   (a) _Hifʻil_

and to establish (cause to stand) Jerusalem (1 Kgs. 15:4)   (b) _עָמַד_

XXII.7 Each of the following contains a participle of a Pe Guttural verb. Indicate the stem (a), root (b), gender (c), and number (d) of each.

חַטַּאת יְהוּדָה חֲרוּשָׁה עַל־לוּחַ לִבָּם

The sin of Judah is engraved upon the tablet of their heart. (Jer. 17:1)

(a) _Qal_ (b) _חָרַשׁ_ (c) _Fem._ (d) _Sing._

(1) וְלֹא־(k)רָאִיתִי צַדִּיק נֶעֱזָב

And I have not seen a righteous man forsaken. (Ps. 37:25)

(a) _Nifʻal_ (b) _עָזַב_ (c) _Masc._ (d) _Sing._

(2) כִּי (l)עַזָּה עֲזוּבָה תִהְיֶה

For Gaza shall be forsaken. (Zeph. 2:4)

(a) _Qal_ (b) _עָזַב_ (c) _Fem._ (d) _Sing._

(3) כִּי הַמָּקוֹם אֲשֶׁר אַתָּה עוֹמֵד עָלָיו אַדְמַת־קֹדֶשׁ הוּא

For the place where you are standing is holy ground. (Exod. 3:5)

(a) _Qal_ (b) _עָמַד_ (c) _Masc._ (d) _Sing._

(4) לֹא־יִמָּצֵא בְךָ מַעֲבִיר בְּנוֹ־וּבִתּוֹ בָּאֵשׁ (b)

There shall not be found among you one causing his son or his daughter to pass through the fire. (Deut. 18:10)

(a)   Hif'il   (b)   עָבַר   (c)   Masc.   (d)   Sing.

(5) בְּכָל־בֵּיתִי נֶאֱמָן הוּא

In all my house he is faithful. (Num. 12:7)

(a)   Nif'al   (b)   [אמן]   (c)   Masc.   (d)   Sing.

Footnotes

(a) A perfect prefixed with vav conjunction will often be translated in the future tense [cf. *G*.31.1(4), p. 86; 63.2(2), pp. 212ff.].

(b) "To cause someone to pass through fire" is idiomatic for offering a human sacrifice.

(c) Cognate accusatives such as "dreaming a dream," "vowing a vow," "sacrificing a sacrifice," etc., are fairly common in Biblical Hebrew.

(d) This word is prefixed with an interrogative ה (cf. *G*.34.1, p. 94).

(e) כּוּשׁ is the biblical name for Ethiopia. כּוּשִׁי is the gentilic adjective used to describe a citizen of כּוּשׁ (cf. *G*. "Gentilic Adjective," Glossary, pp. 431f.).

(f) For the form and function of vav consecutive prefixed to the imperfect, cf. *G*.43, pp. 145f.; 63.1(2), p. 211.

(g) Imperfects third masculine plural and second masculine plural, which end in וּ, may sometimes appear with final nun following וּ (וּן) [cf. *G*.39.3(4), p. 128]. The added nun does not affect the meaning of the form.

(h) The comparative degree ("more than") is expressed in Biblical Hebrew by prefixing מִן to a noun or pronoun preceded by an adjective or some form of a stative verb (cf. *G*, "Comparative Degree," Glossary, p. 427).

(i) The form of this Qal imperative is determined by the fact that עָלָה is a doubly weak verb (Pe Guttural and Lamed He). For the final ṣere, cf. *G*.72.3(1)(c), p. 287.

(j) מִי ("who") is sometimes used in a rhetorical question aimed not so much at gaining information but rather at giving information. This pattern often involves self-abasement or insult (cf. 1 Sam. 17:26, 18:18, 25:10; Exod. 5:2; etc.).

(k) For the form of רָאִיתִי, a Lamed He verb, cf. *G*.72.3(2)(a), p. 288; Verb Chart 7, pp. 412f.

(l) The writer's skill is evident in the juxtapositioning of עַזָּה and עֲזוּבָה, which creates a phonetic effect. Such a play on sounds is lost in translation.

Suggestions for Further Testing

1. Complete the translation by giving the meaning of the verb. In the space marked (a) give its stem (Qal, Nif'al, etc.), in (b) its form (perfect, imperfect, etc.), in (c) its person, gender, and number, and in (d) its root.

(1) וְלֹא הֶאֱמַנְתִּי לַדְּבָרִים

But I did not _____ the reports (words). (1 Kgs. 10:7)

(a) _____ (b) _____ (c) _____ (d) _____

(2) הֵן בַּעֲבָדָיו לֹא יַאֲמִין

Behold, in his servants he does not _____. (Job 4:18)

(a) _____ (b) _____ (c) _____ (d) _____

(3) וַיַּאֲמִינוּ אַנְשֵׁי נִינְוֵה בֵּאלֹהִים

And the men of Nineveh _____ (in) God. (Jon. 3:5)

(a) _____ (b) _____ (c) _____ (d) _____

(4) נַעְבְּרָה־נָּא בְאַרְצֶךָ

Now let us _____ through your land. (Num. 20:17)

(a) _____ (b) _____ (c) _____ (d) _____

(5) לֹא נַעֲבֹר בְּשָׂדֶה וּבְכֶרֶם

We will not _____ through field or vineyard. (Num. 20:17)

(a) _____ (b) _____ (c) _____ (d) _____

(6) הֵן אֲדֹנָי יהוה יַעֲזָר־לִי

Behold, the Lord GOD will _____ me. (Isa. 50:9)

(a) _____ (b) _____ (c) _____ (d) _____

(7) תַּעַבְדוּן אֶת־הָאֱלֹהִים עַל הָהָר הַזֶּה

You shall _____ God on this mountain. (Exod. 3:12)

(a) _____ (b) _____ (c) _____ (d) _____

(8) וַיַּעַזְבוּ אֶת־יְהוָה אֱלֹהֵי אֲבוֹתָם

And they _____ the LORD, the God of their ancestors. (Judg. 2:12)

(a) _____ (b) _____ (c) _____ (d) _____

(9) גַּם אֲנַחְנוּ נַעֲבֹד אֶת־יְהוָה

We also will _____ the LORD. (Josh. 24:18)

(a) _____ (b) _____ (c) _____ (d) _____

(10) עָזַבְנוּ אֶת־אֱלֹהֵינוּ

We have _____ our God. (Judg. 10:10)

(a) _____ (b) _____ (c) _____ (d) _____

(11) אֵינְכֶם מַאֲמִינִם בַּיהוָה אֱלֹהֵיכֶם

None of you are _____ in the LORD your God. (Deut. 1:32)

(a) _____ (b) _____ (c) _____ (d) _____

(12) אֲבוֹתָם לֹא הֶאֱמִינוּ יְהוָה אֱלֹהֵיהֶם

Their ancestors did not _____ in the LORD their God. (2 Kgs. 17:14)

(a) _____ (b) _____ (c) _____ (d) _____

(13) עָזְרֵנִי יְהוָה אֱלֹהָי

_____ me, O LORD my God! (Ps. 109:26)

(a) _____ (b) _____ (c) _____ (d) _____

(14) וּבֵית צַדִּיקִים יַעֲמֹד

But the house of the righteous (ones) shall _____. (Prov. 12:7)

(a) _____ (b) _____ (c) _____ (d) _____

(15) לֹא־יַעֲלֶה עִמָּנוּ בַּמִּלְחָמָה

He shall not _____ _____ with us to the battle. (1 Sam. 29:9)

(a) _____ (b) _____ (c) _____ (d) _____

(16) זִקְנֵיכֶם חֲלֹמוֹת יַחֲלֹמוּן

Your old men shall _____ dreams. (Joel 3:1)

(a) _____ (b) _____ (c) _____ (d) _____

(17) כִּי אֵין אָדָם אֲשֶׁר לֹא־יֶחֱטָא

For there is no one who does not _____. (2 Chr. 6:36)

(a) _____ (b) _____ (c) _____ (d) _____

(18) רֵעֲךָ וְרֵעַה אָבִיךָ אַל־תַּעֲזֹב

Do not _____ your friend or the friend of your father. (Prov. 27:10)

(a) _____ (b) _____ (c) _____ (d) _____

2. Match the following:

(1)	( )	אָהַב	(A)	he overturned
(2)	( )	[אמן]	(B)	he was strong
(3)	( )	הָפַךְ	(C)	he helped
(4)	( )	הָרַג	(D)	he passed over
(5)	( )	חָזַק	(E)	he loved
(6)	( )	עָבַד	(F)	he abandoned
(7)	( )	עָבַר	(G)	he stood
(8)	( )	עָזַב	(H)	he served
(9)	( )	עָזַר	(I)	he believed
(10)	( )	עָמַד	(J)	he killed

LESSON XXIII

Answer Key
(Cf. *G*, pp. 242ff.)

XXIII.1 Underline the participial form that belongs in each of the following entries.

(1) וּמְפִיבֹשֶׁת (יֹשֵׁב / יָשַׁב / יֹשֶׁבֶת) בִּירוּשָׁלַ͏ִם כִּי עַל־שֻׁלְחַן הַמֶּלֶךְ תָּמִיד

הוּא (אֹכֵל / אָכַל / אֹכֶלֶת)

So Mephibosheth dwelt in Jerusalem; for he ate always at the king's table. (2 Sam. 9:13)

(2) (וְהָאֹכֵל / וְהָאֹכְלִים) בַּבַּיִת יְכַבֵּס אֶת־בְּגָדָיו

And he who eats in the house shall wash his clothes. (Lev. 14:47)

(3) כִּי יְהוָה אֱלֹהֶיךָ אֵשׁ (אֹכֵל / אָכְלָה / הוּא)[a]

For the LORD your God is a devouring fire. (Deut. 4:24)

(4) וּמַרְאֵה כְּבוֹד יְהוָה כְּאֵשׁ (אֹכֶלֶת / אוֹכְלוֹת) בְּרֹאשׁ הָהָר

Now the appearance of the glory of the LORD was like a devouring fire on the top of the mountain. (Exod. 24:17)

(5) אֶרֶץ (אֹכֵל / אֹכֶלֶת / יוֹשְׁבֶיהָ הוּא)

It is a land that devours its inhabitants. (Num. 13:32)

(6) אֲשֶׁר לֹא־נְטַעְתֶּם אַתֶּם (אֹכְלִים / אוֹכְלוֹת)

That which you did not plant you are eating. (Josh. 24:13)

(7) וּבָנָיו וּבְנֹתָיו (אֹכְלִים[b] / אוֹכְלוֹת) וְשֹׁתִים יַיִן בְּבֵית אֲחִיהֶם הַבְּכוֹר

And his sons and his daughters were eating and drinking wine in the house of their elder brother. (Job 1:13)

(8) וְזֹאת (אֹמֶרֶת / אוֹמְרוֹת)

But this one said. (1 Kgs. 3:26)

(9) (הָאֹמְרָה / הָאֹמֵר) בִּלְבָבָהּ

the one saying in her heart (Isa. 47:8)

(10) כֵּן נַעֲשֶׂה כַּאֲשֶׁר אַתָּה (אֹמֶרֶת / אוֹמֵר)

Thus we will do according as you are saying. (Neh. 5:12)

(11) (אֹמְרָה / אֹמֵר) אֲדֹנָי אֶת־קוֹל וָאֶשְׁמַע

And I heard the voice of the Lord saying. (Isa. 6:8)

(12) אֶת־יַעֲקֹב (אָהֲבָה / אֹהֵב) וְרִבְקָה

And Rebekah loved Jacob. (Gen. 25:28)

XXIII.2 Each of the following entries contains a Pe ʾAlef verb form. In the space marked (a) identify the stem, in (b) the form (perfect, imperfect, imperative, etc.), in (c) the person, gender, and number, and in (d) the root. Ignore verb forms that are not Pe ʾAlef.

וָאֹכֵל מִן־הָעֵץ נָתְנָה־לִּי הוּא she gave to me from the tree, and I ate. (Gen. 3:12)

    (a) __Qal__   (b) __Imperfect__   (c) __1 cs__   (d) __אָכַל__

(1) אֶל־הַנָּחָשׁ הָאִשָּׁה וַתֹּאמֶר And the woman said to the serpent. (Gen. 3:2)

    (a) __Qal__   (b) __Imperfect__   (c) __3 fs__   (d) __אָמַר__

(2) נֹאכֵל עֵץ־הַגָּן מִפְּרִי From the fruit of the tree(s) of the garden we may eat. (Gen. 3:2)

    (a) __Qal__   (b) __Imperfect__   (c) __1 cp__   (d) __אָכַל__

(3) יְהוָה יִבְחַר(d) אֲשֶׁר בַּמָּקוֹם תֹּאכְלֶנּוּ(c) You shall eat it in the place that the LORD chooses. (Deut. 12:18)

    (a) __Qal__   (b) __Imperfect__   (c) __2 ms__   (d) __אָכַל__

(4) וְאֶת־הַלֶּחֶם אֹתוֹ תֹאכְלוּ וְשָׁם And there you shall eat it and the bread. (Lev. 8:31)

    (a) __Qal__   (b) __Imperfect__   (c) __2 mp__   (d) __אָכַל__

(5) יֹאכְלֻהוּ(e) וּבָנָיו אַהֲרֹן Aaron and his sons shall eat it. (Lev. 8:31)

    (a) __Qal__   (b) __Imperfect__   (c) __3 mp__   (d) __אָכַל__

(6) בַּמִּדְבָּר אֶתְכֶם הֶאֱכַלְתִּי I fed you (caused you to eat) in the wilderness. (Exod. 16:32)

    (a) __Hifʿil__   (b) __Perfect__   (c) __1 cs__   (d) __אָכַל__

(7) יֵאָכֵל אֶחָד בְּבַיִת In one house it shall be eaten. (Exod. 12:46)

    (a) __Nifʿal__   (b) __Imperfect__   (c) __3 ms__   (d) __אָכַל__

(8) אֶת־הַמָּן וַיַּאֲכִלְךָ(f) And he fed you with manna. (Deut. 8:3)

    (a) __Hifʿil__   (b) __Imperfect__   (c) __1 cs__   (d) __אָכַל__

(9) וַיְהִי דְבַר־יְהוָה אֵלַי (g)לֵאמֹר And the word of the LORD came (was) to me saying. (Jer. 18:5)

    (a) ___Qal___ (b) ___Inf. Const.___ (c) ___X X X___ (d) ___אָמַר___

(10) (h)בְּאָמְרִי לְרָשָׁע מוֹת תָּמוּת when I say (in my saying) to the wicked, "You shall surely die." (Ezek. 3:18)

    (a) ___Qal___ (b) ___Inf. Const.___ (c) ___X X X___ (d) ___אָמַר___

(11) (h)בְּאָמְרָם אֵלַי כָּל־הַיּוֹם אַיֵּה אֱלֹהֶיךָ through their saying to me all the day (every day), "Where is your God?" (Ps. 42:11; Eng. 42:10)

    (a) ___Qal___ (b) ___Inf. Const.___ (c) ___X X X___ (d) ___אָמַר___

(12) כֹּל אֲשֶׁר־תֹּאמְרִי [אֵלַי] אֶעֱשֶׂה־לָּךְ All that you say [to me], I will do to you. (Ruth 3:11)

    (a) ___Qal___ (b) ___Imperfect___ (c) ___2 fs___ (d) ___אָמַר___

(13) (i)וַתֹּאמַרְנָה הֲזֹאת נָעֳמִי And they said, "Is this Naomi?" (Ruth 1:19)

    (a) ___Qal___ (b) ___Imperfect___ (c) ___3 fp___ (d) ___אָמַר___

(14) אֱמֹר לִבְנֵי־יִשְׂרָאֵל אֲנִי יְהוָה Say to the sons of Israel, "I am the LORD." (Exod. 6:6)

    (a) ___Qal___ (b) ___Imperative___ (c) ___2 ms___ (d) ___אָמַר___

(15) אִמְרִי לְעָרֵי יְהוּדָה הִנֵּה אֱלֹהֵיכֶם Say to the cities of Judah, "Behold your God!" (Isa. 40:9)

    (a) ___Qal___ (b) ___Imperative___ (c) ___2 fs___ (d) ___אָמַר___

(16) אִמְרוּ בַגּוֹיִם יְהוָה (j)מָלָךְ Say among the nations, "The LORD reigns" (Ps. 96:10)

    (a) ___Qal___ (b) ___Imperative___ (c) ___2 mp___ (d) ___אָמַר___

(17) אֶת־הָאֹבֶדֶת אֲבַקֵּשׁ And I will seek that which is lost. (Ezek. 34:16)

    (a) ___Qal___ (b) ___Participle___ (c) ___fs___ (d) ___אָבַד___

(18) כִּי לֹא־תֹאבַד תּוֹרָה מִכֹּהֵן For the law shall not perish from the priest. (Jer. 18:18)

    (a) ___Qal___ (b) ___Imperfect___ (c) ___3 fs___ (d) ___אָבַד___

(19) וְאַתְּ וּבֵית־אָבִיךְ (k)תֹּאבֵדוּ But you and your father's house shall perish. (Est. 4:14)

    (a) ___Qal___ (b) ___Imperfect___ (c) ___2 mp___ (d) ___אָבַד___

(20) וַיְשַׁלְּחֵם בִּיהוּדָה לְהַאֲבִידוֹ And he sent them against Judah to destroy it.
(2 Kgs. 24:2)

    (a) Hif'il   (b) Inf. Const.   (c) X X X   (d) אָבַד

XXIII.3 Each of the following entries contains a plural construct form of a participle. Match each entry with its correct translation.

(1)	(G)	אֹהֲבַי	(A)	those who eat it (Lev. 17:14)
(2)	(K)	אֹהֲבֶיךָ	(B)	all who seek you (Ps. 40:17; Eng. 40:16)
(3)	(N)	אֹהֲבָיו	(C)	all who serve (worship) him (2 Kgs. 10:19)
(4)	(R)	אֹהֲבֶיהָ	(D)	all who forsake you (Jer. 17:13)
(5)	(I)	אֹכְלַיִךְ	(E)	all who help her (Ezek. 30:8)
(6)	(A)	אֹכְלָיו	(F)	from those that pursue (persecute) me (Ps. 142:7; Eng. 142:6)
(7)	(O)	מְבַקְשֵׁי נַפְשָׁם	(G)	those who love me (Prov. 8:17)
(8)	(M)	מְבַקְשֵׁי נַפְשֶׁךָ	(H)	all those who seek her (Jer. 2:24)
(9)	(B)	כָּל־מְבַקְשֶׁיךָ	(I)	those who devour you (Jer. 30:16)
(10)	(P)	כָּל־מְבַקְשָׁיו	(J)	all those that pursue her (Lam. 1:3)
(11)	(H)	כָּל־מְבַקְשֶׁיהָ	(K)	those who love you (Jer. 20:6)
(12)	(C)	כָּל־עֹבְדָיו	(L)	those that pursue us (Lam. 4:19)
(13)	(D)	כָּל־עֹזְבֶיךָ	(M)	those who seek your life (soul) (Jer. 22:25)
(14)	(Q)	כָּל־עֹזְבָיו	(N)	those who love him (Ps. 145:20)
(15)	(E)	כָּל־עֹזְרֶיהָ	(O)	those who seek their life (soul) (Jer. 19:7)
(16)	(F)	מֵרֹדְפַי	(P)	all who seek him (Ezr. 8:22)
(17)	(J)	כָּל־רֹדְפֶיהָ	(Q)	all who forsake him (Ezr. 8:22)
(18)	(L)	רֹדְפֵינוּ	(R)	those who love her (it) (Prov. 18:21)

XXIII.4 In the following clauses and sentences, identify (a) the verb sequence (cf. XXI.63, pp. 210–216), (b) the verb stems, and (c) the verb roots.

Example:

הֵמָּה כָּשְׁלוּ וְנָפָלוּ They shall stumble and fall. (Ps. 27:2)

(a) __Perfect__ + __Perfect__ Sequence (b) __Qal__ , __Qal__

(c) __נָפַל__ , __כָּשַׁל__

(1) שָׁמְעָה וַתִּשְׂמַח צִיּוֹן Zion heard and was glad. (Ps. 97:8)

(a) __Perfect__ + __Imperfect__ Sequence (b) __Qal__ , __Qal__

(c) __שָׁמַע__ , __שָׂמַח__

(2) יִזְכֹּר עֲוֺנָם וְיִפְקֹד חַטֹּאתָם He will remember their iniquity and punish (visit) their sins. (Jer. 14:10)

(a) __Imperfect__ + __Imperfect__ Sequence (b) __Qal__ , __Qal__

(c) __זָכַר__ , __פָּקַד__

(3) נִמְצָא־חֵן בְּעֵינֵי אֲדֹנִי וְהָיִינוּ עֲבָדִים לְפַרְעֹה[(1)] Let us find favor in the eyes of my lord, and let us become slaves (servants) to Pharaoh. (Gen. 47:25)

(a) __Imperfect__ + __Perfect__ Sequence (b) __Qal__ , __Qal__

(c) __מָצָא__ , __הָיָה__

(4) לֹא־תִשְׂנָא אֶת־אָחִיךָ בִּלְבָבֶךָ וְאָהַבְתָּ לְרֵעֲךָ כָּמוֹךָ You shall not hate your brother in your heart, but you shall love your neighbor as yourself. (Lev. 19:17,18)

(a) __Imperfect__ + __Perfect__ Sequence (b) __Qal__ , __Qal__

(c) __שָׂנֵא__ , __אָהֵב__

(5) בַּקֵּשׁ שָׁלוֹם וְרָדְפֵהוּ Seek peace and pursue it. (Ps. 34:15; Eng. 34:14)

(a) __Imperative__ + __Perfect__ Sequence (b) __Pi‘el__ , __Qal__

(c) __בָּקַשׁ__ , __רָדַף__

(6) שִׂנְאוּ־רָע[(m)] וְאֶהֱבוּ טוֹב Hate evil, and love good. (Amos 5:15)

(a) __Imperative__ + __Imperative__ Sequence (b) __Qal__ , __Qal__

(c) __שָׂנֵא__ , __אָהֵב__

(7) שְׁמַע בְּקוֹלָם וְהִמְלַכְתָּ לָהֶם מֶלֶךְ Harken to their voice, and make for them a king. (1 Sam. 8:22)

(a) __Imperative__ + __Perfect__ Sequence (b) __Qal__ , __Hif‘il__

(c) __שָׁמַע__ , __מָלַךְ__

(8) שַׁלַּח אֶת־עַמִּי (e)וְיַעַבְדֻנִי Send my people away, that they may serve me. (Exod. 7:26)

    (a) <u>Imperative + Imperfect</u> Sequence (b) <u>Piʿel</u> , <u>Qal</u>

    (c) <u>שָׁלַח</u> , <u>עָבַד</u>

(9) הָלוֹךְ(n) וְדִבַּרְתָּ אֶל־דָּוִד Go and speak to David. (2 Sam. 24:12)

    (a) <u>Inf. Abs. + Perfect</u> Sequence (b) <u>Qal</u> , <u>Piʿel</u>

    (c) <u>הָלַךְ</u> , <u>[דבר]</u>

(10) הוא נָתְנָה־לִּי מִן־הָעֵץ (o)וָאֹכֵל She gave to me from the tree, and I ate. (Gen. 3:12)

    (a) <u>Perfect + Imperfect</u> Sequence (b) <u>Qal</u> , <u>Qal</u>

    (c) <u>נָתַן</u> , <u>אָכַל</u>

Footnotes

(a) An alternate rendering: "As for the LORD your God, a consuming fire is he."

(b) A compound subject of mixed gender will take a masculine plural participle. The accompanying participle, וְשֹׁתִים (from שָׁתָה), is also masculine plural.

(c) Sometimes a variant form of the pronominal suffix occurs with verbs ending in consonants [cf. *G*.47.3(1), p. 159].

(d) For a synopsis of the ʿAyin Guttural verb בָּחַר, "he chose," cf. *G*.69.3, p. 253.

(e) On the occurrence of defective šureq before a pronominal suffix, cf. *G*.47.1(1), p. 157.

(f) The characteristically long ḥireq-yod in this Hifʿil imperfect form is written defectively (as ḥireq). It is still to be considered a long vowel. Note that the sheva under the following consonant is vocal, joining the pronominal suffix to the verb form.

(g) The infinitive construct לֵאמֹר serves roughly the same purpose as quotation marks in modern usage.

(h) The infinite construct may be prefixed with a preposition. It may also receive a pronominal suffix. Here the suffix is the subject of the infinitive.

(i) The interrogative ה is prefixed to this demonstrative pronoun.

(j) מָלָךְ is the pausal form (with secondary accent) for מָלַךְ.

(k) תֹּאבֵדוּ is the pausal form (with 'atnaḥ, תֹּאבֵדוּ) for תֹּאבְדוּ.

(l) A first person cohortative imperfect is the governing verb in this coordinate relationship, determining that the following first person perfect with vav conjunction should also be translated as a cohortative.

(m) The accent on וְאָהֲבוּ has been retracted one syllable before the heavily accented (pausal) טוֹב. Hebrew resists juxtaposing two heavily accented syllables, except where it is unavoidable.

(n) For the use of the infinitive absolute with the force of an imperative, cf. G.57.3(4), p. 185.

(o) For the contraction of אֹאכַל (Qal imperfect, first common singular) to אֹכַל, cf. G.67.4(c), p. 238. The stem vowel pataḥ becomes ṣere after vav consecutive (וָאֹאכַל becomes וָאֹכַל).

Suggestions for Further Testing

1. Circle the word that is out of place in each of the following categories.

(1)	Marks of good character	אֱמוּנָה	חַטָּאת	חָכְמָה
(2)	Food products	דְּבַשׁ	שֶׁמֶן	אֶבֶן
(3)	Parts of the body	הֵיכָל	עַיִן	אֹזֶן
(4)	Animals	אַיִל	צֹאן	עֵץ
(5)	Sources of water	נָהָר	יַבָּשָׁה	בְּאֵר
(6)	Religious legislation	עָנָן	מִשְׁפָּט	תּוֹרָה
(7)	Religious functionaries	נָבִיא	מַלְכָּה	רוֹאֶה
(8)	Dry areas	נֶגֶב	בְּאֵר	מִדְבָּר
(9)	Things constructed	כּוֹכָב	מִזְבֵּחַ	חוֹמָה
(10)	Sources of fruit	גַּן	כֶּרֶם	שָׁמַיִם

2. Translate the following sentences and clauses, and locate fully all verbs having
א as their initial root consonant.

(1)   וַתֹּאמֶר אֵלֶיהָ כֹּל אֲשֶׁר־תֹּאמְרִי אֵלַי
אֶעֱשֶׂה   (Ruth 3:5)

(2)   וַיֹּאמֶר אַל־נָא תַּעֲזֹב אֹתָנוּ   (Num. 10:31)

(3)   וַיֹּאמֶר הָאָדָם הָאִשָּׁה אֲשֶׁר נָתַתָּה עִמָּדִי
הִוא נָתְנָה־לִּי מִן־הָעֵץ וָאֹכֵל   (Gen. 3:12)

(4)   כִּי לֹא־תֹאבַד תּוֹרָה מִכֹּהֵן   (Jer. 18:18)

(5)   וְאָסַפְתָּ אֶת־זִקְנֵי יִשְׂרָאֵל וְאָמַרְתָּ אֲלֵהֶם   (Exod. 3:16)

(6)   וַיֹּאַסְפוּ אֶת־כָּל־זִקְנֵי בְּנֵי יִשְׂרָאֵל   (Exod. 4:29)

(7)   וַיֶּאֱסֹף שִׁבְעִים אִישׁ מִזִּקְנֵי הָעָם   (Num. 11:24)

(8)   וְהַאֲבַדְתָּ אֶת־שְׁמָם מִתַּחַת הַשָּׁמָיִם   (Deut. 7:24)

(9)   וְאִבַּדְתֶּם אֶת־שְׁמָם מִן־הַמָּקוֹם הַהוּא   (Deut. 12:3)

(10)   אַבֵּד תְּאַבְּדוּן אֶת־כָּל־הַמְּקֹמוֹת אֲשֶׁר
עָבְדוּ־שָׁם הַגּוֹיִם אֶת־אֱלֹהֵיהֶם   (Deut. 12:2)

(11)   וַתֹּאמֶר אֶל־הָעֶבֶד מִי־הָאִישׁ הַהֹלֵךְ
בַּשָּׂדֶה לִקְרָאתֵנוּ   (Gen. 24:65)

(12)   נֶאֶסְפוּ מֵעָרֵיהֶם   (1 Chr. 19:7)

(13)   אֶסְפָה־לִּי שִׁבְעִים אִישׁ מִזִּקְנֵי יִשְׂרָאֵל   (Num. 11:16)

(14)   אָהַבְתָּ רָע מִטּוֹב   (Ps. 52:5; Eng. 52:4)

(15)   אָמַרְתִּי לַיהוָה אֵלִי אָתָּה   (Ps. 140:7; Eng. 140:6)

LESSON XXIV

Answer Key
(Cf. *G*, pp. 255ff.)

XXIV.1 Observe the ʿAyin Guttural verb forms as they occur in the following sentences. Fill in the blanks with the correct pronouns.

(1) אָז ^(a)יִזְעֲקוּ אֶל־יְהֹוָה וְלֹא יַעֲנֶה אוֹתָם Then __they__ will cry to the LORD, but he will not answer __them__ . (Mic. 3:4)

(2) ^(a)וַיִּמְאֲסוּ אֶת־חֻקָּיו וְאֶת־בְּרִיתוֹ אֲשֶׁר כָּרַת אֶת־אֲבוֹתָם And __they__ rejected __his__ statutes and __his__ covenant which __he__ made with __their__ ancestors. (2 Kgs. 17:15)

(3) וַנִּצְעַק אֶל־יְהֹוָה וַיִּשְׁמַע קֹלֵנוּ Then __we__ cried to the LORD, and he heard __our__ voice. (Num. 20:16)

(4) וְרָחֲצוּ יְדֵיהֶם וְרַגְלֵיהֶם And __they__ shall wash __their__ hands and __their__ feet (Exod. 30:21)

(5) ^(b)אַל־תַּעַזְבֵנִי יְהֹוָה אֱלֹהָי Do not forsake __me__ , O LORD __my__ God. (Ps. 38:22; Eng. 38:21)

(6) וּבֵרַכְתָּ אֶת־יְהֹוָה אֱלֹהֶיךָ And __you__ shall bless the LORD __your__ God. (Deut. 8:10)

(7) בֵּרַכְנוּ אֶתְכֶם בְּשֵׁם יְהֹוָה __We__ bless __you__ in the name of the LORD. (Ps. 129:8)

(8) בֵּרַכְנוּכֶם מִבֵּית יְהֹוָה __We__ bless __you__ from the house of the LORD. (Ps. 118:26)

(9) ^(c)וַאֲבָרֶכְךָ ^(c)וַאֲגַדְּלָה שְׁמֶךָ And __I__ will bless __you__ , and __I__ will make __your__ name great. (Gen. 12:2)

(10) ^(b)יְבָרְכֵנוּ אֱלֹהִים אֱלֹהֵינוּ May God __our__ God bless __us__ . (Ps. 67:7; Eng. 67:6)

(11) זָכָר וּנְקֵבָה בְּרָאָם וַיְבָרֶךְ אֹתָם וַיִּקְרָא אֶת־שְׁמָם אָדָם Male and female __he__ created __them__ , and __he__ blessed __them__ , and __he__ called __their__ name Humankind. (Gen. 5:2)

138

(12) עָשִׂיתִים‎(d) כִּי נִחַמְתִּי כִּי For ___I___ am sorry that ___I___ have made ___them___. (Gen. 6:7)

XXIV.2 Each of the following sentences contains a form of an 'Ayin Guttural verb. In the space numbered (a) identify the verb form (perfect, imperfect, etc.), in (b) the verb stem (Qal, Nif'al, etc.), in (c) the person, gender, and number of the form, and in (d) the verb root.

Example:

וַיִּזְעֲקוּ אִישׁ אֶל־אֱלֹהָיו And they cried, each unto his God. (Jon. 1:5)
(a) Imperfect (b) Qal (c) 3 mp (d) זָעַק

(1) וְעַתָּה הִנֵּה הַמֶּלֶךְ אֲשֶׁר בְּחַרְתֶּם And now behold the king whom you have chosen. (1 Sam. 12:13)
(a) Perfect (b) Qal (c) 2 mp (d) בָּחַר

(2) אֶחָד מֵאֶחָיו יִגְאָלֶנּוּ‎(e) One of his brothers shall redeem him. (Lev. 25:48)
(a) Imperfect (b) Qal (c) 3 ms (d) גָּאַל

(3) וְלֹא־זָעֲקוּ אֵלַי בְּלִבָּם But they do not cry to me with (in) their heart. (Hos. 7:14)
(a) Perfect (b) Qal (c) 3 cp (d) זָעַק

(4) וַיִּזְעַק הַמֶּלֶךְ קוֹל גָּדוֹל בְּנִי אַבְשָׁלוֹם אַבְשָׁלוֹם בְּנִי בְנִי And the king cried with a loud voice, "O my son Absalom, O Absalom, my son, my son." (2 Sam. 19:5; Eng. 19:4)
(a) Imperfect (b) Qal (c) 3 ms (d) זָעַק

(5) גַּם־אֲנִי אֶמְאַס‎(c) בְּכָל־זֶרַע יִשְׂרָאֵל Also I will reject all the seed (descendants) of Israel. (Jer. 31:37)
(a) Imperfect (b) Qal (c) 1 cs (d) מָאַס

(6) וְאִשָּׁה צָעֲקָה אֵלָיו And a woman cried out to him. (2 Kgs. 6:26)
(a) Perfect (b) Qal (c) 3 fs (d) צָעַק

(7) וַיִּצְעֲקוּ‎(a) בְנֵי־יִשְׂרָאֵל אֶל־יְהוָה And the children (sons) of Israel cried out to the LORD. (Exod. 14:10)
(a) Imperfect (b) Qal (c) 3 mp (d) צָעַק

(8) וַיִּרְחֲצוּ‎(a) רַגְלֵיהֶם And they washed their feet. (Gen. 43:24)
(a) Imperfect (b) Qal (c) 3 mp (d) רָחַץ

(9) וָאֶשְׁאַל אֹתָהּ בַּת־מִי אַתְּ And I asked her, "Whose daughter are you?" (Gen. 24:47)

    (a) Imperfect (b) ____ Qal (c) ____ 1 cs (d) שָׁאַל

(10) שַׁאֲלוּ שְׁלוֹם יְרוּשָׁלָ͏ִם Pray (ask) for the peace of Jerusalem. (Ps. 122:6)

    (a) Imperative (b) ____ Qal (c) ____ 2 mp (d) שָׁאַל

(11) יְהֹוָה (b)יְבָרֵךְ אֶת־עַמּוֹ בַשָּׁלוֹם May the LORD bless his people with peace! (Ps. 29:11)

    (a) Imperfect (b) ____ Pi'el (c) ____ 3 ms (d) [ברך]

(12) וַאֲנַחְנוּ (c)נְבָרֵךְ יָהּ מֵעַתָּה וְעַד־עוֹלָם But we will bless the LORD from now until eternity. (Ps. 115:18)

    (a) Imperfect (b) ____ Pi'el (c) ____ 1 cp (d) [ברך]

(13) וַיְבָרֲכוּ אֱלֹהִים בְּנֵי יִשְׂרָאֵל And the people (sons) of Israel blessed God. (Josh. 22:33)

    (a) Imperfect (b) ____ Pi'el (c) ____ 3 mp (d) [ברך]

(14) בָּרֲכִי נַפְשִׁי אֶת־יְהוָה Bless the LORD, O my soul! (Ps. 103:1)

    (a) Imperative (b) ____ Pi'el (c) ____ 2 fs (d) [ברך]

(15) וַיְנַחֵם דָּוִד אֵת בַּת־שֶׁבַע אִשְׁתּוֹ And David comforted Bathsheba his wife. (2 Sam. 12:24)

    (a) Imperfect (b) ____ Pi'el (c) ____ 3 ms (d) [נחם]

(16) שִׁבְטְךָ (a)וּמִשְׁעַנְתֶּךָ הֵמָּה (f)יְנַחֲמֻנִי Your rod and your staff, they comfort me. (Ps. 23:4)

    (a) Imperfect (b) ____ Pi'el (c) ____ 3 mp (d) [נחם]

(17) וּבְתוֹךְ בְּנֵי יִשְׂרָאֵל לֹא (a)יִנְחֲלוּ (g)נַחֲלָה And among (in the midst of) the people (sons) of Israel they shall not receive (inherit) an inheritance. (Num. 18:23)

    (a) Imperfect (b) ____ Qal (c) ____ 3 mp (d) נָחַל

(18) וְהִתְנַחַלְתֶּם אֶת־הָאָרֶץ בְּגוֹרָל And you shall inherit the land by lot. (Num. 33:54)

    (a) Perfect (b) ____ Hitpa'el (c) ____ 2 mp (d) נָחַל

XXIV.3 Each of the following sentences contains an infinitive construct. In the space numbered (a) list its stem, and in (b) its root.

(1) וְאָכַלְתָּ לִפְנֵי יְהוָה אֱלֹהֶיךָ בַּמָּקוֹם אֲשֶׁר־יִבְחַר (h)לְשַׁכֵּן שְׁמוֹ שָׁם

And you shall eat before the LORD your God in the place which he will choose, to make his name dwell there. (Deut. 14:23)

(a) ___Pi'el___ (b) ___שָׁכֵן___

(2) וָאֶבְחַר בִּירוּשָׁלַ͏ִם (d)לִהְיוֹת שְׁמִי שָׁם

But I have chosen Jerusalem in order that my name might be there. (2 Chr. 6:6)

(a) ___Qal___ (b) ___הָיָה___

(3) וְאִם רַע בְּעֵינֵיכֶם לַעֲבֹד אֶת־יְהוָה בַּחֲרוּ לָכֶם הַיּוֹם אֶת־מִי תַעֲבֹדוּן

And if it be evil in your eyes to serve the LORD, choose for yourselves this day whom you will serve. (Josh. 24:15)

(a) ___Qal___ (b) ___עָבַד___

(4) כִּי־אֹתִי מָאָסוּ מִמְּלֹךְ עֲלֵיהֶם

But they have rejected me from being king over them. (1 Sam. 8:7)

(a) ___Qal___ (b) ___מָלַךְ___

(5) אֵלֶּה יַעַמְדוּ לְבָרֵךְ אֶת־הָעָם עַל־הַר גְּרִזִים

These shall stand upon Mount Gerizim to bless the people. (Deut. 27:12)

(a) ___Pi'el___ (b) ___[בּרךְ]___

(6) כִּי לֹא אָדָם הוּא לְהִנָּחֵם

For he is not a mortal, that he should repent. (1 Sam. 15:29)

(a) ___Nif'al___ (b) ___[נחם]___

(7) וַיְמָאֵן לְהִתְנַחֵם

But he refused to be comforted. (Gen. 37:35)

(a) ___Hitpa'el___ (b) ___[נחם]___

(8) כָּבֵד לֵב פַּרְעֹה (i)מֵאֵן לְשַׁלַּח הָעָם

Pharaoh's heart is hardened; he refuses to let the people go. (Exod. 7:14)

(a) ___Pi'el___ (b) ___שָׁלַח___

(9) מֵאֲנוּ (j)לָשׁוּב

They refuse to return (repent). (Jer. 5:3)

(a) ___Qal___ (b) ___שׁוּב___

(10) וַיְמָאֲנוּ הָעָם לִשְׁמֹעַ בְּקוֹל שְׁמוּאֵל

And the people refused to harken (listen) to the voice of Samuel. (1 Sam. 8:19)

(a) ___Qal___ (b) ___שָׁמַע___

XXIV.4 Each of the following sentences contains a participle. In the space numbered (a) write the participle, in (b) give its stem, in (c) its gender and number, and in (d) its root.

Example:

וּבָעֲרוּ שְׁנֵיהֶם יַחְדָּו וְאֵין מְכַבֶּה And both of them shall burn together, and no one quenching (them). (Isa. 1:31)

(a) מְכַבֶּה (b) Piʻel (c) ms (d) כָּבָה

(1) וְהָיָה בְלִבִּי כְּאֵשׁ בֹּעֶרֶת And there is in my heart as a burning fire (as if it were a burning fire). (Jer. 20:9)

(a) בֹּעֶרֶת (b) Qal (c) fs (d) בָּעַר

(2) וְהִנֵּה (k)יִצְחָק מְצַחֵק אֵת רִבְקָה אִשְׁתּוֹ And behold, Isaac was fondling Rebekah his wife. (Gen. 26:8)

(a) מְצַחֵק (b) Piʻel (c) ms (d) צָחַק

(3) וַיְהִי מֶלֶךְ יִשְׂרָאֵל עֹבֵר עַל־הַחֹמָה And the king of Israel was passing by upon the wall. (2 Kgs. 6:26)

(a) עֹבֵר (b) Qal (c) ms (d) עָבַר

(4) מֶה עָשִׂיתָ קוֹל (l)דְּמֵי אָחִיךָ צֹעֲקִים אֵלַי מִן־הָאֲדָמָה What have you done? The voice of your brother's blood(s) is crying out to me from the ground. (Gen. 4:10)

(a) צֹעֲקִים (b) Qal (c) mp (d) צָעַק

(5) וְדָוִיד וְכָל־יִשְׂרָאֵל מְשַׂחֲקִים לִפְנֵי הָאֱלֹהִים בְּכָל־עֹז And David and all Israel were making merry (celebrating) before God with all their might. (1 Chr. 13:8)

(a) מְשַׂחֲקִים (b) Piʻel (c) mp (d) שָׂחַק

(6) וַאֲבָרֲכָה מְבָרְכֶיךָ(c) And I will bless the ones who bless you. (Gen. 12:3)

(a) מְבָרְכֶיךָ (b) Piʻel (c) mp (d) [ברך]

(7) כִּי יָדַעְתִּי אֵת אֲשֶׁר־תְּבָרֵךְ מְבֹרָךְ For I know that the one whom you bless is blessed. (Num. 22:6)

(a) מְבֹרָךְ (b) Puʻal (c) ms (d) [ברך]

(8) אֵין מְנַחֵם לָהּ There is no comforter for her. (Lam. 1:9)

(a) מְנַחֵם (b) Piʻel (c) ms (d) [נחם]

(9) מֵאַיִן אֲבַקֵּשׁ מְנַחֲמִים לָךְ Whence shall I seek comforters for you? (Nah. 3:7)

(a) מְנַחֲמִים (b) Piʻel (c) mp (d) [נחם]

(10) אָנֹכִי אָנֹכִי הוּא מְנַחֶמְכֶם I, I am he that comforts you. (Isa. 51:12)

(a) מְנַחֶמְכֶם (b) Pi'el (c) _____ ms (d) [נחם]

Footnotes

(a) When two shevas stand side by side within the word, the first will be silent and the second vocal. A sheva placed under a guttural (ר generally excepted) will be compound. Note that compound shevas are always vocal.

(b) תַּעַזְבֵנִי is a jussive, i.e., an imperfect (either second or third person), used to express the speaker's desire, wish, or command directed toward another person (cf. G.41.1, p. 131). אַל with the jussive expresses a mild prohibition, a wish or desire that a specific action not be done (cf. G.55.2, p. 174).

(c) A first person imperfect that is classified as a cohortative is used to express the speaker's desire or strong determination to perform a given action. Cohortatives are sometimes lengthened by the addition of הָ as a suffix (cf. G.41.2, p. 132). וַאֲבָרֶכְךָ has the second masculine singular pronominal suffix as its direct object, while וַאֲגַדְּלָה has the cohortative הָ suffix and שְׁמֶךָ as its direct object.

(d) עָשִׂיתִים comes from עָשָׂה, "he did, made," a weak verb (Lamed He), which will be studied in Lesson XXVII (cf. G.72.7, p. 291).

(e) For the variant form of the pronominal suffix found on the imperfect verb יִגְאָלֶנּוּ, cf. G.47.3, p. 159.

(f) For the defective writing of וּ (as qibbuṣ) before pronominal suffixes, cf. G.47.1(1), p. 157.

(g) Biblical authors seem to have been fond of using cognate accusatives such as this one: "yinhᵃlu nahᵃlah."

(h) A verb is sometimes used in the Pi'el stem to express a causative sense [cf. G.36.2(2), p. 109].

(i) מֵאֵן is the Pi'el perfect third masculine singular form of the 'Ayin Guttural [מאן], "he refused" (cf. Verb Chart 4 in G, p. 406).

(j) For the form of the Qal infinitive construct שׁוּב, cf. G.74, p. 316ff.

(k) There is a play on words between Isaac's name (yiṣḥaq) and the succeeding participle (mᵉṣaḥeq). Both are from the same root, צָחַק.

(l) When the word for blood occurs in the plural (דָּמִים, of which the construct form is דְּמֵי), it usually refers to blood shed through some act of violence.

Suggestions for Further Testing

1. Match the following:

(1) ( ) יְבָרְכֵנוּ אֱלֹהִים   (A) And the LORD blessed him. (Gen. 26:12)

(2) ( ) וַיְבָרֶךְ אֹתוֹ   (B) And bless your people. (Deut. 26:15)

(3) ( ) וַיְבָרְכֵהוּ יְהוָה   (C) And he blessed them. (Gen. 5:2)

(4) ( ) וַיְבָרֶךְ יְהוָה אֹתְךָ   (D) The LORD your God has blessed you. (Deut. 2:7)

(5) ( ) וַיְבָרֶךְ אֹתָם   (E) For I will surely bless you. (Gen. 22:17)

(6) ( ) וַאֲנִי אֲבָרְכֵם   (F) God will bless us. (Ps. 67:6)

(7) ( ) יְהוָה אֱלֹהֶיךָ בֵּרַכְךָ   (G) And I will bless you. (Exod. 20:24)

(8) ( ) כִּי־בָרֵךְ אֲבָרֶכְךָ   (H) And I will bless her. (Gen. 17:16)

(9) ( ) וּבֵרַכְתִּיךָ   (I) And they blessed the people. (2 Chr. 30:27)

(10) ( ) וּבֵרַכְתִּי אֹתָהּ   (J) And he blessed him. (Gen. 28:1)

(11) ( ) וּבָרֵךְ אֶת־עַמֶּךָ   (K) And I will bless them. (Num. 6:27)

(12) ( ) וַיְבָרְכוּ אֶת־הָעָם   (L) And the LORD has blessed you. (Gen. 30:30)

2. Translate the following sentences and clauses and locate fully all ʿAyin Guttural verb forms.

(1)   הַמִּתְבָּרֵךְ בָּאָרֶץ יִתְבָּרֵךְ בֵּאלֹהֵי אָמֵן (Isa. 65:16)

     [אָמֵן, "faithfulness"]

(2)   וַיִּזְעֲקוּ בְּנֵי יִשְׂרָאֵל אֶל־יְהוָה לֵאמֹר חָטָאנוּ לָךְ (Judg. 10:10)

(3)   יְהוָה נָתַן וַיהוָה לָקָח יְהִי שֵׁם יְהוָה מְבֹרָךְ (Job 1:21)

(4)   וַיִּשְׁאַל יַעֲקֹב [proper name] וַיֹּאמֶר [מַה] שְּׁמֶךָ (Gen. 32:30)

     וַיֹּאמֶר לָמָּה זֶּה תִּשְׁאַל לִשְׁמִי וַיְבָרֶךְ אֹתוֹ שָׁם

(5)   וַיִּצְעַק צְעָקָה גְדֹלָה וּמָרָה עַד־מְאֹד (Gen. 37:34)

(6)   כִּי לֵאלֹהִים זָעֲקוּ בַּמִּלְחָמָה (1 Chr. 5:20)

(7)   וַאֲבָרְכָה שִׁמְךָ לְעוֹלָם וָעֶד (Ps. 145:1)

LESSON XXV

Answer Key
(Cf. *G*, pp. 267ff.)

XXV.1 Fill in the blanks with the proper verb translations.

(1) וַיְמָאֲנוּ הָעָם ^(a)לִשְׁמֹעַ בְּקוֹל שְׁמוּאֵל And the people __refused__ to __listen__ to the voice of Samuel. (1 Sam. 8:19)

(2) וּכְשָׁמְעִי אֶת־הַדָּבָר הַזֶּה קָרַעְתִּי אֶת־בִּגְדִי^(b) And when I __heard__ this word, I __tore__ my garment. (Ezr. 9:3)

(3) בָּרוּךְ הַגֶּבֶר אֲשֶׁר יִבְטַח בַּיהוָה __Blessed__ is the man who __trusts__ in the LORD. (Jer. 17:7)

(4) כִּי־יָדְעוּ הָאֲנָשִׁים כִּי־מִלִּפְנֵי יְהוָה הוּא ^(a)בֹרֵחַ For the men __knew__ that he was __fleeing__ from the presence of the LORD. (Jon. 1:10)

(5) אֶשְׁלַח אֵלֶיךָ אִישׁ מֵאֶרֶץ בִּנְיָמִן I will __send__ to you a man from the land of Benjamin. (1 Sam. 9:16)

(6) לֹא אֶשְׁכַּח ^(c)דְּבָרֶךָ I will not __forget__ your word. (Ps. 119:16)

(7) בְּרִית עוֹלָם לֹא ^(a)תִשָּׁכֵחַ An everlasting covenant (which) shall not be __forgotten__ . (Jer. 50:5)

(8) וְשֵׁשׁ שָׁנִים תִּזְרַע אֶת־^(c)אַרְצֶךָ For six years you shall __sow__ your land. (Exod. 23:10)

(9) כִּי ^(a)כִגְבֹהַּ שָׁמַיִם עַל־הָאָרֶץ for as the heavens are __high__ above the earth (Ps. 103:11)

(10) כִּי בַיהוָה אֱלֹהֶיךָ ^(c)פָּשַׁעַתְּ For you have __rebelled__ against the LORD your God. (Jer. 3:13)

XXV.2 Each of the following sentences contains a perfect form of a Lamed Guttural verb. In the space marked (a) give its stem, in (b) its person, gender, and number, and in (c) its root.

(1) הֵן בְּנֵי־יִשְׂרָאֵל לֹא־שָׁמְעוּ אֵלַי
Behold, the people of Israel have not listened to me.
(Exod. 6:12)

(a) __Qal__

(b) __3 cp__

(c) __שָׁמַע__

145

(2) אֲשֶׁר שָׁלַחְתִּי מִירוּשָׁלַ‍ם (d)בָּבֶלָה

whom I sent from Jerusalem to Babylon (Jer. 29:20)

(a)	Pi‘el
(b)	1 cs
(c)	שָׁלַח

(3) יְהוָה אֱלֹהֵי הָעִבְרִים שְׁלָחַנִי אֵלֶיךָ

The LORD God of the Hebrews has sent me to you.

(Exod. 7:16)

(a)	Qal
(b)	3 ms
(c)	שָׁלַח

(4) כַּאֲשֶׁר שָׁכְחוּ אֲבוֹתָם אֶת־שְׁמִי (c)בַּבָּעַל

just as their ancestors forgot my name for Baal (Jer. 23:27)

(a)	Qal
(b)	3 cp
(c)	שָׁכַח

(5) וְגַם־בְּזֹאת לֹא (c)שָׂבָעַתְּ

And even with this you were not satisfied. (Ezek. 16:29)

(a)	Qal
(b)	2 fs
(c)	שָׂבַע

XXV.3 Each of the following entries contains an imperfect form of a Lamed Guttural verb. In the space marked (a) give its stem, in (b) its person, gender, and number, and in (c) its root.

(1) וְגַם אֶת־יִשְׂרָאֵל לֹא (a)אֲשַׁלֵּחַ

And moreover I will not set Israel free (let Israel go).

(Exod. 5:2)

(a)	Pi‘el
(b)	1 cs
(c)	שָׁלַח

(2) וְאֵיךְ יִשְׁמַע אֵלַי פַּרְעֹה

How then shall Pharaoh listen to me? (Exod. 6:30)

(a)	Qal
(b)	3 ms
(c)	שָׁמַע

(3) כִּי נִשְׁמַע בְּקוֹל יְהוָה אֱלֹהֵינוּ

For we will listen to (obey) the voice of the LORD our God. (Jer. 42:6)

(a)	Qal
(b)	1 cp
(c)	שָׁמַע

(4) וְלֹא־יִשָּׁמַע בָּהּ עוֹד קוֹל בְּכִי

There shall no more be heard in her (it) the voice (sound) of weeping. (Isa. 65:19)

(a)	Nif‘al
(b)	3 ms
(c)	שָׁמַע

(5) לְךָ־(e)אֶזְבַּח זֶבַח תּוֹדָה

To you I will sacrifice a sacrifice of thanksgiving. (Ps. 116:17)

(a)	Qal
(b)	1 cs
(c)	זָבַח

(6) וָאֶשְׁלַח לְפָנֶיךָ אֶת־מֹשֶׁה אַהֲרֹן וּמִרְיָם

And I sent before you Moses, Aaron, and Miriam. (Mic. 6:4)

(a)	Qal
(b)	1 cs
(c)	שָׁלַח

(7) וְלֹא יְשַׁלַּח אֶת־הָעָם

And he will not let the people go (set the people free). (Exod. 4:21)

(a)	Pi'el
(b)	3 ms
(c)	שָׁלַח

(8) בְּנִי תּוֹרָתִי אַל־תִּשְׁכָּח

My son, do not forget my law (my instruction). (Prov. 3:1)

(a)	Qal
(b)	2 ms
(c)	שָׁכַח

(9) כִּי לֹא לָנֶצַח יִשָּׁכַח אֶבְיוֹן

For the needy shall never be forgotten. (Ps. 9:19; Eng. 9:18)

(a)	Nif'al
(b)	3 ms
(c)	שָׁכַח

(10) וְהַמֶּלֶךְ יִשְׂמַח בֵּאלֹהִים

But the king shall rejoice in God. (Ps. 63:12; Eng. 63:11)

(a)	Qal
(b)	3 ms
(c)	שָׂמַח

(11) וְיַיִן יְשַׂמַּח לְבַב־אֱנוֹשׁ

And wine shall gladden the heart of man. (Ps. 104:15)

(a)	Pi'el
(b)	3 ms
(c)	שָׂמַח

(12) וַיִּגְבַּה(f) יְהוָה צְבָאוֹת בַּמִּשְׁפָּט

But the LORD of hosts is exalted in justice. (Isa. 5:16)

(a)	Qal
(b)	3 ms
(c)	גָּבַה

XXV.4 Each of the following entries contains an imperative form of a Lamed Guttural verb. In the space marked (a) give its stem, in (b) its person, gender, and number, and in (c) its root.

(1) אֱלֹהִים שְׁמַע תְּפִלָּתִי

O God, hear my prayer. (Ps. 54:4; Eng. 54:2)

(a)	Qal
(b)	2 ms
(c)	שָׁמַע

(2) כִּי־שְׁמַעְנָה נָשִׁים דְּבַר־יְהוָה

Hear, O women, the word of the LORD! (Jer. 9:19; Eng. 9:20)

(a)	Qal
(b)	2 fp
(c)	שָׁמַע

(3) אֶרֶץ אֶרֶץ (c)אָרֶץ שִׁמְעִי דְּבַר־יְהוָה

O earth, earth, earth, hear the word of the LORD! (Jer. 22:29)

(a)	Qal
(b)	2 fs
(c)	שָׁמַע

(4) הַשְׁמִיעִינִי אֶת־קוֹלֵךְ

Let me hear (cause me to hear) your voice. (Song of Sol. 2:14)

(a)	Hif'il
(b)	2 fs
(c)	שָׁמַע

(5)	בְּטַח אֶל־יְהוָה בְּכָל־(c)לִבֶּךָ	(a)	Qal
	Trust in the LORD with all your heart. (Prov. 3:5)	(b)	2 ms
		(c)	בְּטַח

(6)	סְלַח־נָא לַעֲוֹן הָעָם הַזֶּה	(a)	Qal
	Forgive the iniquity of this people. (Num. 14:19)	(b)	2 ms
		(c)	סְלַח

(7)	וְאַתֶּם שִׁמְעוּ דְבַר־יְהוָה	(a)	Qal
	Hear the word of the LORD! (Jer. 29:20)	(b)	2 mp
		(c)	שָׁמַע

(8)	וְעַתָּה שְׁלַח־לִי אִישׁ־חָכָם	(a)	Qal
	And now send me a wise man (a skilled man).	(b)	2 ms
	(2 Chr. 2:6; Eng. 2:7)	(c)	שְׁלַח

(9)	שַׁלַּח אֶת־עַמִּי (g)וְיַעַבְדֻנִי בַּמִּדְבָּר	(a)	Piʿel
	Let my people go (send my people) that they may serve	(b)	2 ms
	(worship) me in the wilderness. (Exod. 7:16)	(c)	שָׁלַח

(10)	חֲכַם בְּנִי וְשַׂמַּח לִבִּי	(a)	Piʿel
	Be wise, my son, and make my heart glad. (Prov. 27:11)	(b)	2 ms
		(c)	שָׂמַח

XXV.5 Each of the following entries contains either an infinitive construct or an infinitive absolute from a Lamed Guttural verb. In the space marked (a) indicate whether it is construct or absolute, in (b) give its stem, and in (c) its root.

(1)	וַיְהִי (b)כִשְׁמֹעַ הָעָם אֶת־קוֹל הַשּׁוֹפָר	(a)	Construct
	and so it was that when the people heard the sound of	(b)	Qal
	the trumpet (Josh. 6:20)	(c)	שָׁמַע

(2)	אָזְנַיִם לָהֶם (a)לִשְׁמֹעַ וְלֹא (c)שָׁמֵעוּ	(a)	Construct
	They have ears to hear, but they do not hear. (Ezek. 12:2)	(b)	Qal
		(c)	שָׁמַע

(3)	(h)מִי יְהוָה אֲשֶׁר אֶשְׁמַע בְּקֹלוֹ לְשַׁלַּח אֶת־יִשְׂרָאֵל	(a)	Construct
	Who is the LORD that I should obey (listen to) his voice	(b)	Piʿel
	to let Israel go? (Exod. 5:2)	(c)	שָׁלַח

(4)	(i)שִׁמְעוּ (a)שָׁמוֹעַ אֵלַי וְאִכְלוּ־טוֹב	(a)	Absolute
	Hearken diligently to me, and eat what is good. (Isa. 55:2)	(b)	Qal
		(c)	שָׁמַע

(5) ‏אִם־שָׁמוֹעַ תִּשְׁמַע לְקוֹל יְהוָה אֱלֹהֶיךָ‏(i)

if you will diligently hearken to the voice of the LORD
your God (Exod. 15:26)

(a)	Absolute
(b)	Qal
(c)	‏שָׁמַע‏

(6) ‏שַׁלֵּחַ תְּשַׁלַּח אֶת־הָאֵם‏(i)

You shall surely let the mother go free. (Deut. 22:7)

(a)	Absolute
(b)	Pi‘el
(c)	‏שָׁלַח‏

(7) ‏וְהָיָה אִם־‏(i)‏שָׁכֹחַ תִּשְׁכַּח אֶת־יְהוָה אֱלֹהֶיךָ‏

and it shall be (that) if you totally forget the LORD
your God (Deut. 8:19)

(a)	Absolute
(b)	Qal
(c)	‏שָׁכַח‏

(8) ‏הַחֹשְׁבִים‏ (a)‏לְהַשְׁכִּיחַ אֶת־עַמִּי שְׁמִי בַּחֲלוֹמֹתָם‏

the ones thinking (intending) to cause my people to forget
my name through their dreams (Jer. 23:27)

(a)	Construct
(b)	Hif‘il
(c)	‏שָׁכַח‏

(9) ‏כִּי‏ (a)‏כִגְבֹהַּ שָׁמַיִם עַל־הָאָרֶץ‏

for as the heavens are high above the earth (Ps. 103:11)

(a)	Construct
(b)	Qal
(c)	‏גָּבַהּ‏

(10) ‏(a)‏לִזְבֹּחַ לַיהוָה אֱלֹהֶיךָ בַּגִּלְגָּל‏

to sacrifice to the LORD your God in Gilgal (1 Sam. 15:21)

(a)	Construct
(b)	Qal
(c)	‏זָבַח‏

XXV.6 Each of the following entries contains a participle from a Lamed Guttural
verb. In the space marked (a) give its stem, in (b) its gender and number, and
in (c) its root.

(1) ‏וַיֹּאמֶר שְׁמוּאֵל דַּבֵּר כִּי‏ (a)‏שֹׁמֵעַ‏ (c)‏עַבְדֶּךָ‏

And Samuel said, "Speak, for your servant is listening."
(1 Sam. 3:10)

(a)	Qal
(b)	ms
(c)	‏שָׁמַע‏

(2) ‏בְּזֹאת אֲנִי‏ (a)‏בוֹטֵחַ‏

(Even) in this I will trust (be confident). (Ps. 27:3)

(a)	Qal
(b)	ms
(c)	‏בָּטַח‏

(3) ‏מִפְּנֵי שָׂרַי גְּבִרְתִּי אָנֹכִי‏ (j)‏בֹּרַחַת‏

I am fleeing from Sarai my mistress. (Gen. 16:8)

(a)	Qal
(b)	fs
(c)	‏בָּרַח‏

(4) ‏בֶּן־אָדָם‏ (a)‏שׁוֹלֵחַ אֲנִי אוֹתְךָ אֶל־בְּנֵי יִשְׂרָאֵל‏

Son of man, I am sending you to the people (sons)
of Israel. (Ezek. 2:3)

(a)	Qal
(b)	ms
(c)	‏שָׁלַח‏

(5) הִנְנִי (a)מְשַׁלֵּחַ בָּם אֶת־הַחֶרֶב אֶת־הָרָעָב וְאֶת־(c)הַדָּבֶר

Behold, I am sending against them sword, famine, and

pestilence. (Jer. 29:17)

(a) ___Pi'el___

(b) ___ms___

(c) שָׁלַח

Footnotes

(a) For the rules governing the use of pataḥ furtive before a strong guttural (ה, ח, ע) standing at the end of a word, cf. *G*.13.2, p. 23.

(b) The infinitive construct governed by a preposition is often used as the equivalent of a temporal clause, expressing ideas such as "when," "while," "as soon as," etc.

(c) The vowel change in this word is to be explained by its being "in pause" (cf. *G*.68, pp. 240f.).

(d) The הָ ending on this noun is called a "He-directive." It may be added to nouns or directional adverbs to indicate motion or direction toward a place or a thing (never a person). The He-directive ending never takes the accent. (Cf. *G*.44, pp. 146f.)

(e) Cognate accusatives are fairly common in Hebrew. "To sacrifice a sacrifice" is a good example. Compare the English, "Speak a speech."

(f) Final ה is sometimes pointed with mappiq (הּ), in which case it retains its full consonantal value, instead of serving merely as a vowel letter. Final ה with mappiq (הּ) belongs to the same class of strong gutturals as ח and ע, and thus closes the syllable to which it belongs. Like ח and ע, it also may have a pataḥ furtive written before it to compensate for the lack of an "a" class vowel (cf. *G*.11, pp. 18f.).

(g) For the occasional occurrence of the defective šureq (written as qibbuṣ) before pronominal suffixes, cf. *G*.47.1(1), p. 157.

(h) The interrogative pronoun מִי ("who?") is sometimes used to introduce a question with an implied insult. The questioner does not wish for information, but uses this means to attack another's integrity or adequacy.

(i) The infinitive absolute may stand either before or after a finite form of its cognate verb, thus serving to strengthen, reinforce, and intensify the verbal idea [cf. *G*.57.3(2)(3), p. 185].

(j) בֹּרַחַת is Qal active participle, feminine singular, from בָּרַח, "he fled." Trans. "(I am) fleeing." The subject is Hagar.

Suggestions for Further Testing

1. Circle the word that does not belong to the category indicated.

(1)	Violent acquisition	אָחַז	נָחַל	גָּנַב
(2)	Division or separation	קָרַב	עָזַב	[בדל]
(3)	Expression of anger	אָרַר	עָזַר	שָׂנֵא
(4)	Ingestion of food	בָּלַע	אָכַל	יָצַר
(5)	What could be done with water	רָחַץ	שָׁפַךְ	שָׁכַח
(6)	Source of light	כּוֹכָב	מַיִם	שֶׁמֶשׁ
(7)	Response to adversity	חָפֵץ	אָבַל	יָרֵא
(8)	Questionable behavior	פָּשַׁע	חָטָא	בָּטַח
(9)	Disposition of property	נָתַן	מוּת	מָכַר
(10)	Movement upward	קוּם	עָלָה	יָרַד
(11)	Acts of belligerency	רָפָא	[נכה]	[לחם]
(12)	Destroy by fire	שָׂרַף	זָרַע	בָּעַר

2. Match the following:

(1) ( )	קוֹלִי שְׁמָעָה	(A) Your (sing.) eyes are open. (Jer. 32:19)
(2) ( )	כִּי שֹׁמֵעַ עַבְדֶּךָ	(B) And he sent them. (Num. 13:17)
(3) ( )	שְׁמַע בְּקוֹלָם	(C) My people have forgotten me. (Jer. 2:32)
(4) ( )	עֵינֶיךָ פְּקֻחוֹת	(D) Have I not sent you? (Judg. 6:14)
(5) ( )	וְנִפְקְחוּ עֵינֵיכֶם	(E) For your servant is listening. (1 Sam. 3:10)
(6) ( )	וְעַמִּי שְׁכֵחוּנִי	(F) And he sent them (by) night. (Josh. 8:3)
(7) ( )	הֲלֹא שְׁלַחְתִּיךָ	(G) I have not sent them. (Jer. 14:14)
(8) ( )	לֹא שְׁלַחְתִּים	(H) Hear my voice! (Ps. 119:149)
(9) ( )	וַיִּשְׁלַח אֹתָם	(I) And your (pl.) eyes shall be opened. (Gen. 3:5)
(10) ( )	וַיִּשְׁלָחֵם לָיְלָה	(J) Hear their voice! (1 Sam. 8:9)

3. Translate the following sentences and clauses. Locate fully all Lamed Guttural verb forms.

(1) (Exod. 8:24) אָנֹכִי אֲשַׁלַּח אֶתְכֶם וּזְבַחְתֶּם לַיהוָה אֱלֹהֵיכֶם בַּמִּדְבָּר

(2) (Isa. 65:16) וְהַנִּשְׁבָּע בָּאָרֶץ יִשָּׁבַע בֵּאלֹהֵי אָמֵן

(3) (Neh. 4:14) בִּמְקוֹם אֲשֶׁר תִּשְׁמְעוּ אֶת קוֹל הַשּׁוֹפָר שָׁמָּה תִּקָּבְצוּ אֵלֵינוּ

(4) (Zech. 6:15) אִם־שָׁמוֹעַ תִּשְׁמְעוּן בְּקוֹל יְהוָה אֱלֹהֵיכֶם

(5) (Num. 22:37) הֲלֹא שָׁלֹחַ שָׁלַחְתִּי אֵלֶיךָ לִקְרֹא־לָךְ לָמָּה לֹא־הָלַכְתָּ אֵלָי

(6) (1 Sam. 15:22) הִנֵּה שְׁמֹעַ מִזֶּבַח טוֹב

(7) (Gen. 3:7) וַתִּפָּקַחְנָה עֵינֵי שְׁנֵיהֶם

(8) (2 Kgs. 6:17) וַיֹּאמֶר יְהוָה פְּקַח־נָא אֶת־עֵינָיו וַיִּפְקַח יְהוָה אֶת־עֵינֵי הַנַּעַר

(9) (Neh. 8:5) וַיִּפְתַּח הַסֵּפֶר לְעֵינֵי כָל־הָעָם

(10) (Isa. 48:6) הִשְׁמַעְתִּיךָ חֲדָשׁוֹת מֵעַתָּה

LESSON XXVI

Answer Key
(Cf. *G*, pp. 280ff.)

XXVI.1 Fill in the blanks with the correct translation for the verbs in the following entries, noting especially Lamed ʾAlef verbs as they occur.

(1) מֵחֲטוֹא (b)דְּרָכַי אֶשְׁמְרָה(a) אָמַרְתִּי I __said__ , "I will __keep__ my ways, that I might not __sin__ with my tongue." (Ps. 39:2; Eng. 39:1)

(2) רְפָאָה נַפְשִׁי כִּי־חָטָאתִי לָךְ(c) __Heal__ my soul, for I have __sinned__ against thee. (Ps. 41:5; Eng. 41:4)

(3) וַאֲנִי אֶשְׁמַע מִן־הַשָּׁמַיִם וְאֶסְלַח לְחַטָּאתָם וְאֶרְפָּא אֶת־אַרְצָם And I will __hear__ from heaven, and I will __forgive__ their sin, and I will __heal__ their land. (2 Chr. 7:14)

(4) קוֹל אֹמֵר קְרָא וְאָמַר(d) מָה אֶקְרָא A voice saying, " __Cry__ !" And he __said__ , "What shall I __cry__ ?" (Isa. 40:6)

(5) וְדֶרֶךְ הַקֹּדֶשׁ יִקָּרֵא לָהּ And it shall be __called__ the holy way. (Isa. 35:8)

(6) יְהוָה יִשְׁמַע(e) בְּקָרְאִי אֵלָיו The LORD will __hear__ when I __call__ to him. (Ps. 4:4)

(7) סֵפֶר הַתּוֹרָה מָצָאתִי בְּבֵית יְהוָה I have __found__ the book of the law in the house of the LORD. (2 Kgs. 22:8)

(8) וַיִּקְרָא אֶת־שְׁמָם(f) אָדָם בְּיוֹם(g) הִבָּרְאָם And he __called__ their name Humankind in the day they were __created__ . (Gen. 5:2)

(9) מָה אוֹת כִּי־יִרְפָּא יְהוָה לִי What is the sign that the LORD will __heal__ me? (2 Kgs. 20:8)

(10) בְּצֵל יָדוֹ הֶחְבִּיאָנִי In the shadow (shade) of his hand he __hid__ me. (Isa. 49:2)

(11) וְהִנֵּה מָלֵא כְבוֹד־יְהוָה הַבָּיִת And behold the glory of the LORD __filled__ the house. (Ezek. 43:5)

(12) מַלֵּא קַרְנְךָ שֶׁמֶן __Fill__ your horn with oil. (1 Sam. 16:1)

(13) עֵת לֶאֱהֹב וְעֵת לִשְׂנֹא a time to ___love___ and a time to ___hate___
(Eccl. 3:8)

(14) שָׂנֵאתָ כָּל־פֹּעֲלֵי אָוֶן You ___hate___ all workers of iniquity (evil).
(Ps. 5:6; Eng. 5:5)

(15) חָטָאנוּ כִּי־דִבַּרְנוּ בַיהוָה וָבָךְ We have ___sinned___ for we have
___spoken___ against the LORD and against you. (Num. 21:7)

(16) וַיַּחֲטִיאָם חֲטָאָה גְדוֹלָה And he caused them to ___sin___ a great sin.
(2 Kgs. 17:21)

XXVI.2 Fill in the blanks with the correct pronouns, noting especially Lamed ʾAlef
verb forms as they occur.

(1) פֶּן־יַחֲטִיאוּ אֹתְךָ לִי Lest ___they___ cause ___you___ to sin against
___me___. (Exod. 23:33)

(2) חָטָאתִי לַיהוָה אֱלֹהֵיכֶם וְלָכֶם ___I___ have sinned against the
LORD ___your___ God and against ___you___. (Exod. 10:16)

(3) כִּי־יָרֵא אָנֹכִי אֹתוֹ For ___I___ fear ___him___. (Gen. 32:12;
Eng. 32:11)

(4) הוּא יִקְרָא בִשְׁמִי וַאֲנִי (h)אֶעֱנֶה אֹתוֹ ___He___ will call on ___my___
name and ___I___ will answer ___him___. (Zech. 13:9)

(5) יִקְרָאֵנִי (h)וְאֶעֱנֵהוּ ___He___ will call on ___me___ and ___I___
will answer ___him___ (Ps. 91:15)

(6) וְקָרָאת שְׁמוֹ עִמָּנוּ אֵל And ___you___ shall call ___his___ name
Immanuel. (Isa. 7:14)

(7) וַתִּקְרָא לְאַנְשֵׁי בֵיתָהּ And ___she___ called to the men of ___her___
house. (Gen. 39:14)

(8) קְרָאתִיו וְלֹא (h)עָנָנִי ___I___ called ___him___ but ___he___ did
not answer ___me___. (Song of Sol. 5:6)

(9) בִּקַּשְׁתִּיו וְלֹא מְצָאתִיו ___I___ sought ___him___ but did not find
___him___. (Song of Sol. 3:1)

(10) וְגַם־מָצָאתָ חֵן בְּעֵינָי And also ___you___ have found favor in
___my___ eyes. (Exod. 33:12)

(11) וּבִקַּשְׁתֶּם אֹתִי וּמְצָאתֶם (אֹתִי) And ___you___ shall seek ___me___,
and ___you___ shall find (___me___). (Jer. 29:13)

(12) זָכָר וּנְקֵבָה בְּרָאָם וַיְבָרֶךְ אֹתָם   Male and female __he__ created
__them__ , and __he__ blessed __them__ . (Gen. 5:2)

(13) וּמִלֵּאתִי אֶת־הַבַּיִת הַזֶּה כָּבוֹד   And __I__ will fill __this__ house
with glory. (Hag. 2:7)

(14) אֲמַלֵּא(i) אֶת־מִסְפַּר יָמֶיךָ   __I__ will fulfil the number of __your__
days. (Exod. 23:26)

(15) כָּל־רָעָתָם בַּגִּלְגָּל כִּי־שָׁם שְׂנֵאתִים   All __their__ evil is in Gilgal, for
there __I__ have hated __them__ . (Hos. 9:15)

(16) וַיֹּאמֶר אָבִיהָ אָמֹר אָמַרְתִּי כִּי־(j)שָׂנֹא שְׂנֵאתָהּ   And __her__ father
said, "__I__ surely said that __you__ utterly hated __her__ ."
(Judg. 15:2)

(17) יָרֵא אֲנִי אֶת־אֲדֹנִי הַמֶּלֶךְ   __I__ fear __my__ lord the king.
(Dan. 1:10)

(18) לְמַעַן לֹא אֶחֱטָא־לָךְ   In order that __I__ might not sin against
__you__ . (Ps. 119:11)

XXVI.3   Each of the following entries contains a participle from a Lamed 'Alef
verb. In the space marked (a) give its stem, in (b) tell whether it is *active* or
passive, in (c) give its gender and number, and in (d) list its root.

(1) כִּי־הִנְנִי בוֹרֵא שָׁמַיִם חֲדָשִׁים   For behold, I am creating new heavens.
(Isa. 65:17)

    (a) __Qal__ (b) __Active__ (c) __ms__ (d) __בָּרָא__

(2) הָרֹפֵא לִשְׁבוּרֵי לֵב   the one healing the brokenhearted (Ps. 147:3)

    (a) __Qal__ (b) __Active__ (c) __ms__ (d) __רָפָא__

(3) שֹׂנְאֵי טוֹב וְאֹהֲבֵי רָע   those who hate good and love evil (Mic. 3:2)

    (a) __Qal__ (b) __Active__ (c) __mp__ (d) __שָׂנֵא__

(4) הָאַחַת אֲהוּבָה וְהָאַחַת שְׂנוּאָה   the one loved, and the one hated
(Deut. 21:15)

    (a) __Qal__ (b) __Passive__ (c) __fs__ (d) __שָׂנֵא__

(5) הֲלוֹא־מְשַׂנְאֶיךָ יְהוָה אֶשְׂנָא(k)   O LORD, do I not hate the ones hating
you? (Ps. 139:21)

    (a) __Pi‹el__ (b) __Active__ (c) __mp__ (d) __שָׂנֵא__

(6) וְאֶת־יְהוָה אֱלֹהֵי הַשָּׁמַיִם אֲנִי יָרֵא And the LORD, the God of the heavens I fear. (Jon. 1:9)

(a) _____ Qal (b) _____ Active (c) _____ ms (d) _____ יָרֵא

(7) וְשׁוּלָיו מְלֵאִים אֶת־הַהֵיכָל And his skirts were filling the temple. (Isa. 6:1)

(a) _____ Qal (b) _____ Active (c) _____ mp (d) _____ מָלֵא

(8) הוֹי גּוֹי חֹטֵא Woe to the nation that sins (the sinful nation). (Isa. 1:4)

(a) _____ Qal (b) _____ Active (c) _____ ms (d) _____ חָטָא

(9) הַנֶּפֶשׁ הַחֹטֵאת הִיא תָמוּת The person who sins, this one shall die. (Ezek. 18:4)

(a) _____ Qal (b) _____ Active (c) _____ fs (d) _____ חָטָא

(10) תְּהוֹם־אֶל־תְּהוֹם קוֹרֵא Deep calls unto deep. (Ps. 42:8; Eng. 42:7)

(a) _____ Qal (b) _____ Active (c) _____ ms (d) _____ קָרָא

XXVI.4 Each of the following entries contains a verb form from a Lamed ʾAlef verb. In (a) identify the form (perfect, imperfect, or imperative), in (b) give its stem, in (c) its person, gender, and number, and in (d) its root.

(1) קְרָא שְׁמוֹ לֹא עַמִּי Call his name "Not-My-People." (Hos. 1:9)

(a) Imperative (b) _____ Qal (c) _____ 2 ms (d) _____ קָרָא

(2) לֹא־יִקָּרֵא שִׁמְךָ עוֹד יַעֲקֹב Your name shall no longer be called Jacob. (Gen. 35:10)

(a) Imperfect (b) _____ Nifʿal (c) _____ 3 ms (d) _____ קָרָא

(3) אֲנִי יְהוָה קְרָאתִיךָ בְצֶדֶק I the LORD have called you in righteousness. (Isa. 42:6)

(a) Perfect (b) _____ Qal (c) _____ 1 cs (d) _____ קָרָא

(4) וַתִּקְרֶאנָה שְׁמוֹ עוֹבֵד הוּא אֲבִי־יִשַׁי אֲבִי דָוִד And they called his name Obed; he was the father of Jesse, the father of David. (Ruth 4:17)

(a) Imperfect (b) _____ Qal (c) _____ 3 fp (d) _____ קָרָא

(5) הַמְצָאתַנִי[k] אֹיְבִי Have you found me, O my enemy? (1 Kgs. 21:20)

(a) Perfect (b) _____ Qal (c) _____ 2 ms (d) _____ מָצָא

(6) אוּלַי יִמָּצְאוּן שָׁם אַרְבָּעִים Perhaps forty shall be found there. (Gen. 18:29)

(a) Imperfect (b) _____ Nifʿal (c) _____ 3 mp (d) _____ מָצָא

(7) אֲנִי יְהוָה בְּרָאתִיו I the LORD have created it. (Isa. 45:8)

    (a) Perfect   (b)   Qal   (c)   1 cs   (d) בָּרָא

(8) לֵב טָהוֹר בְּרָא־לִי אֱלֹהִים Create for me a clean heart, O God! (Ps. 51:12)

    (a) Imperative   (b)   Qal   (c)   2 ms   (d) בָּרָא

(9) וְהַבַּיִת יִמָּלֵא עָשָׁן And the house was filled with smoke. (Isa. 6:4)

    (a) Imperfect   (b)   Nifʻal   (c)   3 ms   (d) מָלֵא

(10) וָאֲמַלֵּא אֹתוֹ רוּחַ אֱלֹהִים[i] And I have filled him (with) the spirit of God. (Exod. 31:3)

    (a) Imperfect   (b)   Piʻel   (c)   1 cs   (d) מָלֵא

(11) וְאֶת־עֵשָׂו שָׂנֵאתִי But Esau have I hated. (Mal. 1:3)

    (a) Perfect   (b)   Qal   (c)   1 cs   (d) שָׂנֵא

(12) חָדְשֵׁיכֶם וּמוֹעֲדֵיכֶם שָׂנְאָה[l] נַפְשִׁי Your new moon (festivals) and your appointed feasts my soul hates. (Isa. 1:14)

    (a) Perfect   (b)   Qal   (c)   3 fs   (d) שָׂנֵא

Footnotes

(a) For הָ ending on first person cohortative imperfects, cf. *G*.41.2, p. 132.

(b) The preposition מִן prefixed to an infinitive construct sometimes expresses a negative outcome or consequence, "so as not to," "so that not."

(c) The הָ suffix often occurs with the second masculine singular form of the Qal imperative (cf. *G*.53, pp. 172f.).

(d) A slight change from וְאָמַר (Qal perfect, third masculine singular) to וָאֹמַר (Qal imperfect, first common singular, plus vav consecutive) would give the meaning "And I said," which agrees with the following verb, "What shall I say?" Some authorities have proposed this change.

(e) When the preposition בְּ is prefixed to an infinitive construct, it serves as a temporal conjunction ("when," "as," "while") or as a causal conjunction ("through," "because of," "on account of").

(f) אָדָם is a collective noun, as indicated by the plural pronominal suffix on the following verb (הִבָּרְאָם).

(g) The Nif'al infinitive construct with a third masculine plural pronominal suffix (הִבָּרְאָם) is immediately preceded by the preposition בְּ prefixed to יוֹם and produces the same effect as if בְּ were attached directly to the infinitive [cf. fn.(e) above]. The two words serve as a temporal clause: "in the day of their being created," i.e., "when they were created."

(h) The verb עָנָה is doubly weak (Pe Guttural/Lamed He). For Pe Guttural rules, cf. G.66, pp. 223ff. For Lamed He, cf. G.72, pp. 286ff.

(i) Verbs in the Pi'el stem frequently have a causative meaning [cf. G.36.2(2), p. 109].

(j) An infinitive absolute may stand either before or after a finite form of its cognate verb root, thus serving to strengthen, reinforce, and intensify the verbal idea [cf. G.57.3(2)(3), p. 185]. Having two occurrences of this construction in the same sentence is unusual.

(k) Questions requiring a simple "yes" or "no" answer are usually introduced by interrogative הַ, which is prefixed to the initial word in the sentence (cf. G.34.1, pp. 94f.).

(l) שָׂנְאָה is the third feminine singular since its subject (נַפְשִׁי) is also feminine.

Suggestions for Further Testing

1. Translate the following interrogative sentences.

   (1) מָה יְהוָה אֱלֹהֶיךָ שֹׁאֵל מֵעִמָּךְ (Deut. 10:12)

   (2) הֲשָׁלוֹם אֲבִיכֶם הַזָּקֵן (Gen. 43:27)

   (3) הֲלֹא־הוּא אָבִיךָ (Deut. 32:6)

   (4) הֲתַחַת אֱלֹהִים אָנִי (Gen. 50:19)

   (5) הֲלוֹא לָנוּ הֵם (Gen. 34:23)

   (6) הֲיֵשׁ בָּהּ עֵץ אִם אַיִן (Num. 13:20)

   (7) וְלָמָּה דִּבַּרְתָּ אֵלַי כַּדָּבָר הַזֶּה (1 Sam. 9:21)

2. Translate the following sentences and clauses. Locate fully all Lamed 'Alef verbs.

(1) (Eccl. 3:3) עֵת לַהֲרוֹג וְעֵת לִרְפּוֹא

(2) (Num. 12:13) וַיִּצְעַק מֹשֶׁה אֶל־יְהוָה לֵאמֹר
אֵל נָא רְפָא נָא לָהּ

(3) (Isa. 40:26) לְכֻלָּם בְּשֵׁם יִקְרָא

(4) (1 Kgs. 8:43) כִּי־שִׁמְךָ נִקְרָא עַל־הַבַּיִת הַזֶּה

(5) (Isa. 4:1) רַק יִקָּרֵא שִׁמְךָ עָלֵינוּ

(6) (Isa. 43:1) קָרָאתִי בְשִׁמְךָ לִי־אָתָּה

(7) (Exod. 12:21) וַיִּקְרָא מֹשֶׁה לְכָל־זִקְנֵי יִשְׂרָאֵל

(8) (Ps. 119:64) חַסְדְּךָ יְהוָה מָלְאָה הָאָרֶץ

(9) (Zech. 8:3) וְנִקְרְאָה יְרוּשָׁלַם עִיר־הָאֱמֶת

(10) (Gen. 1:28) וּמִלְאוּ אֶת־הָאָרֶץ

(11) (Jer. 15:16) נִמְצְאוּ דְבָרֶיךָ וָאֹכְלֵם

(12) (Jer. 17:14) רְפָאֵנִי יְהוָה וְאֵרָפֵא

LESSON XXVII

Answer Key
(Cf. *G*, pp. 293ff.)

XXVII.1 Each of the following entries contains a Lamed He verb form. In the space marked (a) give its stem, in (b) its form (perfect, imperfect, or imperative), in (c) its person, gender, and number, and in (d) its root. *Ignore all verb forms that are not Lamed He.*

(1) וַיֹּאמְרוּ כֹּל אֲשֶׁר־דִּבֶּר יְהוָה נַעֲשֶׂה וְנִשְׁמָע And they said, "All that the LORD has spoken we will do, and we will obey (listen)." (Exod. 24:7)

    (a) ___Qal___ (b) ___Imperfect___ (c) ___1 cp___ (d) ___עָשָׂה___

(2) בְּטַח בַּיהוָה וַעֲשֵׂה־טוֹב Trust in the LORD and do good. (Ps. 37:3)

    (a) ___Qal___ (b) ___Imperative___ (c) ___2 ms___ (d) ___עָשָׂה___

(3) לָמָּה לֹא־בְנִיתֶם לִי בֵּית אֲרָזִים Why have you not built for me a house of cedar (cedars)? (2 Sam. 7:7)

    (a) ___Qal___ (b) ___Perfect___ (c) ___2 mp___ (d) ___בָּנָה___

(4) וַיַּעֲלוּ עֹלוֹת וּשְׁלָמִים⁽ᵃ⁾ And they offered up (caused to go up) whole burnt offerings and peace offerings. (Judg. 21:4)

    (a) ___Hifʻil___ (b) ___Imperfect___ (c) ___3 mp___ (d) ___עָלָה___

(5) וַיִּבֶן נֹחַ מִזְבֵּחַ לַיהוָה And Noah built an altar to the LORD. (Gen. 8:20)

    (a) ___Qal___ (b) ___Imperfect___ (c) ___3 ms___ (d) ___בָּנָה___

(6) בֵּיתִי ⁽ᵇ⁾יִבָּנֶה בָּהּ My house shall be built in her (it). (Zech. 1:16)

    (a) ___Nifʻal___ (b) ___Imperfect___ (c) ___3 ms___ (d) ___בָּנָה___

(7) כֻּלָּם לְדַרְכָּם פָּנוּ They have all turned to their (own) way. (Isa. 56:11)

    (a) ___Qal___ (b) ___Perfect___ (c) ___3 cp___ (d) ___פָּנָה___

(8) בְּנוֹת יִשְׂרָאֵל אֶל־שָׁאוּל בְּכֶינָה Daughters of Israel, weep over Saul. (2 Sam. 1:24)

    (a) ___Qal___ (b) ___Imperative___ (c) ___2 fp___ (d) ___בָּכָה___

(9) צִיּוֹן בְּמִשְׁפָּט תִּפָּדֶה Zion shall be redeemed in justice. (Isa. 1:27)

    (a) ___Nifʻal___ (b) ___Imperfect___ (c) ___3 fs___ (d) ___פָּדָה___

160

(10) וְנִגְלָה כְּבוֹד יְהוָה And the glory of the LORD shall be revealed. (Isa. 40:5)

    (a) __Nifʻal__ (b) __Perfect__ (c) __3 ms__ (d) גָּלָה

(11) וְרָאוּ כָל־בָּשָׂר יַחְדָּו And all flesh shall see it together. (Isa. 40:5)

    (a) __Qal__ (b) __Perfect__ (c) __3 cp__ (d) רָאָה

(12) אֶרֶץ (c)אַל־תְּכַסִּי דָמִי O earth, do not cover my blood! (Job 16:18)

    (a) __Piʻel__ (b) __Imperfect__ (c) __2 fs__ (d) כָּסָה

(13) (d)וְיִתְכַּסּוּ שַׂקִּים הָאָדָם וְהַבְּהֵמָה And let them cover themselves with sackcloth, both men and cattle. (Jon. 3:8)

    (a) __Hitpaʻel__ (b) __Imperfect__ (c) __3 mp__ (d) כָּסָה

(14) כְּרֹעֶה עֶדְרוֹ יִרְעֶה Like a shepherd he will feed his flock. (Isa. 40:11)

    (a) __Qal__ (b) __Imperfect__ (c) __3 ms__ (d) רָעָה

(15) לֶחֶם לֹא אָכַלְתִּי וּמַיִם לֹא שָׁתִיתִי I did not eat bread, and I did not drink water. (Deut. 9:9)

    (a) __Qal__ (b) __Perfect__ (c) __1 cs__ (d) שָׁתָה

(16) וַתֹּאמֶר שְׁתֵה אֲדֹנִי And she said, "Drink, my lord." (Gen. 24:18)

    (a) __Qal__ (b) __Imperative__ (c) __2 ms__ (d) שָׁתָה

(17) (d)וְתֵרָאֶה הַיַּבָּשָׁה And let dry land appear (be seen). (Gen. 1:9)

    (a) __Nifʻal__ (b) __Imperfect__ (c) __3 fs__ (d) רָאָה

(18) יְהוָה הֶעֱלִיתָ מִן־שְׁאוֹל נַפְשִׁי O LORD, you have brought up (caused to go up) my soul from Sheol. (Ps. 30:4; Eng. 30:3)

    (a) __Hifʻil__ (b) __Perfect__ (c) __2 ms__ (d) עָלָה

XXVII.2 Each of the following entries contains a Qal form of הָיָה, "he was." In the space marked (a) identify each form (perfect, imperfect, etc.), in (b) give its person, gender, and number, and if the verb form has a prefixed vav, indicate in (c) whether it is a vav conjunction (vav conj.) or a vav consecutive (vav cons.). *Ignore verb forms not derived from* הָיָה.

(1) וְהָאָרֶץ הָיְתָה תֹהוּ (e)וָבֹהוּ Now the earth was without form and empty. (Gen. 1:2)

    (a) __Perfect__ (b) __3 fs__

(2) וַיֹּאמֶר אֱלֹהִים (f)יְהִי אוֹר And God said, "Let there be light." (Gen. 1:3)

    (a) __Imperfect__ (b) __3 ms__

(3) וַיְהִי־אוֹר And there was light. (Gen. 1:3)

    (a) __Imperfect__ (b) __3 ms__ (c) __Vav Cons.__

(4) וְהָיוּ לְאֹתֹת וּלְמוֹעֲדִים וּלְיָמִים וְשָׁנִים (f) And let them be for signs and for appointed seasons, and for days and years. (Gen. 1:14)

(a) __Perfect__ (b) __3 cp__ (c) __Vav Conj.__

(5) לֹא־טוֹב הֱיוֹת הָאָדָם לְבַדּוֹ It is not good for the man to be alone. (Gen. 2:18)

(a) __Inf. Const.__

(6) וֶהְיֵה־לָנוּ לְאָב וּלְכֹהֵן And be to us a father and a priest. (Judg. 18:19)

(a) __Imperative__ (b) __2 ms__ (c) __Vav Conj.__

(7) וַיֹּאמֶר אֱלֹהִים אֶל־מֹשֶׁה אֶהְיֶה אֲשֶׁר אֶהְיֶה And God said to Moses, "I am who I am" (or, "I will be who I will be"). (Exod. 3:14)

(a) __Imperfect__ (b) __1 cs__

(8) תְּהִי נָא יָדְךָ בִּי וּבְבֵית אָבִי (f) I pray, let your hand be upon me and upon my father's house. (2 Sam. 24:17) (a) __Imperfect__ (b) __3 fs__

(9) כִּי־תִהְיֶיןָ לְאִישׁ שְׁתֵּי נָשִׁים if there shall be two wives to a man (if a man has two wives) (Deut. 21:15) (a) __Imperfect__ (b) __3 fp__

(10) וַיִּהְיוּ שְׁנֵיהֶם עֲרוּמִּים הָאָדָם וְאִשְׁתּוֹ And the two of them were naked, the man and his wife. (Gen. 2:25)

(a) __Imperfect__ (b) __3 mp__ (c) __Vav Cons.__

(11) וִיהִי חֹשֶׁךְ עַל־אֶרֶץ מִצְרָיִם (f) And let there be darkness over the land of Egypt. (Exod. 10:21) (a) __Imperfect__ (b) __3 ms__ (c) __Vav Conj.__

(12) וְהָיוּ לְבָשָׂר אֶחָד (f) And they shall become (be) one flesh. (Gen. 2:24)

(a) __Perfect__ (b) __3 cp__ (c) __Vav Conj.__

(13) וְאַתֶּם תִּהְיוּ־לִי (f) מַמְלֶכֶת כֹּהֲנִים וְגוֹי קָדוֹשׁ And you shall be to me a kingdom of priests and a holy nation. (Exod. 19:6)

(a) __Imperfect__ (b) __2 mp__

(14) הֱיֵה־עֹזֵר לִי Be my helper (be a helper to me). (Ps. 30:11; Eng. 30:10)

(a) __Imperative__ (b) __2 ms__

(15) הִתְחַזְּקוּ וִהְיוּ לַאֲנָשִׁים Make yourselves strong and be men! (1 Sam. 4:9)

(a) __Imperative__ (b) __2 mp__ (c) __Vav Conj.__

(16) וַתְּהִי־לִי לְאִשָּׁה And she became my wife. (Gen. 20:12)

(a) __Imperfect__ (b) __3 fs__ (c) __Vav Cons.__

(17) לְמַעַן תִּהְיֶה תּוֹרַת יְהוָה בְּפִיךָ In order that the law of the LORD may be in your mouth. (Exod. 13:9) (a) __Imperfect__ (b) __3 fs__

(18) לִהְיוֹת־שְׁמִי שָׁם עַד־עוֹלָם that my name may be there for ever
(2 Chr. 7:16)   (a) <u>Inf. Const.</u>

XXVII.3 Each of the following entries contains a participle of a Lamed He verb.
Underscore the correct form for each entry.

(1) הַבַּיִת הַזֶּה אֲשֶׁר־אַתָּה (<u>בֹּנֶה</u> / בָּנָה)
the house which you are building (1 Kgs. 6:12)

(2) וַיֹּאמֶר חֲזָאֵל מַדּוּעַ אֲדֹנִי (בֹּכֶה / <u>בּוֹכִים</u>)
And Hazael said, "Why is my lord weeping?" (2 Kgs. 8:12)

(3) רָחֵל (מְבַכֶּה / <u>מְבַכָּה</u>) עַל־בָּנֶיהָ
Rachel weeping for her children (Jer. 31:15)

(4) וְיַעֲקֹב (רֹעֶה / <u>רֹעִים</u>) אֶת־צֹאן לָבָן
And Jacob was tending the flock of Laban. (Gen. 30:36)

(5) מָה־אַתָּה (רֹאֶה / <u>רֹאֶה</u>) עָמוֹס
What are you seeing, Amos? (Amos 7:8)

(6) כַּאֲשֶׁר אַתֶּם (<u>רֹאִים</u> / רֹאֶה) בְּעֵינֵיכֶם
as you are seeing with your (own) eyes (2 Chr. 29:8)

(7) וַיֹּאמֶר אֶל־הַשֹּׁפְטִים רְאוּ מָה־אַתֶּם (עֹשֶׂה / <u>עֹשִׂים</u>)
And he said to the judges, "See (consider) what you are doing." (2 Chr. 19:6)

(8) עֲבָדֶיךָ יַעֲשׂוּ כַּאֲשֶׁר אֲדֹנִי (^(g)<u>מְצַוֶּה</u> / מְצַוִּים)
Your servants will do as my lord commands. (Num. 32:25)

(9) מִי זֹאת (עֹלֶה / <u>עֹלָה</u>) מִן־הַמִּדְבָּר
Who is this going up from the desert? (Song of Sol. 3:6)

(10) וְהִנֵּה מִן־הַיְאֹר (עֹלִים / <u>עֹלֹת</u>) שֶׁבַע פָּרוֹת
And behold, seven cows were coming up out of the Nile (river). (Gen. 41:2)

(11) וַיְהִי שְׁמוּאֵל (<u>מַעֲלֶה</u> / מַעֲלָה) הָעוֹלָה
And Samuel was offering up the whole burnt offering. (1 Sam. 7:10)

(12) כִּי אֲנִי יְהוָה (<u>הַמַּעֲלֶה</u> / הַמַּעֲלִים) אֶתְכֶם מֵאֶרֶץ מִצְרַיִם
For I (am) the LORD, the one bringing you up from the land of Egypt.
(Lev. 11:45)

(13) וַיִּהְיוּ (<u>מַעֲלִים</u> / מַעֲלוֹת) ^(a)עֹלוֹת בְּבֵית־יְהוָה תָּמִיד
And they were offering up whole burnt offerings in the house of the LORD
continually. (2 Chr. 24:14)

(14) וַיֹּאמֶר אֲלֵיהֶם הַכֹּהֵן מָה אַתֶּם (עֹשֶׂה / <u>עֹשִׂים</u>)

And the priest said to them, "What are you doing?" (Judg. 18:18)

(15) הוֹי (<u>הַמַּרְבֶּה</u> / הַמַּרְבֶּה) לֹּא־לוֹ

Woe to the one heaping up (making much, multiplying) what is not his own. (Hab. 2:6)

XXVII.4 Supply the correct pronouns in the translations of the Hebrew in the following examples of Lamed He verbs.

(1) וַיֹּאמְרוּ אֵלָיו מַה־זֹּאת עָשִׂיתָ And ___they___ said to ___him___, "What is this ___you___ have done?" (Jon. 1:10)

(2) וְאָמְרוּ לֶהָרִים כַּסּוּנוּ And ___they___ shall say to the mountains, "Cover ___us___!" (Hos. 10:8)

(3) (h)וָאֹמַר אֲלֵיהֶם שְׁתוּ־יָיִן And ___I___ said to ___them___, "Drink wine!" (Jer. 35:5)

(4) (i)וַיַּרְא אֹתָם אֶת־בֶּן־הַמֶּלֶךְ And ___he___ showed ___them___ the king's son. (2 Kgs. 11:4)

(5) וַיַּרְאוּם אֶת־פְּרִי הָאָרֶץ And ___they___ showed ___them___ the fruit of the land. (Num. 13:26)

(6) (j)וַיֹּאמַר הַרְאֵנִי נָא אֶת־כְּבֹדֶךָ And ___he___ said, "Show ___me___ ___your___ glory." (Exod. 33:18)

(7) לֹא־תִרְאֶה אֶת־פָּנַי ___You___ shall not see ___my___ face. (2 Sam. 3:13)

(8) לַעֲשׂוֹת כְּכֹל אֲשֶׁר צִוִּיתִךָ to do according to all that ___I___ commanded ___you___ (1 Kgs. 9:4)

(9) וּכְבוֹדוֹ עָלַיִךְ יֵרָאֶה And ___his___ glory will be seen upon ___you___. (Isa. 60:2)

(10) עָשִׂיתִי כְּכֹל אֲשֶׁר צִוִּיתָנִי ___I___ have done according to all that ___you___ commanded ___me___. (Deut. 26:14)

(11) (k)וְלָהּ אָמַר עֲלִי לְשָׁלוֹם לְבֵיתֵךְ And ___he___ said to ___her___, "Go up in peace to ___your___ house." (1 Sam. 25:35)

(12) וַיֹּאמְרוּ זֶה אֱלֹהֶיךָ אֲשֶׁר הֶעֶלְךָ מִמִּצְרָיִם And ___they___ said, "This is ___your___ God who brought ___you___ up from Egypt." (Neh. 9:18)

(13) וַיֹּאמְרוּ אֵלֶּה אֱלֹהֶיךָ אֲשֶׁר הֶעֱלוּךָ מֵאֶרֶץ מִצְרָיִם And ___they___ said, " ___These___ are ___your___ gods which brought ___you___ up from the land of Egypt." (Exod. 32:4)

(14) וָאֶקְרָא לָהֶם וְלֹא עָנוּ And ___I___ called to ___them___ but ___they___ did not answer. (Jer. 35:17)

(15) עַמִּי מֶה־עָשִׂיתִי לְךָ עֲנֵה בִי O ___my___ people, what have ___I___ done to ___you___ ? Answer ___me___ ! (Mic. 6:3)

(16) עֲשֵׂה־לָנוּ אֱלֹהִים אֲשֶׁר יֵלְכוּ לְפָנֵינוּ Make for ___us___ gods which shall go before ___us___ . (Exod. 32:1)

(17) וַיֹּאמֶר לוֹ עֲשֵׂה כָּל־אֲשֶׁר בִּלְבָבֶךָ And ___he___ said to ___him___ , "Do all that is in ___your___ heart." (1 Sam. 14:7)

(18) וְלֹא אָבִיתִי לִשְׁלֹחַ יָדִי בִּמְשִׁיחַ יְהוָה And ___I___ was not willing to put forth ___my___ hand against the LORD's anointed. (1 Sam. 26:23)

Footnotes

(a) (וַיַּעֲלוּ עֹלֹת) In this construction, עֹלֹת is a feminine plural noun (singular: עֹלָה), designating whole burnt offerings. The translation would be "to offer up offerings," an example of the use of a cognate accusative, which means that the verb form (וַיַּעֲלוּ) and its object (עֹלֹת) are derived from the same root (עָלָה).

(b) The accent has moved backward one syllable on יְבַנֶּה. This was done to avoid juxtaposing two tone syllables.

(c) אַל, "not," with the imperfect indicates the jussive use of the imperfect (cf. G.41.1, p. 131). The jussive expresses a negative wish, a negative exhortation, or a mild prohibition (cf. G.55, pp. 173f.).

(d) A second or third person form of the imperfect may be used as a jussive, except when the form is prefixed with vav consecutive. The vav used here (וְיִתְכַּסּוּ) is vav conjunction. (Cf. G.41.1, p. 131.)

(e) Vav conjunction may be pointed as וָ before the accented syllable of the word to which it has been prefixed (cf. G.62.5, p. 209).

(f) Imperfect second person and third person forms of הָיָה, either with or without vav conjunction, are frequently used as jussives.

165

(g) צַוָּה is unusual in that vav (ו) continues to function as a consonant instead of combining with the preceding vowel to form a diphthong (cf. *G*.74.1, p. 316).

(h) On the inflection of the Qal imperfect forms of אָמַר (with vav consecutive), cf. *G*.67.5, pp. 238f.

(i) Forms of רָאָה, "he saw," in the Qal imperfect third masculine singular plus vav consecutive and the Hifʻil imperfect third masculine singular plus vav consecutive are written alike (וַיַּרְא) [cf. *G*.72.8(10), p. 292]. Only the context will enable students to distinguish between the two.

(j) הַרְאֵנִי is the Hifʻil imperative, second masculine singular, plus first common singular pronominal suffix, from רָאָה, "he saw." Translated: "Cause me to see" i.e., "Show me."

(k) עֲלִי is the Qal imperative, second feminine singular (feminine subject indicated by pronominal suffixes), from עָלָה, "he went up." Translated: "Go up."

Suggestions for Further Testing

1. Translate the following and locate all forms of Lamed He verbs.

(1)	עֲשׂוּ־לִי כַּטּוֹב בְּעֵינֵיכֶם	(Jer. 26:14)
(2)	וַיַּעַל יוֹסֵף לִקְבֹּר אֶת־אָבִיו וַיַּעֲלוּ אִתּוֹ כָּל־עַבְדֵי פַרְעֹה	(Gen. 50:7)
(3)	צַדִּיק הוּא חָיֹה יִחְיֶה	(Ezek. 18:9)
(4)	הוּא יִקְרָא בִשְׁמִי וַאֲנִי אֶעֱנֶה אֹתוֹ	(Zech. 13:9)
(5)	מִלְחָמוֹת גְּדֹלוֹת עָשִׂיתָ לֹא־תִבְנֶה בַיִת לִשְׁמִי	(1 Chr. 22:8)
(6)	וּרְאוּ אֶת־הַדָּבָר הַגָּדוֹל הַזֶּה אֲשֶׁר יְהוָה עֹשֶׂה לְעֵינֵיכֶם	(1 Sam. 12:16)
(7)	יְהוָה נָתַן וַיהוָה לָקָח יְהִי שֵׁם יְהוָה מְבֹרָךְ	(Job 1:21)
(8)	כִּי אֶת־הַמֶּלֶךְ יְהוָה צְבָאוֹת רָאוּ עֵינָי	(Isa. 6:5)
(9)	כִּי לֹא יָכְלוּ לִשְׁתֹּת מִמֵּימֵי הַיְאֹר	(Exod. 7:24)
(10)	כֹּל אֲשֶׁר תִּמְצָא יָדְךָ לַעֲשׂוֹת בְּכֹחֲךָ עֲשֵׂה	(Eccl. 9:10)

2. Match the following:

(1) ( )   וְאֶעֶשְׂךָ לְגוֹי גָּדוֹל   (A) Has this happened in your days? (Joel 1:2)

(2) ( )   כִּי־בֵן הָיִיתִי לְאָבִי   (B) Be not wise in your (own) eyes. (Prov. 3:7)

(3) ( )   הֶהָיְתָה זֹּאת בִּימֵיכֶם   (C) And you did (what was) evil in my eyes. (Isa. 65:12)

(4) ( )   וַיְמַהֵר לַעֲשׂוֹת אֹתוֹ   (D) to do the commandments of the LORD (Neh. 10:30)

(5) ( )   אַל־תְּהִי חָכָם בְּעֵינֶיךָ   (E) The hand of the LORD has done this. (Isa. 41:20)

(6) ( )   לַעֲשׂוֹת אֶת־מִצְוֺת יְהוָה   (F) Your hands made me. (Ps. 119:73)

(7) ( )   אֲדַבֵּר דָּבָר וַעֲשִׂיתִיו   (G) And I will make you a great nation. (Gen. 12:2)

(8) ( )   יַד־יְהוָה עָשְׂתָה זֹּאת   (H) Do what is good in your eyes. (1 Sam. 14:36)

(9) ( )   מַה־זֹּאת עֲשִׂיתֶם   (I) I will speak a word and I will do it. (Ezek. 12:25)

(10) ( )   יָדֶיךָ עָשׂוּנִי   (J) What is this you have done? (Judg. 2:2)

(11) ( )   וַתַּעֲשׂוּ הָרַע בְּעֵינַי   (K) And he hastened to do (prepare) it. (Gen. 18:7)

(12) ( )   הַטּוֹב בְּעֵינֶיךָ עֲשֵׂה   (L) For I was a son to my father. (Prov. 4:3)

LESSON XXVIII

Answer Key
(Cf. *G*, pp. 308ff.)

XXVIII1. Each of the following entries contains a Pe Nun verb form. Supply the correct translation of the verb form. In the space marked (a) give its stem, in (b) the identification of the form (perfect, imperfect, etc.), in (c) its person, gender, and number, and in (d) its root. *Ignore verb forms that are not Pe Nun, except for* לָקַח, *"he took."*

(1) לֹא־יִשָּׂא גוֹי אֶל־גּוֹי חֶרֶב Nation shall not ___lift___ ___up___ sword against nation. (Isa. 2:4)

    (a) ___Qal___ (b) ___Imperfect___ (c) ___3 ms___ (d) ___נָשָׂא___

(2) כִּי אֶת־כָּל־הָאָרֶץ אֲשֶׁר אַתָּה רֹאֶה לְךָ ^(a)אֶתְּנֶנָּה For all the land that you see, to you I will ___give___ it. (Gen. 13:15)

    (a) ___Qal___ (b) ___Imperfect___ (c) ___1 cs___ (d) ___נָתַן___

(3) שְׂאוּ שְׁעָרִים רָאשֵׁיכֶם ___Lift___ up your heads, O gates! (Ps. 24:7)

    (a) ___Qal___ (b) ___Imperative___ (c) ___2 mp___ (d) ___נָשָׂא___

(4) וַיִּפֹּל הַגּוֹרָל עַל־יוֹנָה And the lot ___fell___ upon Jonah. (Jon. 1:7)

    (a) ___Qal___ (b) ___Imperfect___ (c) ___3 ms___ (d) ___נָפַל___

(5) וַיִּתְפַּלֵּל אֵלָיו וְיֹאמַר הַצִּילֵנִי כִּי אֵלִי אָתָּה And he prays to it and says, " ___Deliver___ me, for you are my god." (Isa. 44:17)

    (a) ___Hif'il___ (b) ___Imperative___ (c) ___2 ms___ (d) ___[נצל]___

(6) לָמָּה לֹא־הִגַּדְתָּ לִי כִּי אִשְׁתְּךָ הִוא Why did you not ___tell___ me that she was your wife? (Gen. 12:18)

    (a) ___Hif'il___ (b) ___Perfect___ (c) ___2 ms___ (d) ___[נגד]___

(7) וַיִּשְׁלַח יְהוָה אֶת־יָדוֹ וַיַּגַּע עַל־פִּי And the LORD put forth (sent) his hand and ___touched___ my mouth. (Jer. 1:9)

    (a) ___Hif'il___ (b) ___Imperfect___ (c) ___3 ms___ (d) ___נָגַע___

(8) וַיֹּאמֶר יְהוָה אֵלַי הִנֵּה ^(b)נָתַתִּי דְבָרַי בְּפִיךָ And the LORD said to me, "Behold, I have ___put___ my words in your mouth." (Jer. 1:9)

    (a) ___Qal___ (b) ___Perfect___ (c) ___1 cs___ (d) ___נָתַן___

(9) וַיִּטַּע יְהוָה אֱלֹהִים גַּן־בְּעֵדֶן   And the LORD God ___planted___ a garden in Eden. (Gen. 2:8)

    (a) Qal   (b) Imperfect   (c) 3 ms   (d) נָטַע

(10) הַבֵּט מִשָּׁמַיִם וּרְאֵה   ___Look___ from heaven and see! (Isa. 63:15)

    (a) Hif'il   (b) Imperative   (c) 2 ms   (d) נָבַט

(11) וּבַמָּקוֹם הַזֶּה אֶתֵּן שָׁלוֹם   And in this place I will ___give___ peace. (Hag. 2:9)

    (a) Qal   (b) Imperfect   (c) 1 cs   (d) נָתַן

(12) (c)וְהִכֵּיתִי כָל־בְּכוֹר בְּאֶרֶץ מִצְרַיִם   And I will ___smite___ all the firstborn in the the land of Egypt. (Exod. 12:12)

    (a) Hif'il   (b) Perfect   (c) 1 cs   (d) [נכה]

(13) וְרוּחַ קָדְשְׁךָ אַל־(d)תִּקַּח מִמֶּנִּי   And ___take___ not your holy spirit from me. (Ps. 51:13; Eng. 51:11)

    (a) Qal   (b) Imperfect   (c) 2 ms   (d) לָקַח

(14) (d)וַתִּקַּח מִפִּרְיוֹ וַתֹּאכַל   And she ___took___ from its fruit, and she ate. (Gen. 3:6)

    (a) Qal   (b) Imperfect   (c) 3 fs   (d) לָקַח

(15) (e)יִשָּׂא יְהוָה פָּנָיו אֵלֶיךָ   May the LORD ___lift___ ___up___ his countenance (face) upon you. (Num. 6:26)

    (a) Qal   (b) Imperfect   (c) 3 ms   (d) נָשָׂא

XXVIII.2 Each of the following entries contains an infinitive form from a Pe Nun verb. In the space marked (a) give its stem, in (b) tell whether it is *construct* or *absolute*, and in (c) give its root.

(1) (f)לָתֵת לָהֶם לֵב אֶחָד
to give to them one heart (2 Chr. 30:12)

    (a) Qal
    (b) Const.
    (c) נָתַן

(2) וַיְבַקְשׁוּ אֶת־נַפְשִׁי (d)לְקַחְתָּהּ
And they seek my soul (life) to take it. (1 Kgs. 19:10)

    (a) Qal
    (b) Const.
    (c) לָקַח

(3) וְעַתָּה אָרוּר אָתָּה מִן־הָאֲדָמָה אֲשֶׁר פָּצְתָה אֶת־פִּיהָ
(d)לָקַחַת אֶת־(g)דְּמֵי אָחִיךָ מִיָּדֶךָ
And now cursed are you from the ground which has opened its mouth to receive (take) the blood (bloods) of your brother from your hand. (Gen. 4:11)

    (a) Qal
    (b) Const.
    (c) לָקַח

(4) בִּנְטֹתִי אֶת־יָדִי עַל־מִצְרַיִם (h)

when I stretch out my hand against Egypt (Exod. 7:5)

(a) ___ Qal
(b) ___ Const.
(c) ___ נָטָה

(5) וַיְמָאֵן הָאִישׁ (i) לְהַכֹּתוֹ

But the man refused to smite him. (1 Kgs. 20:35)

(a) ___ Hifʻil
(b) ___ Const.
(c) ___ [נכה]

(6) וַיֹּאמְרוּ אֶל־בָּרוּךְ (j) הַגֵּיד נַגִּיד לַמֶּלֶךְ אֵת כָּל־ הַדְּבָרִים הָאֵלֶּה

And they said to Baruch, "We must surely report (declare) all these words to the king." (Jer. 36:16)

(a) ___ Hifʻil
(b) ___ Abs.
(c) ___ [נגד]

(7) לְהַגִּיד לְיַעֲקֹב פִּשְׁעוֹ וּלְיִשְׂרָאֵל חַטָּאתוֹ

to declare to Jacob his transgression and to Israel his sin (Mic. 3:8)

(a) ___ Hifʻil
(b) ___ Const.
(c) ___ [נגד]

(8) כִּי־אִתְּךָ אֲנִי לְהַצִּלֶךָ

For I am with you to deliver you. (Jer. 1:8)

(a) ___ Hifʻil
(b) ___ Const.
(c) ___ [נצל]

(9) וְאַל־יַבְטַח אֶתְכֶם חִזְקִיָּהוּ אֶל־יְהוָה לֵאמֹר (j) הַצֵּל יַצִּילֵנוּ יְהוָה

And do not let Hezekiah cause you to trust in the LORD saying, "The LORD will surely deliver us." (Isa. 36:15)

(a) ___ Hifʻil
(b) ___ Abs.
(c) ___ [נצל]

(10) וְשָׁאוּל חָשַׁב לְהַפִּיל אֶת־דָּוִד בְּיַד־פְּלִשְׁתִּים

And Saul thought to make David fall by the hand of the Philistines. (1 Sam. 18:25)

(a) ___ Hifʻil
(b) ___ Const.
(c) ___ נָפַל

(11) (j) הַכֵּה תַכֶּה אֶת־יֹשְׁבֵי הָעִיר הַהוּא לְפִי־חָרֶב

You shall surely smite the inhabitants of that city by the edge (mouth) of the sword. (Deut. 13:16)

(a) ___ Hifʻil
(b) ___ Abs.
(c) ___ [נכה]

XXVIII.3 Fill in the blanks with the correct pronouns.

(1) אֶשָּׂא עֵינַי אֶל־הֶהָרִים ___ I ___ will lift up ___ my ___ eyes to the mountains. (Ps. 121:1)

(2) וְרוּחַ יְהוָה יִשָּׂאֲךָ And the spirit of the LORD shall lift ___ you ___ up. (1 Kgs. 18:12)

(3) וְאַתָּה נָשָׂאתָ עֲוֹן חַטָּאתִי But ___ you ___ have forgiven (lifted up) the iniquity of ___ my ___ sin. (Ps. 32:5)

170

(4) אָכֵן חֲלָיֵנוּ הוּא נָשָׂא Surely ___he___ has carried (lifted up) ___our___ sicknesses. (Isa. 53:4)

(5) וָאֶפֹּל עַל־פָּנָי And ___I___ fell on ___my___ face. (Ezek. 3:23)

(6) וְהִפַּלְתִּים בַּחֶרֶב לִפְנֵי אֹיְבֵיהֶם And ___I___ caused ___them___ to fall by the sword before ___their___ enemies. (Jer. 19:7)

(7) כִּי הִצַּלְתָּ נַפְשִׁי מִמָּוֶת For ___you___ delivered ___my___ soul from death. (Ps. 56:14; Eng. 56:13)

(8) לְמַעַן הַצִּיל אֹתוֹ מִיָּדָם In order to deliver ___him___ from ___their___ hand. (Gen. 37:22)

(9) בְּצִדְקָתְךָ תַצִּילֵנִי In ___your___ righteousness ___you___ will deliver ___me___ . (Ps. 71:2)

(10) וַיֹּאמֶר מִי הִגִּיד לְךָ כִּי עֵירֹם אָתָּה And ___he___ said, "___Who___ told ___you___ that ___you___ were naked?" (Gen. 3:11)

(11) וְהִגִּידוּ אֶת־כְּבוֹדִי בַּגּוֹים And ___they___ shall declare ___my___ glory among the nations. (Isa. 66:19)

(12) (c)וַיַּכּוּ אֹתוֹ וְאֶת־בָּנָיו וְאֶת־כָּל־עַמּוֹ And ___they___ smote ___him___ and ___his___ sons and all ___his___ people. (Num. 21:35)

(13) וְנָטִיתִי אֶת־יָדִי עֲלֵיהֶם And ___I___ will stretch out ___my___ hand against ___them___ . (Ezek. 6:14)

(14) הַטּוּ אָזְנְכֶם וּלְכוּ אֵלַי שִׁמְעוּ וּתְחִי נַפְשְׁכֶם Incline (stretch out) ___your___ ears and come to ___me___ ; hear that ___your___ soul may live. (Isa. 55:3)

(15) (k)תְּנָה־לָּנוּ מֶלֶךְ לְשָׁפְטֵנוּ Give to ___us___ a king to judge ___us___ . (1 Sam. 8:6)

XXVIII.4 Each of the following entries contains an imperative form of a Pe Nun verb. Fill in the correct translation for each form. In the space marked (a) give its stem, in (b) its person, gender, and number, and in (c) its root. *Ignore verb forms that are not Pe Nun.*

(1) שָׂא נָא עֵינֶיךָ וּרְאֵה מִן־הַמָּקוֹם אֲשֶׁר אַתָּה שָׁם

    ___Lift___ up your eyes and look from the place where you are. (Gen. 13:14)

  (a)   Qal
  (b)   2 ms
  (c)   נָשָׂא

(2) וְעַתָּה הַצִּילֵנוּ מִיַּד אֹיְבֵינוּ

    And now ___deliver___ us from the hand of our enemies. (1 Sam. 12:10)

  (a)   Hifʿil
  (b)   2 ms
  (c)   נָצַל

171

(3) הַגֵּד אֶת־כָּל־אֲשֶׁר־אַתָּה רֹאֶה לְבֵית יִשְׂרָאֵל

___Tell___ all that you are seeing to the house of Israel. (Ezek. 40:4)

(a)   Hifʻil
(b)   2 ms
(c)   נָגַד

(4) וַיֹּאמֶר הַגִּידָה־נָּא שְׁמֶךָ

And he said, "___Tell___ me, I pray, your name!" (Gen. 32:30)

(a)   Hifʻil
(b)   2 ms
(c)   נָגַד

(5) וַיֹּאמֶר אֵלָיו יִצְחָק אָבִיו גְּשָׁה־נָּא וַיִּגַּשׁ

And Isaac his father said to him, "___Draw___ ___near___," and he drew near. (Gen. 27:26–27)

(a)   Qal
(b)   2 ms
(c)   נָגַשׁ

(6) שְׁלַח־נָא יָדְךָ וְגַע בְּכָל־אֲשֶׁר־לוֹ

Put forth (send) your hand and ___touch___ all that which is his. (Job 1:11)

(a)   Qal
(b)   2 ms
(c)   נָגַע

(7) וַיֹּאמֶר הַבֶּט־נָא (l)הַשָּׁמַיְמָה

And he said, "___Look___ to the heavens." (Gen. 15:5)

(a)   Hifʻil
(b)   2 ms
(c)   נָבַט

(8) וַיֹּאמְרוּ (f)תְּנוּ־לָנוּ מַיִם וְנִשְׁתֶּה

And they said, "___Give___ us water that we may drink." (Exod. 17:2)

(a)   Qal
(b)   2 mp
(c)   נָתַן

(9) לֹא לָנוּ יְהוָה לֹא לָנוּ כִּי־לְשִׁמְךָ (f)תֵּן כָּבוֹד

"Not to us, O LORD, not to us, but to your name ___give___ glory." (Ps. 115:1)

(a)   Qal
(b)   2 ms
(c)   נָתַן

(10) תְּנָה־אֶת־בִּתְּךָ(k) לִבְנִי לְאִשָּׁה

___Give___ your daughter to my son for a wife. (2 Kgs. 14:9)

(a)   Qal
(b)   2 ms
(c)   נָתַן

(11) וַיֹּאמֶר יְהוָה אֶל־מֹשֶׁה אֱמֹר אֶל־אַהֲרֹן נְטֵה אֶת־מַטֶּךָ

And the LORD said to Moses, "Say to Aaron, ___stretch___ out your rod." (Exod. 8:12; Eng. 8:16)

(a)   Qal
(b)   2 ms
(c)   נָטָה

(12) וְעַתָּה יְהוָה (d)קַח־נָא אֶת־נַפְשִׁי מִמֶּנִּי כִּי טוֹב מוֹתִי מֵחַיָּי

And now, O LORD, ___take___ from me my soul (life), for better is my death than my life. (Jon. 4:3)

(a)   Qal
(b)   2 ms
(c)   לָקַח

(13) וְעַתָּה (d)קְחוּ לָכֶם שְׁנֵי עָשָׂר אִישׁ מִשִּׁבְטֵי יִשְׂרָאֵל

And now ___take___ for you twelve men from the tribes of Israel. (Josh. 3:12)

(a)   Qal
(b)   2 mp
(c)   לָקַח

(14) הַצִּילֵנִי נָא מִיַּד אָחִי מִיַּד עֵשָׂו   (a) Hif'il

___Deliver___ me, I pray, from the hand of my brother,   (b) 2 ms

from the hand of Esau. (Gen. 32:12)   (c) נָצַל

(15) הַגִּידָה לִּי מֶה עָשִׂיתָ(k)   (a) Hif'il

___Tell___ me what you have done. (1 Sam. 14:43)   (b) 2 ms

  (c) נָגַד

Footnotes

(a) Verbs ending in consonants often occur with an alternate set of forms for pronominal suffixes (cf. *G*.47.3, p. 159). אֶתְּנֶנָּה is the Qal imperfect, first common singular form of נָתַן (אֶתֵּן), plus the third masculine singular pronominal suffix. A simplified form of this word, and one with basically the same meaning, is אֶתְּנֶהוּ (cf. Ps. 89:28; *G*.47.2, pp. 157f.).

(b) The full unassimilated form of נָתַתִּי would be נָתַנְתִּי. The final nun that is supported by a silent sheva drops out and a compensating dagesh forte is placed in the following consonant (ת). This change regularly takes place before consonantal afformatives in verbs whose root forms end in nun [cf. *G*.73.2(6), pp. 305f.]. Such verbs are too rare, however, to be treated as a separate class of weak verbs.

(c) Doubly weak verbs that are both Pe Nun and Lamed He involve a number of changes. Not only is initial נ assimilated when supported by a syllable divider (silent sheva), but an imperfect form ending in ה will lose its final syllable and undergo certain internal vowel changes when it serves as a jussive (cf. *G*.41.1, p. 131) or is prefixed with a vav consecutive. Such changes are especially notable when verbs of this class occur in the Hif'il stem [cf. *G*.73.2(7), p. 306].

(d) לָקַח, "he took," is inflected as if it were a Pe Nun verb [cf. *G*.73.2(8), p. 307; Verb Chart 8, pp. 414f.].

(e) נָשָׂא, "he lifted up," is doubly weak (Pe Nun/Lamed 'Alef). Here the Qal imperfect third masculine singular form of this verb is used as a jussive.

(f) For the full Qal inflection of נָתַן, "he gave," cf. *G*, Verb Chart 8 (Pe Nun), pp. 414f.

(g) The plural form of the noun דָּם, "blood," is used to indicate blood that has been shed by violent means. דְּמֵי is the plural construct, "blood(s) of."

(h) בִּנְטֹתִי is the Qal infinitive construct of נָטָה, "he stretched out," a doubly weak verb in the same class with [נכה]. The first common singular pronominal suffix

173

(יָ) serves as the subject of the infinitive. The preposition בְּ functions as a temporal conjunction and should be translated "when," "as," "while."

(i) For the Hifʻil inflection of [נכה], cf. *G*.73.2(7), p. 306.

(j) An infinitive absolute, standing either before or after a finite form of its cognate verb root, serves to reinforce or intensify the verbal idea [cf. *G*.57.3(2)(3), p. 185].

(k) The הָ suffix is often added to the second masculine singular form of imperatives. The suffix may serve to reinforce the verbal idea (cf. *G*.53, p. 172f.).

(l) The הָ ending on this noun is the "He-directive," indicating motion or direction toward a place or thing (never a person). The accent never falls on the "He-directive" (cf. *G*.44, pp. 146f.).

Suggestions for Further Testing

1. Match the following:

(1) ( )	נָתְנָה אֱלֹהִים בְּיֶדְכֶם	(A) in order to rescue him from their hand (Gen. 37:22)
(2) ( )	וְלֹא־נְתָנוֹ אֱלֹהִים בְּיָדוֹ	(B) Give her to him for a wife. (Gen. 34:8)
(3) ( )	לְמַעַן הַצִּיל אֹתוֹ מִיָּדָם	(C) But let me not fall into the hand of man. (1 Chr. 21:13)
(4) ( )	אֶפְּלָה־נָּא בְּיַד־יְהוָה	(D) And she lifted up her eyes and she saw. (Gen. 24:64)
(5) ( )	וּבְיַד־אָדָם אַל־אֶפֹּל	(E) Lift up your eyes and see. (Zech. 5:5)
(6) ( )	לְמַכֵּה מְלָכִים גְּדֹלִים	(F) My son, give me your heart. (Prov. 23:26)
(7) ( )	שָׂא נָא עֵינֶיךָ וּרְאֵה	(G) But God did not give him into his hand. (1 Sam. 23:14)
(8) ( )	תְּנוּ נָא אֹתָהּ לוֹ לְאִשָּׁה	(H) to the one smiting great kings (Ps. 136:17)
(9) ( )	תְּנָה־בְנִי לִבְּךָ לִי	(I) Let me fall into the hand of the LORD. (1 Chr. 21:13)
(10) ( )	וָאֶשָּׂא אֶת־עֵינַי וָאֵרֶא	(J) And they lifted up their eyes from afar. (Job 2:12)
(11) ( )	וַתִּשָּׂא אֶת־עֵינֶיהָ וַתֵּרֶא	(K) God has given it into your hand. (Judg. 18:10)
(12) ( )	וַיִּשְׂאוּ אֶת־עֵינֵיהֶם מֵרָחוֹק	(L) And I lifted up my eyes and I saw. (Zech. 2:1)

2. Each of the following examples includes a Pe Nun verb or a form of לָקַח,
which shares the characteristics of Pe Nun verbs. Some Pe Nun verbs may also
be doubly weak, thus requiring special attention. Translate each example and
locate the verb form.

(1)   וְנָתַתִּי לָהֶם בְּבֵיתִי וּבְחוֹמֹתַי יָד   (Isa. 56:5)
                וְשֵׁם טוֹב מִבָּנִים וּמִבָּנוֹת

(2)   שֵׁם עוֹלָם אֶתֶּן־לוֹ   (Isa. 56:5)

(3)   הַגִּידָה־נָּא שְׁמֶךָ   (Gen. 32:30)

(4)   וּבִתּוֹ לֹא־תִקַּח לִבְנֶךָ   (Deut. 7:3)

(5)   וְהַךְ אֶת־עֲפַר הָאָרֶץ   (Exod. 8:12)

(6)   וַיֵּט אַהֲרֹן אֶת־יָדוֹ   (Exod. 8:13)

(7)   וַיַּךְ אֶת־עֲפַר הָאָרֶץ   (Exod. 8:13)

(8) יוֹמָם הַשֶּׁמֶשׁ לֹא־יַכֶּכָּה וְיָרֵחַ בַּלָּיְלָה   (Ps. 121:6)

(9)   וַתַּךְ הַשֶּׁמֶשׁ עַל־רֹאשׁ יוֹנָה   (Jon. 4:8)

(10)   וַנַּךְ אֹתוֹ וְאֶת־בָּנוֹ וְאֶת־כָּל־עַמּוֹ   (Deut. 2:33)

3. Fill in the blanks with the correct pronouns.

(1) לְמַעַן הַצִּיל אֹתוֹ מִיָּדָם in order to deliver _____ from _____
hand (Gen. 37:22)

(2) מֶה־עָשִׂיתִי לְךָ כִּי הִכִּיתַנִי What have _____ done to _____
that _____ have smitten _____? (Num. 22:28)

(3) מַדּוּעַ הִכִּיתָנוּ Why have _____ smitten _____? (Jer. 14:19)

(4) וּנְתָנָם יְהוָה אֱלֹהֶיךָ לְפָנֶיךָ וְהִכִּיתָם And the LORD _____ God
will give _____ over to _____, and _____ shall smite
_____. (Deut. 7:2)

(5) בִּתְּךָ לֹא־תִתֵּן לִבְנוֹ וּבִתּוֹ לֹא־תִקַּח לִבְנֶךָ _____ daughter
_____ shall not give to _____ son, and _____ daughter
_____ shall not take for _____ son. (Deut. 7:3)

(6) וְהִכָּם לְעֵינֵיכֶם And _____ shall smite _____ before
_____ eyes. (Jer. 29:21)

(7) וַיַּךְ אוֹתָם And _____ smote _____. (Judg. 15:8)

(8) אֵת אֲשֶׁר־תִּתֵּן עָלַי אֶשָּׂא That which _____ give (place) upon
_____, _____ will bear. (2 Kgs. 18:14)

175

LESSON XXIX

Answer Key
(Cf. *G*, pp. 328ff.)

XXIX.1 Each of the following entries contains an ʿAyin Vav/ʿAyin Yod verb form. Supply the proper translation for the form. In the space marked (a) give its stem, in (b) the identification of the form (perfect, imperfect), in (c) its person, gender, and number, and in (d) its root. Supply this information only for verbs that are ʿAyin Vav/ʿAyin Yod.

(1) יְהוָה בַּשָּׁמַיִם הֵכִין כִּסְאוֹ The LORD has __established__ his throne in the heavens. (Ps. 103:19)

    (a) Hifʿil (b) Perfect (c) 3 ms (d) כּוּן

(2) וְכֹנַנְתִּי אֶת־כִּסְאוֹ עַד־עוֹלָם And I will __establish__ his throne forever. (1 Chr. 17:12)

    (a) Polel (b) Perfect (c) 1 cs (d) כּוּן

(3) לְמַעַן תָּבִינוּ כִּי־אֲנִי הוּא In order that you may __understand__ that I am he. (Isa. 43:10)

    (a) Qal (b) Imperfect (c) 2 mp (d) בִּין

(4) שִׁירוּ לַיהוָה בָּרֲכוּ שְׁמוֹ __Sing__ to the LORD; bless his name. (Ps. 96:2)

    (a) Qal (b) Imperative (c) 2 mp (d) שִׁיר

(5) וְשַׂמְתִּי עֵינִי עֲלֵיהֶם לְטוֹבָה And I will __set__ my eye upon them for good. (Jer. 24:6)

    (a) Qal (b) Perfect (c) 1 cs (d) שׂוּם

(6) וַיַּךְ אֶת־הַפְּלִשְׁתִּי וַיְמִיתֵהוּ And he smote the Philistine and __killed__ him. (2 Sam. 21:17)

    (a) Hifʿil (b) Imperfect (c) 3 ms (d) מוּת

(7) וְאֵין אֱלֹהִים עִמָּדִי אֲנִי אָמִית (a)וַאֲחַיֶּה And there is no god beside me; I __kill__ and I make alive. (Deut. 32:39)

    (a) Hifʿil (b) Imperfect (c) 1 cs (d) מוּת

(8) הַיִחְיֶה (b)גֶּבֶר יָמוּת אִם If a man ___dies___, shall he live (again)? (Job. 14:14)

       (a) __Qal__ (b) __Imperfect__ (c) __3 ms__ (d) __מות__

(9) וָאֶקְרָא קוֹלִי הֲרִימֹתִי I ___raised___ my voice and cried out. (Gen. 39:15)

       (a) __Hifʻil__ (b) __Perfect__ (c) __1 cs__ (d) __רום__

(10) יְשׁוֹבֵב נַפְשִׁי He ___restores___ my soul. (Ps. 23:3)

       (a) __Polel__ (b) __Imperfect__ (c) __3 ms__ (d) __שוב__

(11) וַיַּהַרְגֵהוּ אָחִיו אֶל־הֶבֶל קַיִן וַיָּקָם And Cain ___rose___ against Abel his brother and killed him. (Gen. 4:8)

       (a) __Qal__ (b) __Imperfect__ (c) __3 ms__ (d) __קום__

(12) לְעוֹלָם יָקוּם וּדְבַר־אֱלֹהֵינוּ צִיץ נָבֵל חָצִיר יָבֵשׁ The grass withers, the flower fades; but the word of our God shall ___stand___ for ever. (Isa. 40:8)

       (a) __Qal__ (b) __Imperfect__ (c) __3 ms__ (d) __קום__

(13) אָרֶץ כִּי־עָזַבְנוּ מְאֹד בֹּשְׁנוּ We are utterly ___ashamed___, for we have forsaken the land. (Jer. 9:18)

       (a) __Qal__ (b) __Perfect__ (c) __1 cp__ (d) __בוש__

(14) בָּנוּ לְצַחֶק(c)עִבְרִי אִישׁ לָנוּ הֵבִיא He has ___brought___ to us a Hebrew man to make sport of us. (Gen. 39:14)

       (a) __Hifʻil__ (b) __Perfect__ (c) __3 ms__ (d) __בוא__

(15) עִמִּי לִשְׁכַּב אֵלַי בָּא He ___came___ to me to lie with me. (Gen. 39:14)

       (a) __Qal__ (b) __Perfect__ (c) __3 ms__ (d) __בוא__

XXIX.2 Each of the following entries contains an imperative form of an ʻAyin Vav/ʻAyin Yod verb. Supply the proper translation for the form. In the space marked (a) give its stem, in (b) its person, gender, and number, and in (c) its root.

(1) אוֹרֵךְ בָא כִי קוּמִי   (a) __Qal__

___Arise___, for your light has come. (Isa. 60:1)   (b) __2 fs__

                                   (c) __קום__

(2) הַתֵּבָה אֶל־בֵּיתְךָ וְכָל־ אַתָּה בֹּא לְנֹחַ יְהוָה וַיֹּאמֶר   (a) __Qal__

And the LORD said to Noah, "___Enter___ the ark, you and all your household." (Gen. 7:1)   (b) __2 ms__

                                   (c) __בוא__

(3) בֹּאוּ שְׁעָרָיו בְּתוֹדָה   (a)   Qal

___Enter___ his gates with thanksgiving. (Ps. 100:4)   (b)   2 mp

(c)   **בּוֹא**

(4) קוּמוּ בָּרֲכוּ אֶת־יְהוָה אֱלֹהֵיכֶם   (a)   Qal

___Arise___, bless the LORD your God. (Neh. 9:5)   (b)   2 mp

(c)   **קוּם**

(5) וַיֹּאמֶר לוֹ עֲלֵה הָקֵם לַיהוָה מִזְבֵּחַ   (a)   Hifʻil

And he said to him, "Go up, ___raise___ an altar   (b)   2 ms

to the LORD." (2 Sam. 24:18)   (c)   **קוּם**

(6) וַיֹּאמֶר לֹא־קָרָאתִי בְנִי שׁוּב שְׁכָב   (a)   Qal

And he said, "I did not call, my son; ___return___,   (b)   2 ms

lie down!" (1 Sam. 3:6)   (c)   **שׁוּב**

(7) שׁוּבִי בְּתוּלַת יִשְׂרָאֵל   (a)   Qal

___Return___, O virgin Israel. (Jer. 31:21)   (b)   2 fs

(c)   **שׁוּב**

(8) שֻׁבוּ עָדַי בְּכָל־לְבַבְכֶם   (a)   Qal

___Return___ to me with all your heart. (Joel 2:12)   (b)   2 mp

(c)   **שׁוּב**

(9) הָשִׁיבָה⁽ᵉ⁾⁽ᵈ⁾ לִי שְׂשׂוֹן יִשְׁעֶךָ   (a)   Hifʻil

___Restore___ to me the joy of your salvation. (Ps. 51:14;   (b)   2 ms

Eng. 51:12)   (c)   **שׁוּב**

(10) כַּשּׁוֹפָר הָרֵם קוֹלֶךָ   (a)   Hifʻil

___Lift up___ your voice like the trumpet. (Isa. 58:1)   (b)   2 ms

(c)   **רוּם**

(11) הָרִימִי בַכֹּחַ קוֹלֵךְ   (a)   Hifʻil

___Lift up___ your voice with strength. (Isa. 40:9)   (b)   2 fs

(c)   **רוּם**

(12) שִׂימָה⁽ᵈ⁾⁽ᵉ⁾־לָּנוּ מֶלֶךְ לְשָׁפְטֵנוּ   (a)   Qal

___Set___ for us a king to judge (govern) us.   (b)   2 ms

(1 Sam. 8:5)   (c)   **שִׂים**

(13) כִּי שָׁם שְׁאֵלוּנוּ שִׁירוּ לָנוּ מִשִּׁיר צִיּוֹן   (a)   Qal

For there they requested us, "___Sing___ for us from   (b)   2 mp

the song (one of the songs) of Zion." (Ps. 137:3)   (c)   **שִׁיר**

(14) וְהָבִיאוּ אֶת־אֲחִיכֶם הַקָּטֹן אֵלַי   (a)   Hifʿil

And __bring__ your youngest brother to me.   (b)   2 mp

(Gen. 42:19, 20)   (c)   בּוֹא

(15) הֲשִׁיבֵנִי (f)וְאָשׁוּבָה כִּי אַתָּה יְהוָה אֱלֹהָי   (a)   Hifʿil

__Restore__ me that I may be restored, for you are   (b)   2 ms

the LORD my God. (Jer. 31:18)   (c)   שׁוּב

XXIX.3 Supply the proper translation for the pronouns in the following entries.

(1) וַיִּשָּׂאֵהוּ וַיְבִיאֵהוּ אֶל־אִמּוֹ And __he__ lifted __him__ up and brought __him__ to __his__ mother. (2 Kgs. 4:20)

(2) מִי אַתֶּם וּמֵאַיִן תָּבֹאוּ __Who__ are __you__, and where do __you__ come from? (Josh. 9:8)

(3) וַתָּבוֹא בָהֶם הָרוּחַ וַיִּחְיוּ וַיַּעַמְדוּ עַל־רַגְלֵיהֶם חַיִל גָּדוֹל מְאֹד־מְאֹד And the spirit (breath) entered __them__, and __they__ lived, and stood upon __their__ feet, an exceedingly great army. (Ezek. 37:10)

(4) בָּאנוּ־בָאֵשׁ וּבַמַּיִם __We__ have come through the fire and through the water. (Ps. 66:12)

(5) וְאַתָּה תָּבוֹא אֶל־אֲבֹתֶיךָ בְּשָׁלוֹם And __you__ shall go to __your__ ancestors in peace. (Gen. 15:15)

(6) וַיְבִאֶהָ אֶל־הָאָדָם And __he__ brought __her__ to the man. (Gen. 2:22)

(7) וַיְבִיאֻהוּ יְרוּשָׁלַם וַיָּמָת שָׁם And __they__ brought __him__ to Jerusalem, and __he__ died there. (Judg. 1:7)

(8) לָמָּה תָּבִיאוּ אֹתוֹ אֵלָי Why have __you__ brought __him__ to __me__? (1 Sam. 21:15)

(9) וַהֲקִמֹתִי אֶת־בְּרִיתִי אִתְּכֶם And __I__ will establish __my__ covenant with __you__. (Lev. 26:9)

(10) כִּי־עָפָר אַתָּה וְאֶל־עָפָר תָּשׁוּב For __you__ are dust, and unto dust __you__ shall return. (Gen. 3:19)

(11) וַהֲשִׁבֹתִים עַל־הָאָרֶץ הַזֹּאת And __I__ will bring __them__ back to __this__ land. (Jer. 24:6)

(12) מְבַקֵּשׁ שָׁאוּל אָבִי לַהֲמִיתֶךָ Saul __my__ father is seeking to kill __you__. (1 Sam. 19:2)

(13) הֶעֱלִיתָנוּ מֵאֶרֶץ (g)זָבַת חָלָב וּדְבַשׁ לַהֲמִיתֵנוּ בַּמִּדְבָּר   ____you____
brought ___us___ up from a land flowing with milk and honey to slay ___us___ in the wilderness. (Num. 16:13)

(14) בַּהֲכִינוֹ(h) שָׁמַיִם שָׁם אָנִי   When ___he___ established the heavens, ___I___ was there. (Prov. 8:27)

(15) עַד־עוֹלָם אָכִין זַרְעֶךָ   ___I___ will establish ___your___ seed (descendants) forever. (Ps. 89:5; Eng. 89:4)

XXIX.4 Underscore the correct participial form in each of the following entries.

(1) מָה אֵלֶּה (בָּא / בָּאִים) לַעֲשׂוֹת
What are these coming to do? (Zech. 2:4; Eng. 1:21)

(2) וְהִנֵּה רָחֵל בִּתּוֹ (i)(בָּאָה / בָּאָה) עִם־הַצֹּאן
And behold, Rachel his daughter is coming with the flock. (Gen. 29:6)

(3) וַיַּרְא וְהִנֵּה גְמַלִּים (בָּאוֹת / בָּאִים)
And he saw, and behold, camels were coming. (Gen. 24:63)

(4) הִנֵּה יָמִים (בָּאוֹת / בָּאִים)
Behold, the days are coming. (1 Sam. 2:31)

(5) מִי־זֶה (בָּא / בָּאָה) מֵאֱדוֹם
Who is this coming from Edom? (Isa. 63:1)

(6) הִנְנִי (מְבִיאִים / מֵבִיא) רָעָה עַל־יְרוּשָׁלַםִ
Behold, I am bringing evil against Jerusalem. (2 Kgs. 21:12)

(7) וְלָמָה יְהוָה (מְבִיאָה / מֵבִיא) אֹתָנוּ אֶל־הָאָרֶץ הַזֹּאת
Why is the LORD bringing us to this land? (Num. 14:3)

(8) הִנֵּה (מֵתָה / מֵת) שָׁאוּל
Behold, Saul is dead. (2 Sam. 4:10)

(9) כִּי אָמְרוּ כֻּלָּנוּ (מֵתִים / מֵתוֹת)
For they said, "We are all dead (men)." (Exod. 12:33)

(10) (נָכוֹן / נְכוֹנָה) יִהְיֶה הַר בֵּית־יְהוָה בְּרֹאשׁ הֶהָרִים
The mountain of the house of the LORD shall be established at the head of the mountains. (Isa. 2:2)

XXIX.5 Identify each of the verb sequences in the spaces marked (a). In (b) give the stems of the verbs, and in (c) their roots. (Review Lesson XXI.)

Example:

עֲלוּ הָהָר וַהֲבֵאתֶם עֵץ Go up to the mountain and bring wood. (Hag. 1:8)

(a) _Imperative_ + _Perfect_ sequence (b) _Qal_ , _Hifʻil_

(c) בּוֹא , עָלָה

(1) אָבוֹא אֵלֶיךָ וּבֵרַכְתִּיךָ I will come to you, and I will bless you. (Exod. 20:24)

(a) _Imperfect_ + _Perfect_ sequence (b) _Qal_ , _Piʻel_

(c) בּוֹא , [בָּרַךְ]

(2) בֹּאוּ וְנָבוֹא יְרוּשָׁלָ͏ִם Come, and let us go up to Jerusalem. (Jer. 35:11)

(a) _Imperative_ + _Imperfect_ sequence (b) _Qal_ , _Qal_

(c) בּוֹא , בּוֹא

(3) לְמַעַן תִּזְכְּרִי וָבֹשְׁתְּ In order that you may remember and be put to shame (confounded). (Ezek. 16:63)

(a) _Imperfect_ + _Perfect_ sequence (b) _Qal_ , _Qal_

(c) בּוֹשׁ , זָכַר

(4) וַיֹּאמְרוּ נָקוּם וּבָנִינוּ(j) And they said, "Let us arise and (let us) build." (Neh. 2:18)

(a) _Imperfect_ + _Perfect_ sequence (b) _Qal_ , _Qal_

(c) בָּנָה , קוּם

(5) הִנְנִי נֹתֵן בּוֹ רוּחַ וְשָׁמַע שְׁמוּעָה Behold, I will put a spirit in him, so that he shall hear a rumor (report). (2 Kgs. 19:7)

(a) _Participle_ + _Perfect_ sequence (b) _Qal_ , _Qal_

(c) שָׁמַע , נָתַן

(6) הֲשִׁיבֵנִי וְאָשׁוּבָה(f) כִּי אַתָּה יְהוָה אֱלֹהָי Restore me, that I may be restored, for you are the LORD my God. (Jer. 31:18)

(a) _Imperative_ + _Imperfect_ sequence (b) _Hifʻil_ , _Qal_

(c) שׁוּב , שׁוּב

(7) גַּדְּלוּ לַיהוָה אִתִּי וּנְרוֹמְמָה שְׁמוֹ יַחְדָּו Magnify the LORD with me, and let us exalt his name together. (Ps. 34:4; Eng. 34:3)

(a) _Imperative_ + _Imperfect_ sequence (b) _Piʻel_ , _Polel_

(c) רוּם , גָּדַל

(8) וְהָבִיאוּ אֶת־אֲחִיכֶם הַקָּטֹן אֵלַי וְאֵדְעָה כִּי לֹא מְרַגְּלִים אַתֶּם And bring your youngest brother to me, that I may know you are not spies. (Gen. 42:34)

    (a) <u>Imperative + Imperfect</u> sequence (b) <u>Hifʻil</u> , <u>Qal</u>

          (c) <u>בּוֹא</u> , <u>יָדַע</u>

(9) שִׂים לֶחֶם לִפְנֵיהֶם וְיֹאכֵלוּ Set bread before them, that they may eat. (2 Kgs. 6:22)

    (a) <u>Imperative + Imperfect</u> sequence (b) <u>Qal</u> , <u>Qal</u>

          (c) <u>שִׂים</u> , <u>אָכַל</u>

(10) יָדֶיךָ עָשׂוּנִי וַיְכוֹנְנוּנִי Your hands made me and established me. (Ps. 119:73)

    (a) <u>Perfect + Imperfect</u> sequence (b) <u>Qal</u> , <u>Polel</u>

          (c) <u>כּוּן</u> , <u>עָשָׂה</u>

Footnotes

(a) Piʻel verbs often express a causative meaning [cf. *G.*36.2(2), p. 109]. Thus וָאֲחַיֶּה, Piʻel imperfect first common singular, means "I cause to live," "I make alive."

(b) Interrogative ה is used to introduce questions that may be answered by either yes or no (cf. *G.*34.1, pp. 94f.).

(c) The accent on the Piʻel infinitive construct (with preposition) לְצַחֵק is retracted one syllable away from the end of the word because it is immediately followed by בְּנוֹ with an initial tone (heavily accented) syllable. This also results in the shortening of חֵ to חֶ.

(d) הָ may be added as a suffix to the second masculine singular form of imperatives. It seems to have little effect on the meaning, although it may denote a sense of urgency (cf. *G.*53, pp. 172f.).

(e) A conjunctive dagesh forte is sometimes placed in the initial consonant of a word to link it to the preceding word (cf. *G.*45, p. 147).

(f) הָ added as a suffix to first person imperfects indicates the cohortative use of the imperfect (cf. *G.*41.2, p. 132).

(g) זָבַת, from זוּב, "to flow," is a Qal participle, feminine singular construct, from the absolute זָבָה.

(h) The preposition בְּ, when prefixed to an infinitive construct, functions as a temporal conjunction and should be translated "when," "as," "while."

(i) For a discussion of the distinction between Qal perfect third feminine singular and Qal participle feminine singular of ʿAyin Vav/ʿAyin Yod verbs, cf. *G*.74.3(c), p. 318.

(j) וַיֹּאמְרוּ introduces the sequence of imperfect with coordinated perfect, but is not itself a part of the sequence.

Suggestions for Further Testing

1. Translate and fully locate all ʿAyin Vav/ʿAyin Yod verbs.

(1)	עַד־בֹּאִי אֵלֶיךָ מִצְרַיְמָה	(Gen. 48:5)
(2)	עַד־בֹּאוֹ לְדַבֵּר אִתּוֹ	(Exod. 34:35)
(3)	עַד־בֹּאֵנוּ שָׁמָּה	(Exod. 10:26)
(4)	עַד־בּוֹא אֲדֹנָיו אֶל־בֵּיתוֹ	(Gen. 39:16)
(5)	וּבָאתָ אַתָּה וְזִקְנֵי יִשְׂרָאֵל	(Exod. 3:18)
(6)	עַד־בֹּאָם אֶל־קְצֵה אֶרֶץ כְּנָעַן	(Exod. 16:35)
(7)	שִׁירוּ לַיהוָה שִׁיר חָדָשׁ	(Ps. 96:1)
(8)	כָּל־הַדָּבָר הַגָּדֹל יָבִיאוּ אֵלֶיךָ	(Exod. 18:22)
(9)	וְהִנֵּה רוּחַ גְּדוֹלָה בָּאָה מֵעֵבֶר הַמִּדְבָּר	(Job 1:19)
(10)	לְהָבִיא עָלֵינוּ רָעָה גְדֹלָה	(Dan. 9:12)
(11)	וּמֵתוּ גְדֹלִים וּקְטַנִּים בָּאָרֶץ הַזֹּאת	(Jer. 16:6)
(12)	פֶּן־יָמוּת בַּמִּלְחָמָה	(Deut. 20:5)
(13)	וְאַבְשָׁלוֹם מֵת בַּמִּלְחָמָה	(2 Sam. 19:11)
(14)	עַל־כֵּן הֵבִיא עֲלֵיהֶם אֵת כָּל־הָרָעָה הַזֹּאת	(2 Chr. 7:22)
(15)	מֵתָה רָחֵל בְּאֶרֶץ כְּנָעַן	(Gen. 48:7)
(16)	בְּיוֹם אֶחָד יָמוּתוּ שְׁנֵיהֶם	(1 Sam. 2:34)
(17)	וַיָּבֹאוּ מִכָּל־הָעַמִּים לִשְׁמֹעַ חָכְמַת שְׁלֹמֹה	(1 Kgs. 5:14)
(18)	לְמַעַן הַצִּיל אֹתוֹ מִיָּדָם לַהֲשִׁיבוֹ אֶל־אָבִיו	(Gen. 37:22)

LESSON XXIX

2. Circle the word that seems out of place in the category indicated.

(1)	act of belligerency	[נקם]	הָרַס	בָּחַר	[נכה]
(2)	something possessed	נַחֲלָה	צוּר	בָּקָר	בֶּגֶד
(3)	farmer's place of work	מַחֲנֶה	חוּץ	כֶּרֶם	שָׂדֶה
(4)	verbs of joy	גִּיל	רִיב	שִׁיר	צָחַק
(5)	verbs of sorrow	עָנָה	בָּכָה	[נחם]	חָפֵץ
(6)	verbs of communication	[חבא]	[נגד]	גָּלָה	יָרָה
(7)	verbs of motion	נָסַע	נוּס	שָׁבַת	סוּר
(8)	sources of water	בְּאֵר	שֶׁמֶשׁ	גֶּשֶׁם	נַחַל
(9)	a type of plant	גֶּפֶן	דֶּשֶׁא	כְּלִי	עֵץ
(10)	a preposition	אֲשֶׁר	מִן	בֵּין	עִם

LESSON XXX

Answer Key
(Cf. *G*, pp. 346ff.)

XXX.1 Each of the following entries contains a Pe Vav/Pe Yod verb form. Supply the proper translation for the form. In the space numbered (a) give its stem, in (b) the indentification of the form (perfect, imperfect, imperative), in (c) its person, gender, and number, and in (d) its root.

(1) שׁוּב וְשֵׁב עִם־הַמֶּלֶךְ Return and ___dwell___ with the king. (2 Sam. 15:19)
    (a) ___Qal___ (b) ___Imperative___ (c) ___2 ms___ (d) ___יָשַׁב___

(2) כִּי־אֵשֵׁב בַּחֹשֶׁךְ יְהוָה אוֹר לִי When I ___dwell___ in darkness, the LORD is a light to me. (Mic. 7:8)
    (a) ___Qal___ (b) ___Imperfect___ (c) ___1 cs___ (d) ___יָשַׁב___

(3) וְאָנֹכִי יְהוָה אֱלֹהֶיךָ עֹד אוֹשִׁיבְךָ בָאֳהָלִים I am the LORD your God; once again I will cause you to ___dwell___ in tents. (Hos. 12:10)
    (a) ___Hif'il___ (b) ___Imperfect___ (c) ___1 cs___ (d) ___יָשַׁב___

(4) אָנֹכִי אֵרֵד עִמְּךָ מִצְרַיְמָה (a) I will ___go___ ___down___ with you to Egypt. (Gen. 46:4)
    (a) ___Qal___ (b) ___Imperfect___ (c) ___1 cs___ (d) ___יָרַד___

(5) וְיוֹסֵף הוּרַד מִצְרַיְמָה (a) Now Joseph was ___brought___ ___down___ to Egypt. (Gen. 39:1)
    (a) ___Hof'al___ (b) ___Perfect___ (c) ___3 ms___ (d) ___יָרַד___

(6) כְּעוֹף הַשָּׁמַיִם אוֹרִידֵם Like a bird of the heavens, I will ___bring___ them ___down___ . (Hos. 7:12)
    (a) ___Hif'il___ (b) ___Imperfect___ (c) ___1 cs___ (d) ___יָרַד___

(7) הוֹרֵד אוֹתָם אֶל־הַמַּיִם Bring them down to the water. (Judg. 7:4)
    (a) ___Hif'il___ (b) ___Imperative___ (c) ___2 ms___ (d) ___יָרַד___

(8) אַבְרָהָם הוֹלִיד אֶת־יִצְחָק Abraham ___begot___ Isaac. (Gen. 25:19)
    (a) ___Hif'il___ (b) ___Perfect___ (c) ___3 ms___ (d) ___יָלַד___

185

(9) דְּעוּ כִּי־יְהוָה הוּא אֱלֹהִים   __Know__   that the LORD, he is God.
(Ps. 100:3)

      (a) __Qal__ (b) __Imperative__ (c) __2 mp__ (d) יָדַע

(10) וְיֵדְעוּ כָּל־הָאָרֶץ כִּי יֵשׁ אֱלֹהִים לְיִשְׂרָאֵל That all the earth may
__know__ that there is a God for (in) Israel. (1 Sam. 17:46)

      (a) __Qal__ (b) __Imperfect__ (c) __3 mp__ (d) יָדַע

(11) לֹא־אִירָא(b) רָע כִּי־אַתָּה עִמָּדִי I will __fear__ no evil, for you
are with me. (Ps. 23:4)

      (a) __Qal__ (b) __Imperfect__ (c) __1 cs__ (d) יָרֵא

(12) הִתְיַצְּבוּ וּרְאוּ אֶת־יְשׁוּעַת יְהוָה __Stand__ __still__ and see
the salvation of the LORD. (Exod. 14:13)

      (a) __Hitpaʿel__ (b) __Imperative__ (c) __2 mp__ (d) יָצַב

(13) וַיֹּאמֶר אֵלַי יְהוָה לֵךְ הִנָּבֵא אֶל־עַמִּי יִשְׂרָאֵל And the LORD said to
me, "__Go__, prophesy to my people Israel." (Amos 7:15)

      (a) __Qal__ (b) __Imperative__ (c) __2 ms__ (d) הָלַךְ

(14) וְהוֹשִׁיעַ אֶת־עַמִּי מִיַּד פְּלִשְׁתִּים And he shall __save__ my people
from the hand of the Philistines. (1 Sam. 9:16)

      (a) __Hifʿil__ (b) __Perfect__ (c) __3 ms__ (d) [יָשַׁע]

(15) אֶזְעַק אֵלֶיךָ חָמָס וְלֹא תוֹשִׁיעַ I cry out to you, "Violence!" but you do
not __save__. (Hab. 1:2)

      (a) __Hifʿil__ (b) __Imperfect__ (c) __2 ms__ (d) [יָשַׁע]

XXX.2 Two Pe Vav verbs, יָכֹל, "he was able," and יָסַף, "he added, repeated,"
are frequently followed by infinitives construct, normally prefixed with an
inseparable preposition. The forms of יָכֹל followed by the infinitive construct
express the notion of being able to do (or not to do) something. The forms of
יָסַף followed by the infinitive construct express the notion of repeating an
action. In the following examples various infinitives construct occur in
conjunction with forms of these two Pe Vav verbs. Copy the infinitive construct
in the space marked (a), give its stem in the space marked (b), and list its verb
root in the space marked (c). An example containing more than one infinitive
construct will have additional spaces provided. Note that the infinitives construct
are not necessarily derived from Pe Vav/Pe Yod roots.

וְלֹא־יָסַף שְׁמוּאֵל לִרְאוֹת אֶת־שָׁאוּל עַד־יוֹם מוֹתוֹ   (a) לִרְאוֹת
And Samuel did not see Saul again until the day   (b) __Qal__
of his death. (1 Sam. 15:35)   (c) רָאָה

(1) וַיֹּאמֶר יְהוָה אֶל־לִבּוֹ לֹא־אֹסִף‏(c)‏ עוֹד לְהַכּוֹת
אֶת־כָּל־חַי כַּאֲשֶׁר עָשִׂיתִי

And the LORD said in his heart, "I will never again
destroy (kill) every living creature as I have done." (Gen. 8:21)

(a) לְהַכּוֹת
(b) Hifʿil
(c) [נכה]

(2) לָכֵן לֹא־אוֹסִיף לְהוֹשִׁיעַ אֶתְכֶם

Therefore I will deliver you no more. (Judg. 10:13)

(a) לְהוֹשִׁיעַ
(b) Hifʿil
(c) [ישע]

(3) לֹא אֹסֵף לִשְׁמֹעַ אֶת־קוֹל יְהוָה אֱלֹהָי

Let me not hear again the voice of the LORD my God.
(Deut. 18:16)

(a) לִשְׁמֹעַ
(b) Qal
(c) שָׁמַע

(4) לֹא אוֹסִיף לִהְיוֹת עִמָּכֶם

I will be with you no more. (Josh. 7:12)

(a) לִהְיוֹת
(b) Qal
(c) הָיָה

(5) לֹא־תוֹסִיפוּ לִשְׁתּוֹתָהּ עוֹד

You shall not drink it again. (Isa. 51:22)

(a) לִשְׁתּוֹתָהּ
(b) Qal
(c) שָׁתָה

(6) וַיְשַׁלַּח אֶת־הַיּוֹנָה וְלֹא־יָסְפָה שׁוּב־אֵלָיו עוֹד

And he sent out the dove, but she did not return to him
again. (Gen. 8:12)

(a) שׁוּב
(b) Qal
(c) שׁוּב

(7) וַיֹּסִפוּ‏(c)‏ בְּנֵי יִשְׂרָאֵל לַעֲשׂוֹת הָרַע בְּעֵינֵי יְהוָה

And the Israelites again did what was evil in the eyes
of the LORD. (Judg. 3:12)

(a) לַעֲשׂוֹת
(b) Qal
(c) עָשָׂה

(8) וְלֹא־יָכֹל מֹשֶׁה לָבוֹא אֶל־אֹהֶל מוֹעֵד

And Moses was not able to enter the tent of meeting.
(Exod. 40:35)

(a) לָבוֹא
(b) Qal
(c) בּוֹא

(9) דָּוִד לֹא יָכֹל לִבְנוֹת בַּיִת לְשֵׁם יְהוָה אֱלֹהָיו

David was not able to build a house to the name
of the LORD his God. (1 Kgs. 5:17)

(a) לִבְנוֹת
(b) Qal
(c) בָּנָה

(10) לֹא־אוּכַל עוֹד לָצֵאת וְלָבוֹא

I am no longer able to go out or
to come in. (Deut. 31:2)

(a) לָצֵאת
(b) Qal
(c) יָצָא

(a) וְלָבוֹא
(b) Qal
(c) בּוֹא

187

(11) מִי יוּכַל לַעֲמֹד לִפְנֵי יְהוָה הָאֱלֹהִים הַקָּדוֹשׁ הַזֶּה   (a)   לַעֲמֹד

Who is able to stand before the LORD, this holy God?   (b)   Qal

(1 Sam. 6:20)   (c)   עָמַד

(12) מְלָאכָה גְדוֹלָה אֲנִי עֹשֶׂה וְלֹא אוּכַל לָרֶדֶת   (a)   לָרֶדֶת

I am doing a great work, and I am not able to come   (b)   Qal

down. (Neh. 6:3)   (c)   יָרַד

(13) לֹא נוּכַל דַּבֵּר אֵלֶיךָ רַע אוֹ־טוֹב   (a)   דַּבֵּר

We are not able to speak to you evil or good.   (b)   Piʻel

(Gen. 24:50)   (c)   [דבר]

(14) וְלֹא יָכְלוּ בְּנֵי מְנַשֶּׁה לְהוֹרִישׁ אֶת־הֶעָרִים הָאֵלֶּה   (a)   לְהוֹרִישׁ

But the Manassites were not able to take possession   (b)   Hifʻil

of those cities. (Josh. 17:12)   (c)   יָרַשׁ

(15) כִּי מִי יוּכַל לִשְׁפֹּט אֶת־עַמְּךָ   (a)   לִשְׁפֹּט

For who is able to judge your people? (1 Kgs. 3:9)   (b)   Qal

   (c)   שָׁפַט

XXX.3 Fill in the correct translation for the pronouns in each of the following entries.

(1) וִירַשְׁתֶּם אֹתָם וִישַׁבְתֶּם בְּאַרְצָם And ___you___ shall take possession of ___them___ , and ___you___ shall dwell in ___their___ land. (Deut. 12:29)

(2) לוֹ אֶהְיֶה וְאִתּוֹ אֵשֵׁב I will be ___his___ , and with ___him___ I will dwell (remain). (2 Sam. 16:18)

(3) בָּתֵּי גָזִית בְּנִיתֶם וְלֹא־תֵשְׁבוּ בָם ___You___ have built houses of hewn stone, but ___you___ shall not dwell in ___them___ . (Amos 5:11)

(4) וַיּוֹשִׁיבַנִי עַל־כִּסֵּא דָוִד אָבִי And ___he___ caused ___me___ to sit on the throne of David ___my___ father. (1 Kgs. 2:24)

(5) וַתֹּאמֶר אֶל־עֲבָדֶיךָ הוֹרִדֻהוּ(c) אֵלַי וְאָשִׂימָה עֵינִי עָלָיו And ___you___ said to ___your___ servants, "Bring ___him___ down to ___me___ , that ___I___ may set ___my___ eyes upon ___him___ ." (Gen. 44:21)

(6) אָמַר אֵלַי בְּנִי אַתָּה אֲנִי הַיּוֹם יְלִדְתִּיךָ ___He___ said to ___me___ , "___You___ are ___my___ son, today ___I___ have begotten ___you___ ." (Ps. 2:7)

(7) יְדַעְתִּיךָ בְשֵׁם וְגַם־מָצָאתָ חֵן בְּעֵינָי ___I___ know ___you___ by name, and ___you___ have also found favor in ___my___ eyes. (Exod. 33:12)

(8) וְאֶת־שֵׁם (d)קָדְשִׁי אוֹדִיעַ בְּתוֹךְ עַמִּי יִשְׂרָאֵל And ___my___ holy name ___I___ will make known in the midst of ___my___ people Israel. (Ezek. 39:7)

(9) וַיֹּאמְרוּ לִי עֲשֵׂה־לָנוּ אֱלֹהִים אֲשֶׁר יֵלְכוּ לְפָנֵינוּ And ___they___ said to ___me___, "Make for ___us___ gods who may go before ___us___." (Exod. 32:23)

(10) כִּי־אִתְּךָ אֲנִי לְהוֹשִׁיעֶךָ וּלְהַצִּילֶךָ For ___I___ am with ___you___ to save ___you___ and to deliver ___you___. (Jer. 15:20)

(11) וּמַלְאַךְ פָּנָיו הוֹשִׁיעָם And the angel of ___his___ presence saved ___them___. (Isa. 63:9)

(12) אָנֹכִי יְהוָה אֱלֹהֶיךָ אֲשֶׁר הוֹצֵאתִיךָ מֵאֶרֶץ מִצְרָיִם ___I___ am the LORD ___your___ God, who brought ___you___ up from the land of Egypt. (Exod. 20:2)

(13) וַנִּצְעַק אֶל־יְהוָה וַיִּשְׁמַע קֹלֵנוּ וַיִּשְׁלַח מַלְאָךְ וַיֹּצִאֵנוּ מִמִּצְרָיִם And ___we___ cried out to the LORD, and ___he___ heard ___our___ voice, and ___he___ sent an angel and ___he___ brought ___us___ up from Egypt. (Num. 20:16)

(14) וַיֹּאמֶר אֶת־קֹלְךָ שָׁמַעְתִּי בַּגָּן וָאִירָא כִּי־עֵירֹם אָנֹכִי (e)וָאֵחָבֵא And ___he___ said, "___I___ heard ___your___ voice in the garden, and ___I___ was afraid because ___I___ was naked, and ___I___ hid ___myself___." (Gen. 3:10)

(15) יְהוָה אוֹרִי וְיִשְׁעִי (f)מִמִּי אִירָא The LORD is ___my___ light and ___my___ salvation; of ___whom___ should ___I___ be afraid? (Ps. 27:1)

(16) וְאָזְנֶיךָ תִּשְׁמַעְנָה דָבָר מֵאַחֲרֶיךָ לֵאמֹר זֶה הַדֶּרֶךְ לְכוּ בוֹ And ___your___ ears shall hear a word behind ___you___ saying, " ___This___ is the way, walk in ___it___!" (Isa. 30:21)

(17) וְאֶת־נְבִיאֶיךָ הָרְגוּ בְחָרֶב (g)וָאִוָּתֵר אֲנִי לְבַדִּי וַיְבַקְשׁוּ אֶת־נַפְשִׁי לְקַחְתָּהּ And ___they___ have slain ___your___ prophets with the sword, and ___I___ alone was left, and ___they___ sought ___my___ life to take ___it___. (1 Kgs. 19:10)

(18) כִּי יְהוָה שֹׁפְטֵנוּ יְהוָה מַלְכֵּנוּ הוּא יוֹשִׁיעֵנוּ For the LORD is ___our___ judge; the LORD is ___our___ king; ___he___ will save ___us___. (Isa. 33:22)

XXX.4 Underscore the correct participial form in each of the following entries.

(1) וְהִיא (יוֹשֶׁבֶת / יוֹשֵׁב) בַּשָּׂדֶה

And she was sitting in the field. (Judg. 13:9)

(2) וּבְתוֹךְ עַם־טְמֵא שְׂפָתַיִם אָנֹכִי (יוֹשֵׁב / יוֹשְׁבִים)

And I am dwelling in the midst of a people of unclean lips. (Isa. 6:5)

(3) וְהִנֵּה מַלְאֲכֵי אֱלֹהִים (יֹרְדִים / יֹרְדוֹת) בּוֹ

And behold, the angels of God were descending on it! (Gen. 28:12)

(4) (יוֹרֵד / יוֹרְדֵי (h)) הַיָּם בָּאֳנִיּוֹת הֵמָּה רָאוּ מַעֲשֵׂי יְהוָה

They that go down to the sea in ships, they see the works of the LORD. (Ps. 107:23, 24)

(5) שָׂרָה אִשְׁתְּךָ (יֹלֵד / יֹלֶדֶת (i)) לְךָ בֵּן

Sarah your wife shall bear you a son. (Gen. 17:19)

(6) הִנֵּה־בֵן (נוֹלָד / נוֹלְדִים) לְבֵית־דָּוִד

Behold, a son shall be born to the house of David. (1 Kgs. 13:2)

(7) וִהְיִיתֶם כֵּאלֹהִים (יֹדְעֵי / יֹדְעוֹת (j)) טוֹב וָרָע

And you shall be as God, knowing good and evil. (Gen. 3:5)

(8) מַדּוּעַ אַתְּ (הֹלֵךְ / הֹלֶכֶת) אֵלָיו הַיּוֹם

Why are you going to him today? (2 Kgs. 4:23)

(9) וַיֹּאמֶר עֵשָׂו הִנֵּה אָנֹכִי (הֹלֵךְ / הֹלֶכֶת (i)) לָמוּת

And Esau said, "Behold, I am going to die." (Gen. 25:32)

(10) הָעָם (הַהֹלְכוֹת / הַהֹלְכִים) בַּחֹשֶׁךְ רָאוּ אוֹר גָּדוֹל

The people who walk in darkness have seen a great light. (Isa. 9:1)

XXX.5 Identify each of the verb sequences by filling in the space marked (a). In (b) give the stems of the verbs, and in (c) supply their roots. (Review Lesson XXI).

(1) בְּנוּ־לָכֶם בַּיִת בִּירוּשָׁלַם וִישַׁבְתֶּם שָׁם Build for yourselves a house in Jerusalem, and dwell there. (1 Kgs. 2:36)

(a) ___Imperative___ + ___Perfect___ sequence (b) ___Qal___ , ___Qal___

(c) ___בָּנָה___ , ___יָשַׁב___

(2) קוּם וְיָרַדְתָּ בֵּית הַיּוֹצֵר Arise, and go down to the potter's house. (Jer. 18:2)

    (a) <u>Imperative</u> + <u>Perfect</u> sequence (b) <u>Qal</u> , <u>Qal</u>

                 (c) <u>יָרַד</u> , <u>קוּם</u>

(3) שָׂרָה אִשְׁתְּךָ יֹלֶדֶת לְךָ בֵּן וְקָרָאתָ אֶת־שְׁמוֹ יִצְחָק Sarah your wife shall bear you a son, and you shall call his name Isaac. (Gen. 17:19)

    (a) <u>Participle</u> + <u>Perfect</u> sequence (b) <u>Qal</u> , <u>Qal</u>

                 (c) <u>קָרָא</u> , <u>יָלַד</u>

(4) וְאֶת־בְּנוֹתֵיכֶם תִּתְּנוּ לַאֲנָשִׁים וְתֵלַדְנָה בָּנִים וּבָנוֹת And give your daughters to men, that they may bear sons and daughters. (Jer. 29:6)

    (a) <u>Imperative</u> + <u>Imperfect</u> sequence (b) <u>Qal</u> , <u>Qal</u>

                 (c) <u>יָלַד</u> , <u>נָתַן</u>

(5) כֵּן אוֹשִׁיעַ אֶתְכֶם וִהְיִיתֶם בְּרָכָה So will I save you and you shall be a blessing. (Zech. 8:13)

    (a) <u>Imperfect</u> + <u>Perfect</u> sequence (b) <u>Hifʻil</u> , <u>Qal</u>

                 (c) <u>הָיָה</u> , <u>[יָשַׁע]</u>

(6) צֵא וְעָמַדְתָּ בָהָר לִפְנֵי יְהוָה "Go forth and stand on the mountain before the LORD." (1 Kgs. 19:11)

    (a) <u>Imperative</u> + <u>Perfect</u> sequence (b) <u>Qal</u> , <u>Qal</u>

                 (c) <u>עָמַד</u> , <u>יָצָא</u>

(7) אֶחָד הָיָה אַבְרָהָם וַיִּירַשׁ אֶת־הָאָרֶץ Abraham was one, and he took possession of the land. (Ezek. 33:24)

    (a) <u>Perfect</u> + <u>Imperfect</u> sequence (b) <u>Qal</u> , <u>Qal</u>

                 (c) <u>יָרַשׁ</u> , <u>הָיָה</u>

(8) עָלֹה נַעֲלֶה וְיָרַשְׁנוּ אֹתָהּ(k) "Let us go up at once and (let us) possess it." (Num. 13:30)

    (a) <u>Imperfect</u> + <u>Perfect</u> sequence (b) <u>Qal</u> , <u>Qal</u>

                 (c) <u>יָרַשׁ</u> , <u>עָלָה</u>

(9) לְמַעַן יִיטַב לְךָ וְיָרַשְׁתָּ אֶת־הָאָרֶץ הַטֹּבָה In order that it may be well with you, and that you may inherit the good land. (Deut. 6:18)

    (a) <u>Imperfect</u> + <u>Perfect</u> sequence (b) <u>Qal</u> , <u>Qal</u>

                 (c) <u>יָרַשׁ</u> , <u>יָטַב</u>

(10) פֶּן־יָבוֹא וְהִכַּנִי lest he should come and smite (kill) me (Gen. 32:12)

(a) <u>Imperfect + Perfect</u> sequence (b) <u>Qal</u> , <u>Hif'il</u>

(c) <u>בּוֹא</u> , <u>[נכה]</u>

(11) וְאָנֹכִי אֶהְיֶה עִם־פִּיךָ וְהוֹרֵיתִיךָ And I will be with your mouth and I will teach you. (Exod. 4:12)

(a) <u>Imperfect + Perfect</u> sequence (b) <u>Qal</u> , <u>Hif'il</u>

(c) <u>הָיָה</u> , <u>יָרָה</u>

(12) אִם־תֵּלְכִי עִמִּי וְהָלַכְתִּי "If you go with me, I will go." (Judg. 4:8)

(a) <u>Imperfect + Perfect</u> sequence (b) <u>Qal</u> , <u>Qal</u>

(c) <u>הָלַךְ</u> , <u>הָלַךְ</u>

Footnotes

(a) The הָ ending is the "He-directive." He-directive indicates motion or direction toward a place or thing (never a person). This ending may also be added to directional adverbs such as שָׁם . The ending is never accented (cf. *G*.44, pp. 146f.).

(b) Before the accented monosyllabic רַע , the accent on אִירָא is moved from its normal position on the final syllable to the initial syllable. Hebrew will not ordinarily juxtapose tone syllables in adjacent words.

(c) אֹסֵף is a Hif'il imperfect, first common singular, and וַיֹּסְפוּ is a Hif'il imperfect, third masculine plural. Both verbs are examples of the common occurrence in which a ḥireq-yod (ִי) is written defectively in verb forms. הוֹרִדֵהוּ illustrates the defective writing of šureq (וּ), as well as ḥireq-yod (ִ). The two defective writings (ḥireq and qibbuṣ) are still treated as long vowels for purposes of syllabification.

(d) The noun קֹדֶשׁ , "apartness, sacredness," may function as an adjective when placed after the noun it describes. "My holy name" is literally "the name of my holiness." Note that the pronominal ending is not permitted to separate two words in a construct relationship but is attached to the final word in the relationship.

(e) The ה of this Nif'al imperfect form of [חבא] is doubled by implication (cf. *G*.13.1, p. 23).

(f) מִמִּי is the interrogative pronoun מִי , "who?" with the prefixed preposition מִן , "from."

(g) Note the retention of ו as a regular consonant in the Nif'al forms of Pe Vav verbs such as [יתר] .

(h) **יוֹרְדֵי** is a form of the masculine plural construct participle. Its literal meaning is "the goers down to the sea."

(i) When participles are used in the place of regular verb forms, they often describe an action expected to occur in the near future.

(j) **יֹדְעֵי** is a masculine plural construct participle (Qal) that could be translated "knowers of."

(k) The infinitive absolute functions to intensify the action specified by its cognate verb. The two verbs (**עָלֹה נַעֲלֶה**) are treated as a unit. The coordinate relationship, however, involves two verbs, i.e., the imperfect (comprising the unit **עָלֹה נַעֲלֶה**) followed by the perfect (**וִירִשְׁנוּ**).

Suggestions for Further Testing

1. Translate the following sentences and locate fully all Pe Vav/Pe Yod verb forms.

(1) וְיִרְאוּ צַדִּיקִים וְיִירָאוּ (Ps. 52:8; Eng. 52:6)

(2) וַיּוֹשִׁיעֵם לְמַעַן שְׁמוֹ לְהוֹדִיעַ אֶת־גְּבוּרָתוֹ (Ps. 106:8)

(3) וְהוֹשַׁעְתִּים בַּיהוָה אֱלֹהֵיהֶם וְלֹא אוֹשִׁיעֵם בְּקֶשֶׁת וּבְחֶרֶב וּבְמִלְחָמָה (Hos. 1:7)

(4) הֲיוּכַל אֵל לַעֲרֹךְ שֻׁלְחָן בַּמִּדְבָּר (Ps. 78:19)

(5) וַיִּירְאוּ הָעָם אֶת־יְהוָה וַיַּאֲמִינוּ בַּיהוָה וּבְמֹשֶׁה עַבְדּוֹ (Exod. 14:31)

(6) וְעַתָּה בִּתִּי אַל־תִּירְאִי כֹּל אֲשֶׁר־תֹּאמְרִי אֶעֱשֶׂה־לָּךְ (Ruth 3:11)

(7) הַאוֹסִף עוֹד לָצֵאת לַמִּלְחָמָה (Judg. 20:28)

(8) לֹא תוּכְלוּ לַעֲבֹד אֶת־יְהוָה כִּי־אֱלֹהִים קְדֹשִׁים הוּא (Josh. 24:19)

(9) הוֹשִׁיעֵנִי וְאִוָּשֵׁעָה כִּי תְהִלָּתִי אָתָּה (Jer. 17:14)

(10) לְמַעַן הוֹדִעֲךָ כִּי לֹא עַל־הַלֶּחֶם לְבַדּוֹ יִחְיֶה הָאָדָם (Deut. 8:3)

2. Match the following:

(1) (   ) הוֹדִעֵנִי אֶת־דְּרָכֶךְ   (A) Do not make yourself known to the man. (Ruth 3:3)

(2) (   ) בְּשִׁמְךָ הוֹשִׁיעֵנִי   (B) In his days Judah shall be saved. (Jer. 23:6)

(3) (   ) וָאֵדָעֲךָ בְּשֵׁם   (C) And make know to them the way. (Exod. 18:20)

(4) (   ) צַדִּיקִים יִירְשׁוּ אָרֶץ   (D) Never speak to me again. (Deut. 3:26)

(5) (   ) וְהוֹדַעְתָּ לָהֶם אֶת הַדֶּרֶךְ   (E) Know what you have done. (Jer. 2:23)

(6) (   ) אַל־תִּוָּדְעִי לָאִישׁ   (F) Save me by your name. (Ps. 54:3; Eng. 54:1)

(7) (   ) אַל־תּוֹסֶף דַּבֵּר אֵלַי עוֹד   (G) The righteous shall inherit the land. (Ps. 37:29)

(8) (   ) דְּעִי מֶה עָשִׂית   (H) to the one leading his people through the wilderness (Ps. 136:16)

(9) (   ) בְּיָמָיו תִּוָּשַׁע יְהוּדָה   (I) Teach me to know your way. (Exod. 33:13)

(10) (   ) לְמוֹלִיךְ עַמּוֹ בַּמִּדְבָּר   (J) And I know you by name. (Exod. 33:17)

LESSON XXXI

Answer Key
(Cf. *G*, pp. 364ff.)

XXXI.1 Each of the following entries contains a perfect form of a Double ʿAyin verb. In the space marked (a) give its stem, in (b) its person, gender, and number, and in (c) its root.

(1) בַּיּוֹם הַשְּׁבִיעִי סָבְבוּ אֶת־הָעִיר שֶׁבַע פְּעָמִים	(a)	Qal
On the seventh day they marched around the city	(b)	3 cp
seven times. (Josh. 6:15)	(c)	סָבַב
(2) תַּמּוּ דִּבְרֵי אִיּוֹב	(a)	Qal
The words of Job are completed (ended). (Job 31:40)	(b)	3 cp
	(c)	תָּמַם
(3) וְשַׁדַּי הֵרַע לִי	(a)	Hifʿil
And the Almighty (Shaddai) has brought evil (calamity)	(b)	3 ms
upon me. (Ruth 1:21)	(c)	רָעַע
(4) לָמָה הֲרֵעֹתָ לְעַבְדֶּךָ	(a)	Hifʿil
Why have you caused evil to your servant? (Num. 11:11)	(b)	2 ms
	(c)	רָעַע
(5) וְלֹא־הֵסֵב יֹאשִׁיָּהוּ פָנָיו מִמֶּנּוּ	(a)	Hifʿil
But Josiah would not turn away his face from him.	(b)	3 ms
(2 Chr. 35:22)	(c)	סָבַב
(6) חַתּוּ וַיֵּבֹשׁוּ	(a)	Qal
They are dismayed and confounded (ashamed).	(b)	3 cp
(2 Kgs. 19:26)	(c)	חָתַת
(7) נָשַׁמָּה כָל־הָאָרֶץ	(a)	Nifʿal
All the earth is made desolate. (Jer. 12:11)	(b)	3 fs
	(c)	שָׁמַם
(8) וְנָשַׁמּוּ הַכֹּהֲנִים (a)	(a)	Nifʿal
And the priests shall be appalled. (Jer. 4:9)	(b)	3 cp
	(c)	שָׁמַם

195

(9) וַהֲשִׁמֹּתִי אֲנִי אֶת־הָאָרֶץ(a)	(a)	Hif'il
And I will devastate the land. (Lev. 26:32)	(b)	1 cs
	(c)	שָׁמֵם
(10) שֶׁבַע בַּיּוֹם הִלַּלְתִּיךָ	(a)	Pi'el
Seven times in the day I praise you. (Ps. 119:164)	(b)	1 cs
	(c)	[הלל]

XXXI.2   An imperfect form of the Double 'Ayin verb is included in each of the following entries. In the space marked (a) give its stem, in (b) its person, gender, and number, and in (c) its root.

(1) וַיָּסֹבּוּ אֶת־הָעִיר בַּיּוֹם הַשֵּׁנִי פַּעַם אֶחָת	(a)	Qal
And they circled the city once (one time) on the second	(b)	3 mp
day. (Josh. 6:14)	(c)	סָבַב
(2) הַיַּרְדֵּן יִסֹּב לְאָחוֹר	(a)	Qal
The Jordan turned back. (Ps. 114:3)	(b)	3 ms
	(c)	סָבַב
(3) אָקוּמָה נָּא(b) וַאֲסוֹבְבָה בָעִיר(b)	(a)	Polel
I will arise and I will go about in the city.	(b)	1 cs
(Song of Sol. 3:2)	(c)	סָבַב
(4) וַיַּסֵּב חִזְקִיָּהוּ פָּנָיו אֶל־הַקִּיר	(a)	Hif'il
And Hezekiah turned his face to the wall. (Isa. 38:2)	(b)	3 ms
	(c)	סָבַב
(5) וַתִּתְפַּלֵּל חַנָּה	(a)	Hitpa'el
And Hannah prayed. (1 Sam. 2:1)	(b)	3 fs
	(c)	[פלל]
(6) לֹא תָאֹר אֶת־הָעָם(c)	(a)	Qal
You shall not curse the people. (Num. 22:12)	(b)	2 ms
	(c)	אָרַר
(7) בַּמִּדְבָּר הַזֶּה יִתַּמּוּ וְשָׁם יָמֻתוּ(d)	(a)	Qal
In this wilderness they shall be brought to an end	(b)	3 mp
(finished), and there they shall die. (Num. 14:35)	(c)	תָּמַם
(8) וַיַּרְא יְהוָה וַיֵּרַע בְּעֵינָיו	(a)	Qal
And the LORD saw, and it was evil in his eyes.	(b)	3 ms
(Isa. 59:15)	(c)	רָעַע

196

(9) וְהָיָה מִסְפַּר בְּנֵי־יִשְׂרָאֵל כְּחוֹל הַיָּם אֲשֶׁר לֹא־יִמַּד[^a]
וְלֹא יִסָּפֵר

And the number of the children of Israel shall be as the sand of the sea which can not be measured and can not be counted. (Hos. 2:1; Eng. 1:10)

(a) Nif'al
(b) 3 ms
(c) מָדַד

(10) וְלֹא־יִירְאוּ עוֹד וְלֹא־יֵחַתּוּ

And they shall not fear any more and they shall not be dismayed. (Jer. 23:4)

(a) Nif'al
(b) 3 mp
(c) חָתַת

(11) וַיַּרְא כָּל־הָעָם וַיָּרֹנּוּ

And all the people saw and they cried out. (Lev. 9:24)

(a) Qal
(b) 3 mp
(c) רָנַן

(12) יָשֹׁמּוּ יְשָׁרִים עַל־זֹאת

The upright ones are appalled at this. (Job 17:8)

(a) Qal
(b) 3 mp
(c) שָׁמֵם

(13) וָאֶתְפַּלְלָה לַיהוָה אֱלֹהָי

And I prayed to the LORD my God. (Dan. 9:4)

(a) Hitpa'el
(b) 1 cs
(c) [פלל]

(14) וַיֹּאמֶר יְהוָה אֵלַי[^e] אַל־תִּתְפַּלֵּל בְּעַד־הָעָם הַזֶּה לְטוֹבָה

And the LORD said to me, "Do not pray on behalf of this people for good." (Jer. 14:11)

(a) Hitpa'el
(b) 2 ms
(c) [פלל]

(15) וַיַּעֲמֹד פִּינְחָס וַיְפַלֵּל

And Phinehas stood up and prayed. (Ps. 106:30)

(a) Pi'el
(b) 3 ms
(c) [פלל]

(16) אֲהַלְלָה שִׁמְךָ לְעוֹלָם וָעֶד

I will praise your name for ever and ever. (Ps. 145:2)

(a) Pi'el
(b) 1 cs
(c) [הלל]

(17) וַיֹּאמְרוּ כָל־הַקָּהָל אָמֵן וַיְהַלְלוּ אֶת־יְהוָה[^f]

And all the congregation said, "Amen!" And they praised the LORD. (Neh. 5:13)

(a) Pi'el
(b) 3 mp
(c) [הלל]

(18) בַּיהוָה תִּתְהַלֵּל נַפְשִׁי

My soul boasts in the LORD. (Ps. 34:3; Eng. 34:2)

(a) Hitpa'el
(b) 3 fs
(c) [הלל]

XXI.3 Each of the following entries includes an imperative form of a Double ʿAyin verb. In the space marked (a) give its stem, in (b) its person, gender, and number, and in (c) its root.

(1) עִבְרוּ וְסֹבּוּ אֶת־הָעִיר	(a)	Qal
Pass over and march around the city. (Josh. 6:7)	(b)	2 mp
	(c)	סָבַב
(2) הָקֵל מִן־הָעֹל אֲשֶׁר־נָתַן אָבִיךָ עָלֵינוּ	(a)	Hifʿil
Lighten the yoke that your father placed (gave) upon us.	(b)	2 ms
(1 Kgs. 12:9)	(c)	קָלַל
(3) רָנִּי בַּת־צִיּוֹן הָרִיעוּ יִשְׂרָאֵל	(a)	Qal
Sing aloud, O daughter of Zion; Shout, O Israel!	(b)	2 fs
(Zeph. 3:14)	(c)	רָנַן
(4) שֹׁמּוּ שָׁמַיִם עַל־זֹאת	(a)	Qal
Be appalled, O heavens, at this! (Jer. 2:12)	(b)	2 mp
	(c)	שָׁמַם
(5) הִתְפַּלֵּל בַּעֲדֵנוּ אֶל־יְהוָה אֱלֹהֵינוּ	(a)	Hitpaʿel
Pray on our behalf to the LORD our God. (Jer. 42:20)	(b)	2 ms
	(c)	[פלל]
(6) הַלְלוּ אֶת־יְהוָה מִן־הַשָּׁמַיִם	(a)	Piʿel
Praise the LORD from the heavens. (Ps. 148:1)	(b)	2 mp
	(c)	[הלל]
(7) הַלְלוּהוּ שֶׁמֶשׁ וְיָרֵחַ	(a)	Piʿel
Praise him, sun and moon. (Ps. 148:3)	(b)	2 mp
	(c)	[הלל]
(8) הַלְלוּ־אֵל בְּקָדְשׁוֹ	(a)	Piʿel
Praise God in his sanctuary! (Ps. 150:1)	(b)	2 mp
	(c)	[הלל]
(9) הַלְלוּ־יָהּ	(a)	Piʿel
Praise the LORD! (Ps. 104:35)	(b)	2 mp
	(c)	[הלל]
(10) הַלְלִי נַפְשִׁי אֶת־יְהוָה	(a)	Piʿel
Praise the LORD, O my soul! (Ps. 146:1)	(b)	2 fs
	(c)	[הלל]

XXI.4 A participial form of a Double ʻAyin verb is included in each of the following entries. In the space marked (a) give its stem, in (b) its gender and number, and in (c) its root.

(1) וּמְקַלֵּל אָבִיו וְאִמּוֹ מוֹת יוּמָת   (a) __Piʻel__

And the one who makes light of (curses) his father or   (b) __ms__

his mother shall surely be put to death. (Exod. 21:17)   (c) __קלל__

(2) כִּי מְבֹרָכָיו יִירְשׁוּ אָרֶץ וּמְקֻלָּלָיו יִכָּרֵתוּ   (a) __Puʻal__

For those blessed by him shall possess the land, but   (b) __mp__

those cursed by him shall be cut off. (Ps. 37:22)   (c) __קלל__

(3) (b)וַאֲבָרֲכָה מְבָרְכֶיךָ וּמְקַלֶּלְךָ אָאֹר   (a) __Piʻel__

And I will bless the ones blessing you, but the one   (b) __ms__

cursing you I will curse. (Gen. 12:3)   (c) __קלל__

(4) אָרוּר הַיּוֹם אֲשֶׁר יֻלַּדְתִּי בּוֹ   (a) __Qal__

Cursed be the day on which I was born. (Jer. 20:14)   (b) __ms__

    (c) __ארר__

(5) וְצֹרְרֵי יְהוּדָה יִכָּרֵתוּ   (a) __Qal__

And the oppressors of (the ones oppressing) Judah   (b) __mp__

shall be cut off. (Isa. 11:13)   (c) __צרר__

(6) וּמִתְפַּלְלִים אֶל־אֵל לֹא יוֹשִׁיעַ   (a) __Hitpaʻel__

and those who pray to a god who can not save   (b) __mp__

(Isa. 45:20)   (c) __[פלל]__

(7) גָּדוֹל יְהוָה וּמְהֻלָּל מְאֹד   (a) __Puʻal__

Great is the LORD, and one to be praised profusely.   (b) __ms__

(Ps. 145:3)   (c) __[הלל]__

XXXI.5 Supply the correct pronouns in the translation of each of the following entries.

(1) יְהַלְלוּ אֶת־שֵׁם יְהוָה כִּי הוּא צִוָּה וְנִבְרָאוּ Let __them__ praise the name of the LORD, for __he__ commanded and __they__ were created. (Ps. 148:5)

(2) וַנִּתְפַּלֵּל אֶל־אֱלֹהֵינוּ And __we__ prayed to __our__ God. (Neh. 4:3)

(3) וּקְרָאתֶ֣ם אֹתִי ‎(a) וַהֲלַכְתֶּ֖ם ‎(a) וְהִתְפַּלַּלְתֶּ֖ם אֵלָ֑י ‎(a) וְשָׁמַעְתִּ֖י אֲלֵיכֶֽם

_____ you ____ shall call upon __ me __ , and __ you __ shall come, and

_____ you ____ shall pray to __ me __ , and __ I __ will hear

__ you __ . (Jer. 29:12)

(4) וְיִתְפַּלֵּ֣ל אֵלָ֔יו וְיֹאמַ֔ר הַצִּילֵ֖נִי כִּ֥י אֵלִ֖י אָֽתָּה And __ he __ prays to it

and __ he __ says, "Deliver __ me __ , for __ you __ are __ my __

god!" (Isa. 44:17)

(5) הֵ֖מָּה יִשְׂא֣וּ קוֹלָ֖ם יָרֹֽנּוּ _____ They ____ lift up __ their __ voice, ____ they ____

shout aloud. (Isa. 24:14)

(6) וָאֹמַ֗ר אָ֚נָה אַתָּ֣ה הֹלֵ֔ךְ וַיֹּ֣אמֶר אֵלַ֔י ‎(g) לָמֹ֖ד אֶת־יְרוּשָׁלָֽ͏ם And __ I __

said, "Where are __ you __ going?" And __ he __ said to __ me __ ,

"To measure Jerusalem." (Zech. 2:6)

(7) וַיֵּרְד֤וּ אֲבֹתֵ֙ינוּ ‎(h) מִצְרַ֔יְמָה וַנֵּ֥שֶׁב בְּמִצְרַ֖יִם יָמִ֣ים רַבִּ֑ים וַיָּרֵ֧עוּ לָ֛נוּ
מִצְרַ֖יִם וְלַאֲבֹתֵֽינוּ

And ____ our ____ ancestors went down to Egypt, and ____ we ____ dwelt in Egypt

many days, and the Egyptians dealt harshly with ____ us ____ and with

____ our ____ ancestors. (Num. 20:15)

(8) הֵרֵ֖עוּ מֵאֲבוֹתָֽם _____ They ____ did more evil than ____ their ____ ancestors.
(Jer. 7:26)

(9) בְּפִיהֶ֣ם יְבָרֵ֔כוּ וּבְקִרְבָּ֖ם יְקַלְלוּ With ____ their ____ mouths ____ they ____ bless,

but inwardly ____ they ____ curse (belittle). (Ps. 62:5; Eng. 62:4)

(10) חֶבְלֵ֥י שְׁאוֹל ‎(d) סַבֻּ֖נִי The cords of Sheol encircled ____ me __ . (2 Sam. 22:6)

XXXI.6 In the following clauses and sentences, identify (a) the verb sequence (cf. XXI.63, pp. 213ff.), (b) the verb stems, and (c) the verb roots.

Example:

אָנֹכִ֣י עָשִׂ֤יתִי אֶת־הָאָ֙רֶץ֙ וּנְתַתִּ֔יהָ לַאֲשֶׁ֥ר יָשַׁ֖ר בְּעֵינָֽי I have made the

earth and have given it to the one who is suitable in my sight. (Jer. 27:5)

(a) __ Perfect __ + __ Perfect __ sequence (b) __ Qal __ , __ Qal __

(c) __ נָתַן __ , __ עָשָׂה __

(1) בָּ֣קַע יָ֖ם וַיַּעֲבִירֵ֑ם He divided (split open) the sea, and caused

them to pass over. (Ps. 78:13)

(a) __ Perfect __ + __ Imperfect __ sequence (b) __ Qal __ , __ Hif'il __

(c) __ עָבַר __ , __ בָּקַע __

(2) וְאֶת־מִשְׁפָּטַי תִּשְׁמְרוּ וַעֲשִׂיתֶם אֹתָם You shall keep my ordinances (judgments) and you shall perform them. (Lev. 25:18)

(a) __Imperfect__ + __Perfect__ sequence (b) __Qal__ , __Qal__
(c) עָשָׂה , שָׁמַר

(3) הַאֵלֵךְ וְקָרָאתִי לָךְ אִשָּׁה מֵינֶקֶת מִן הָעִבְרִיֹּת Shall I go and call you a nursing woman from the Hebrew women? (Exod. 2:7)

(a) __Imperfect__ + __Perfect__ sequence (b) __Qal__ , __Qal__
(c) הָלַךְ , קָרָא

(4) לְמַעַן תִּזְכְּרוּ וַעֲשִׂיתֶם אֶת־כָּל־מִצְוֹתָי in order that you may remember and do all my commandments (Num. 15:40)

(a) __Imperfect__ + __Perfect__ sequence (b) __Qal__ , __Qal__
(c) זָכַר , עָשָׂה

(5) שְׁמֹר מִצְוֹתַי וֶחְיֵה Keep my commandments, and live. (Prov. 4:4)

(a) __Imperative__ + __Imperative__ sequence (b) __Qal__ , __Qal__
(c) שָׁמַר , חָיָה

(6) הֲרִימֹתִי קוֹלִי וָאֶקְרָא I lifted up my voice and cried. (Gen. 39:15)

(a) __Perfect__ + __Imperfect__ sequence (b) __Hifʿil__ , __Qal__
(c) רוּם , קָרָא

(7) הַאֶעֱלֶה עַל־פְּלִשְׁתִּים וּנְתַתָּם בְּיָדִי Shall I go up against the Philistines, and will you give them into my hand? (1 Chr. 14:10)

(a) __Imperfect__ + __Perfect__ sequence (b) __Qal__ , __Qal__
(c) עָלָה , נָתַן

(8) שֻׁבוּ אֶל־הַמֶּלֶךְ וְדִבַּרְתֶּם אֵלָיו Return to the king and speak to him. (2 Kgs. 1:6)

(a) __Imperative__ + __Perfect__ sequence (b) __Qal__ , __Piʿel__
(c) שׁוּב , [דבר]

(9) שְׂאוּ שְׁעָרִים רָאשֵׁיכֶם וְיָבוֹא מֶלֶךְ הַכָּבוֹד Lift up your heads, O gates, that the King of glory may come in. (Ps. 24:7)

(a) __Imperative__ + __Imperfect__ sequence (b) __Qal__ , __Qal__
(c) בּוֹא , נָשָׂא

(10) שִׁמְעוּ וּתְחִי נַפְשְׁכֶם Hear, that your soul may live. (Isa. 55:3)

(a) __Imperative__ + __Imperfect__ sequence (b) __Qal__ , __Qal__
(c) חָיָה , שָׁמַע

Footnotes

(a) A perfect prefixed with vav conjunction will often be translated in the future tense [cf. *G*.31.1(4), p. 86].

(b) Cohortatives are first person imperfect verb forms used to express strong determination. They are often written with הָ suffix (cf. *G*.41.2, p. 132).

(c) לֹא before the imperfect expresses a strong prohibition.

(d) Šureq is often written defectively (as qibbuṣ). For purposes of syllabification, the qibbuṣ (.ֻ) is to be treated as a long vowel.

(e) אַל followed by a jussive (an imperfect used as a jussive) expresses a milder form of a prohibition than לֹא with the imperfect.

(f) This form (Piᶜel imperfect, third masculine plural, plus vav consecutive) has lost two dagesh fortes from consonants supported by vocal shevas (וַיְהַלְלוּ becomes וַיְהַלְלוּ). Similar losses occur in other forms in this exercise.

(g) לָמֹד is Qal infinitive construct plus preposition (לְ), from מָדַד, "he measured." Trans. "to measure."

(h) מִצְרַיְמָה has the "He-directive" suffix.

(i) An interrogative הַ is used to introduce a question expecting a simple yes or no answer (cf. *G*.34.1, pp. 94f.).

Suggestions for Further Testing

1. Translate the following sentences and locate fully all Double ᶜAyin verb forms.

(1) לֹא־אֹסִף לְקַלֵּל עוֹד אֶת־הָאֲדָמָה בַּעֲבוּר הָאָדָם (Gen. 8:21)

(2) אָרוּר הַגֶּבֶר אֲשֶׁר יִבְטַח בָּאָדָם (Jer. 17:5)

(3) אֲהַלְלָה שֵׁם אֱלֹהִים בְּשִׁיר (Ps. 69:31; Eng. 69:30)

(4) אַחֲרֵי־כֵן פָּתַח אִיּוֹב אֶת־פִּיהוּ וַיְקַלֵּל אֶת־יוֹמוֹ (Job 3:1)

(5) חָנֻּנִי חָנֻּנִי אַתֶּם רֵעָי (Job 19:21)

(6) וַיהוָה שָׁב אֶת־שְׁבוּת אִיּוֹב בְּהִתְפַּלְלוֹ בְּעַד רֵעֵהוּ (Job 42:10)

(7) הִנְנִי מֵסֵב אֶת־כְּלֵי הַמִּלְחָמָה אֲשֶׁר בְּיֶדְכֶם (Jer. 21:4)

(8) וְהַבּוֹטֵחַ בַּיהוָה חֶסֶד יְסוֹבְבֶנּוּ (Ps. 32:10)

SUGGESTIONS FOR SIMPLIFYING THE TASK
OF VERB LOCATION

Knowing how to locate verb forms is crucial to the understanding of Hebrew. The task of verb location, however, is often baffling to the beginning student. Verb location may seem to be based largely upon guesswork, but this perception is far from the truth. There is order and design in the composition of Hebrew, and this is nowhere more apparent than in the structure of the Hebrew verbal system. The purpose of the following discussion is to take some of the mystery out of the process of verb location by identifying some of the guideposts that the language provides for those making this journey. The following questions provide a starting point.

1. *Does the verb form under consideration have a preformative?*

    If the verb does not have a preformative, then it must belong either to the Qal, Pi‘el, or Pu‘al stem. These three stems are the only verb forms without preformatives. Of course, all stems have preformatives in the imperfect, and all stems except Qal have preformatives in the participle. The Nif‘al, Hitpa‘el, Hif‘il, and Hof‘al stems have preformatives on every verb form.

    The rules regarding preformatives apply to all verb roots, whether they are strong or weak (cf. *G*, pp. 400ff.).

2. *Is the verb form under consideration an imperfect?*

    Imperfects can usually be identified by examining the preformative. The imperfect preformatives are the easiest to recognize since they are the same for all verbs and for all stems. The strong verb imperfect preformatives (consonants and vowels) for all seven stems are:

	Qal	Nif‘al	Pi‘el	Pu‘al	Hitpa‘el	Hif‘il	Hof‘al
3 ms	יִ	יִ	יְ	יְ	יִתְ	יַ	יָ
3 fs	תִּ	תִּ	תְּ	תְּ	תִּתְ	תַּ	תָּ
2 ms	תִּ	תִּ	תְּ	תְּ	תִּתְ	תַּ	תָּ
2 fs	תִּ	תִּ	תְּ	תְּ	תִּתְ	תַּ	תָּ
1 cs	אֶ	אֶ	אֲ	אֲ	אֶתְ	אַ	אָ
3 mp	יִ	יִ	יְ	יְ	יִתְ	יַ	יָ
3 fp	תִּ	תִּ	תְּ	תְּ	תִּתְ	תַּ	תָּ
2 mp	תִּ	תִּ	תְּ	תְּ	תִּתְ	תַּ	תָּ
2 fp	תִּ	תִּ	תְּ	תְּ	תִּתְ	תַּ	תָּ
1 cp	נִ	נִ	נְ	נְ	נִתְ	נַ	נָ

Note that preformative vowels are the same throughout a given stem except when they stand after the guttural א. (א becomes אֶ; א becomes אֲ.) All of the preformative consonants and most of the vowels are repeated in the imperfect of weak verbs.

3. *Is the verb form being located prefixed with a vav consecutive (normally ·וַ)?*

If prefixed with a vav consecutive, the verb form must be the imperfect, for while any verb form, including imperfects, may be prefixed with a vav conjunction, *only an imperfect* may take a vav consecutive.

Identifying vav consecutives on imperfects simplifies the overall task of verb location. Just knowing that the form is an imperfect makes it easier for the student to identify the verb root. The consonant standing immediately after the vav consecutive is always an imperfect preformative and thus not to be considered as part of the verb root.

One may also expect the addition of vav consecutive to result in an occasional apocopated imperfect, especially in Lamed He verbs (יִהְיֶה becomes וַיְהִי). Again, recognizing this simplifies the task of reconstructing the verb root.

4. *Does the form being located have a prefix other than vav consecutive?*

(1) Is the verb prefixed with vav conjunction? Remember that vav conjunction may occur on any verb form, including imperfects. It is distinguishable from the vav consecutive by its pointing.

(2) Is there a stem prefix (other than the imperfect prefixes discussed above)?

(a) The Nif'al stem occurs with prefixed nun (נ) throughout the perfect, in the alternate form of the infinitive absolute (rarely used), and in all participial forms. A he (ה) prefix is found throughout the Nif'al imperative, the Nif'al infinitive construct, and the regular form of the Nif'al infinitive absolute.

(b) The Hitpa'el stem has a prefixed הִת, the longest of all stem prefixes, in all forms of the perfect, the imperative, the infinitive construct, and the infinitive absolute. All Hitpa'el participial forms occur with a מִת prefix.

(c) The Hif'il stem has a he (ה) prefix in all forms of the perfect, the imperative, the infinitive construct, and the infinitive absolute. All participial forms are prefixed with mem (מ).

(d) The Hof'al stem is prefixed with he (ה) in all forms of the prefect, in the infinitive construct, and in the infinitive absolute. The Hif'il participial forms are prefixed with the mem (מ).

(3) Is there a prefixed preposition? The prepositions that may function as verbal prefixes are מִן (with assimilated נ), and the inseparable prepositions בְּ, כְּ, and לְ. These may be prefixed to infinitives construct and to participial forms.

(4) Is there an interrogative הַ prefixed to the verbal form? Theoretically, the interrogative הַ may be prefixed to any form of the verb, although its actual occurrence in this capacity is somewhat rare.

5. *Is there an afformative that functions as an integral part of the verb form?*

(1) The perfect afformatives that fall in this category are the same for all stems and for all verbs.

3 ms	(none)	3 cp	וּ
3 fs	הָ		
2 ms	תָּ	2 mp	תֶּם
2 fs	תְּ	2 fp	תֶּן
1 cs	תִּי	1 cp	נוּ

(2) The imperfect afformatives are also the same for all stems and for all verbs.

3 ms	(none)	3 mp	וּ
3 fs	(none)	3 fp	נָה
2 ms	(none)	2 mp	וּ
2 fs	יִ	2 fp	נָה
1 cs	(none)	1 cp	(none)

(3) The imperative afformatives are the same for all stems in which imperatives occur (Qal, Nifʻal, Piʻel, Hitpaʻel, and Hifʻil) and for all verbs.

2 ms	(none)	2 mp	וּ
2 fs	יִ	2 fp	נָה

6. *Is there an afformative that functions as an occasional part of the verb form?*

(1) A final nun (ן) is added to over three hundred third masculine plural and second masculine plural imperfect forms in the Hebrew Bible (cf. תִּשְׁמָעוּן in Deut. 1:17). This is apparently an archaic ending, and the reason for its survival has never been discovered.

(2) Is there an הָ suffix added to a first person imperfect verb form, indicating that it is to be interpreted as a cohortative (cf. *G.*41.2, p. 132)?

(3) Is there a הָ suffix added to a second masculine singular form of the imperative, perhaps to make it more emphatic (cf. *G*.53, pp. 172f.)?

7. *Does the form being located have a pronominal suffix?*

This question refers to pronominal endings that serve as direct objects of the verbs. Pronominal suffixes are the same for perfects and imperfects that end in vowels, but there are slight differences between those added to perfects and imperfects that end in consonants.

(1) Pronominal suffixes for perfects and imperfects ending in vowels (cf. *G*.46.2, p. 153; 47, pp. 156f.)

1 cs	נִי	me	1 cp	נוּ	us
2 ms	ךָ	you	2 mp	כֶם	you
2 fs	ךְ	you	2 fp	כֶן	you
3 ms	הוּ, וּ	him	3 mp	הֶם, ם	them
3 fs	הָ	her	3 fp	ן	them

(2) Pronominal suffixes for perfects ending in consonants (cf. *G*.46.3, p. 155)

1 cs	נִֽי	(pausal נִֽי) me	1 cp	נֽוּ	us
2 ms	ךְ	(pausal ךָ) you	2 mp	כֶם	you
2 fs	ךְ or ךְ	you	2 fp	כֶן	you
3 ms	וֹ or הֽוּ	him	3 mp	ם	them
3 fs	הָ	her	3 fp	ן	them

(3) Pronominal suffixes for imperfects ending in consonants (cf. *G*.47.2, pp. 157f.)

1 cs	נִי	me	1 cp	נוּ	us
2 ms	ךְ	(pausal ךָ) you	2 mp	כֶם	you
2 fs	ךְ	you	2 fp	כֶן	you
3 ms	הֽוּ	him (it)	3 mp	ם	them
3 fs	הָ, הָ	her (it)	3 fp	ן	them

(4) An alternate form of the pronominal suffix is sometimes used with verbs ending in consonants (cf. *G*.47.3, p. 159). The following forms are found in the Hebrew Bible:

1 cs	נִּי ָ.	(for נְנִי ָ.)	1 cp	נּוּ ָ.	(for נְנוּ ָ.)
2 ms	ךָ ָ.	(for נְךָ ָ.)			
3 ms	נּוּ ָ.	(for נְנוּ ָ.)			
3 fs	נָּה ָ.	(for נְנָה ָ.)			

(5) Pronominal suffixes used with imperatives, infinitives construct, and participles follow the same pattern as those used with imperfects [cf. *G*.48.4, p. 167; 50.3, p. 170; 52.2, pp. 172f.; 56.2(3), p. 183; 60.3(2), p. 202].

Since participles are verbal nouns, they may occur in the singular or plural form, and may be either absolute or construct. Pronominal suffixes may be attached to any participial form that is in the construct state.

8. *Having identified all prefixes and suffixes of the form under consideration, is it now possible to determine what consonants make up the verb root?*

The process is fairly simple where strong verbs are concerned, since their roots always consist of three strong consonants. (For a representative list of strong verbs, cf. *G*.29.8, p. 82.) Most weak verbs likewise contain three root consonants in all their inflected forms, which makes identification of their roots less complicated.

Major problems arise, however, when an inflected form of a weak verb has lost one or more of its root consonants. How is one to reconstruct the verb root when one or more of its consonants is missing? Constant vocabulary building is the surest path to progress in this area. Until that can be achieved, beginning students must resort to a process of trial and error in determining the verb root (and meaning) for abbreviated verb forms.

Root consonants may disappear from the beginning, the middle, or the end of certain weak verb forms.

(1) Weak verbs that sometimes lose their *initial consonants* include Pe Nuns (plus לָקַח) and Pe Vavs (plus הָלַךְ). Representative forms drawn from these two classes of weak verbs are listed below. Some may also have prefixes and suffixes. Practice identifying the prefixes and suffixes, determining what consonants make up the verb root, and fully locating the verb form. When in doubt about a particular form, the student should consult the *Grammar* for the verb charts on Pe Nuns (pp. 414f.) and Pe Vavs (pp. 420f.).

(a)	קַחְתֵּךְ	(Gen. 30:15)	(g)	תֵּת	(Jer. 43:3)
(b)	וָאֶקַּח	(Gen. 12:19)	(h)	לָשֶׁבֶת	(Gen. 19:30)
(c)	וְקַח	(Exod. 17:5)	(i)	וַיֵּשֶׁב	(Gen. 4:16)
(d)	אֶתְּנֶנָּה	(Gen. 13:17)	(j)	נֵשֵׁב	(Jer. 42:14)
(e)	וַתִּתְּנֵם	(Neh. 9:24)	(k)	שְׁבוּ	(Jer. 40:9)
(f)	תְּנוּ	(Exod. 17:2)	(l)	וַיֵּלֶךְ	(Gen. 12:4)

(2) Weak verbs that sometimes lose their *middle consonants* include ʿAyin Vav and ʿAyin Yod verbs (cf. *G*, pp. 416ff.). Representative forms drawn from these weak verbs are listed below, some with prefixes and suffixes. Identify the prefixes and suffixes, determine the verb root (Qal infinitive construct), and fully locate the form.

(a)	בָּא	(Josh. 23:1)	(g)	מֵתוּ	(Josh. 5:4)
(b)	בָּאתִי	(Josh. 23:2)	(h)	הֵמִית	(2 Chr. 25:4)
(c)	הַבָּא	(Ps. 118:26)	(i)	קָם	(2 Sam. 23:10)
(d)	הַבָּאָה	(Gen. 46:26)	(j)	קַמְנוּ	(Ps. 20:9; Eng. 20:8)
(e)	בָּאִים	(Gen. 24:63)	(k)	וַיָּקָם	(Gen. 4:8)
(f)	וּמֵת	(Exod. 11:5)	(l)	מֵקִים	(Gen. 9:9)

(3) Weak verbs that sometimes lose their *final consonants* include Lamed He and Double ʿAyin (Geminate verbs). Lamed He verbs occur so frequently that it is imperative to understand the circumstances under which the ה, the third consonant of the verb root, drops out. For this reason, the student should carefully review the lesson on the Lamed He verb (cf. *G*.72, pp. 286ff.). Special attention should be given to the loss of ה before vocalic afformatives [cf. *G*.72.3(2)(a)(b), p. 287f.], the substitution of yod (י) for ה before consonantal afformatives [cf. *G*.72.3(3)(a)(b)(c), pp. 288f.], and the apocopation of imperfects of Lamed He verbs without afformatives. Apocopation occurs when these imperfects are used as jussives or when prefixed with vav consecutive (cf. *G*.72.8, pp. 292f.).

Representative forms of Lamed He and Double ʿAyin (Geminate) verbs are listed below. Determine the triconsonantal root for each form and give a full location of the form.

(a)	הָיְתָה	(Gen. 1:2)	(g)	פְּרוּ	(Gen. 1:22)
(b)	יְהִי	(Gen. 1:3)	(h)	תַּמּוּ	(Job 31:40)
(c)	וַיְהִי	(Gen. 1:3)	(i)	סֹבּוּ	(Ps. 48:13; Eng. 48:12)
(d)	וַיַּרְא	(Gen. 1:4)	(j)	תִּסֹּב	(Ps. 114:5)
(e)	וַיַּעַשׂ	(Gen. 1:7)	(k)	הֵמַר	(Job 27:2)
(f)	וְהָיוּ	(Gen. 1:14)	(l)	וַיֵּרַע	(Gen. 38:10)

(4) Special difficulties arise when verbs are doubly weak, as, for example, in the case of those that are both Pe Nun and Lamed He. Occurrences of such verbs are rare, but those that do occur are quite significant, especially in the case of נָטָה, "he stretched forth," and [נכה], "he smote, killed," the latter occurring only in the Hifʿil stem.

Representative forms of these verbs are listed below. Give a full location of each form [cf. *G*.59.7:96)(F), pp. 197f.].

(a)	לְהַכּוֹת	(2 Sam. 21:16)	(f)	וַיַּכּוּ	(Josh. 8:24)
(b)	לְהַכֹּתָם	(2 Sam. 21:2)	(g)	נָטוּ	(Isa. 45:12)
(c)	הִכִּיתָ	(Exod. 17:5)	(h)	וְנָטִיתִי	(Ezek. 6:14)
(d)	הִכּוּ	(Josh. 11:14)	(i)	וַיֵּט	(Exod. 10:22)
(e)	וַיַּךְ	(Exod. 2:12)	(j)	וָאַט	(Jer. 15:6)

By way of summary, when a verb form contains only two root consonants, it may have dropped an initial נ (Pe Nun) or an initial י (Pe Yod). Try placing first one and then the other of these consonants to the two remaining root consonants. Then consult a lexicon or vocabulary list to see if such a triconsonantal verb root exists, and, if so, whether or not its meaning fits the context in which the form is found.

If the search thus far has been fruitless, try placing a ו (ʿAyin Vav) or י (ʿAyin Yod) between the two consonants that remain. Then repeat the lexicon search for such a verb root and determine its meaning and suitability for the context.

If this also proves fruitless, try placing a final ה (Lamed He) after the other two root consonants or repeating the second of the two consonants (Double ʿAyin/Geminate). Then test the resulting verb root by checking a lexicon to see if it exists and if it has a meaning that suits the context. As a final precaution, check the appropriate verb chart in the *Grammar* (pp. 400ff.) to see if the form being located would fit into the class of weak verbs to which it has tentatively been assigned.

If this procedure seems cumbersome at first, it will become less so with practice. Mastering it will simplify the task of verb location and make the study of Hebrew much more intelligible.

WORD LIST*

A. Verbs Occurring 200 or More Times

אָהַב	208	he loved	כָּתַב	223	he wrote
אָכַל	807	he ate, devoured	לָקַח	966	he took, seized
אָמַר	5298	he said	מוּת	780	to die
אָסַף	200	he gathered, removed	מָלֵא	250	he (it) was full
בּוֹא	2565	to come, go	מָלַךְ	347	he reigned
בָּנָה	373	he built	מָצָא	455	he found
[בקשׁ]	225	he sought	[נגד]	369	he told, declared
[ברך]	327	he blessed	[נכה]	504	he struck, killed
[דבר]	1137	he spoke	נָפַל	434	he fell
הָיָה	3548	he was, became	[נצל]	213	he delivered, saved
הָלַךְ	1549	he went, walked	נָשָׂא	650	he lifted, carried
זָכַר	222	he remembered	נָתַן	2011	he gave
חָזַק	293	he was strong	סוּר	300	to turn aside, depart
חָטָא	238	he sinned	עָבַד	289	he served, worked
חָיָה	283	he was alive	עָבַר	547	he passed over, through
יָדַע	940	he knew			
יָלַד	468	he begot (children)	עָזַב	208	he abandoned, left, forsook
יָסַף	212	he added	עָלָה	890	he went up
יָצָא	1067	he went out	עָמַד	521	he stood
יָרֵא	336	he feared	עָנָה	316	he answered
יָרַד	379	he descended, went down	עָשָׂה	2627	he made, did
יָרַשׁ	231	he possessed, subdued	פָּקַד	223	he visited, appointed
יָשַׁב	815	he sat, dwelt	[צוה]	496	he commanded
[ישׁע]	205	he saved, delivered	קוּם	629	to rise, stand
כּוּן	217	to be fixed, firm, established	קָרָא	738	he called, read, met
			קָרַב	291	he drew near, approached
כָּלָה	206	he (it) was completed	רָאָה	1299	he saw
כָּרַת	285	he cut			

* The frequency of occurrence of each word is taken from A. Even-Shoshan's *New Concordance of the Old Testament Using the Hebrew and Aramaic Text.* 2nd. ed. Grand Rapids: Baker Book House, 1989.

רָעָה	319	he pastured, tended	שָׁלַח	846	he stretched out, sent
שׁוּב	1059	to turn, return, repent	שָׁמַע	1159	he heard
שִׂים	586	to set, place	שָׁמַר	411	he kept, watched
שָׁכַב	212	he lay down	שָׁתָה	217	he drank

B. Verbs Occurring 100 to 199 Times

אָבַד	184	he perished	כָּבֵד	113	he was (became) heavy, he was honored, glorified
[אמן]	100	he was faithful, he believed			
בּוֹשׁ	109	to be ashamed, confounded	כָּסָה	156	he covered, concealed
			[כפר]	101	he covered, made atonement
בָּטַח	120	he trusted	לָבַשׁ	112	he put on, wore
בִּין	171	to understand, discern	[לחם]	171	he fought
בָּכָה	114	he wept	[נבא]	115	he prophesied
גָּדַל	116	he was (became) great	נָגַע	150	he touched, smote
גָּלָה	187	he uncovered, revealed	נָגַשׁ	125	he approached, drew near
דָּרַשׁ	164	he sought, inquired	נוּס	157	to flee, escape
הָלַל	150	he was boastful, he praised	נָסַע	146	he set out, departed, journeyed
הָרַג	167	he killed, slew	סָבַב	162	he surrounded, turned about
זָבַח	134	he sacrificed, slew			
[חלל]	141	he was polluted, he began	[ספר]	107	he told, related, counted
חָנָה	143	he encamped	פָּנָה	135	he turned toward, faced, prepared
חָשַׁב	123	he thought, devised, reckoned			
			קָבַץ	127	he collected, gathered
טָמֵא	163	he was unclean	קָבַר	133	he buried
[ידה]	111	he praised, confessed, gave thanks	קָדַשׁ	171	he was holy, consecrated, set apart
יָטַב	101	he did well, was good	[קטר]	116	he burned (offered) incense
[יתר]	105	he (it) was left over, remained	רָדַף	144	he pursued, persecuted

שָׂמַח	154	he rejoiced, was glad	[שחת]	140	he destroyed, corrupted
שָׂנֵא	112	he hated	שָׁכַח	102	he forgot
שָׂרַף	117	he burned	שָׁכַן	129	he settled, dwelt
שָׁאַל	172	he asked	[שלך]	125	he cast, threw
שָׁאַר	133	he was left, left over	שָׁלֵם	117	he was whole, complete
[שבע]	185	he swore	שָׁפַט	142	he judged, delivered
שָׁבַר	148	he broke in pieces	שָׁפַך	115	he poured out
[שחה]	172	he bowed down, worshipped			

C. Nouns Occurring 300 or More Times

אָב	1215	father, ancestor	יוֹם	2291	day
אָדָם	561	man, humankind	יָם	392	sea
אֲדֹנָי/אָדוֹן	425	Lord/master, lord	כֹּהֵן	752	priest
אֹהֶל	345	tent	כֹּל/כָּל־	5408	all/all of
אָח	629	brother	כְּלִי	324	tool, weapon, vessel
אִישׁ	2179	man, husband	כֶּסֶף	403	silver
אֱלֹהִים	2603	God, gods	לֵבָב , לֵב	851	heart, mind, will
אֶרֶץ	2504	(f) earth	מִזְבֵּחַ	400	altar, place of sacrifice
אִשָּׁה	782	(f) woman, wife	מַיִם	580	water
בַּיִת/בֵּית	2036	house/house of	מִלְחָמָה	316	(f) war, battle
בֵּן	4891	son	מֶלֶך	2518	king
בַּת	574	(f) daughter	מָקוֹם	401	place
גּוֹי	556	nation, people	מִשְׁפָּחָה	303	(f) family, clan
דָּבָר	1442	word, thing	מִשְׁפָּט	424	judgment, justice
דָּם	360	blood	נְאֻם	373	utterance, oracle
דֶּרֶך	706	(m/f) way, road	נָבִיא	315	prophet
הַר	547	mountain	נֶפֶשׁ	753	(f) life, soul, person
זָהָב	387	gold	עֶבֶד	799	servant, slave, worshiper
חֶרֶב	411	sword			
יָד	1617	hand			

עוֹלָם	437	eternity, long duration, antiquity
עַיִן	868	(f) eye, fountain
עִיר	1042	(f) city
עַם	1850	people
עֵץ	329	tree, trees, wood
פֶּה	502	mouth
פָּנִים	2040	face(s)
צָבָא, צְבָאוֹת	482	host(s), army(ies)
קוֹל	505	voice, sound
קֹדֶשׁ	477	holiness, apartness, sacredness

רֹאשׁ	600	head
רוּחַ	378	(f) spirit, wind, breath
רֵעַ	319	friend, companion
שָׂדֶה	333	field
שַׂר	421	prince, leader, official
שֵׁם	864	name
שָׁמַיִם	421	heavens, sky
שָׁנָה	874	(f) year
שַׁעַר	375	gate
תָּוֶךְ/תּוֹךְ	318	midst/midst of

D. Nouns Occurring 200 to 299 Times

אֶבֶן	269	(f) stone
אֲדָמָה	225	(f) ground, earth
אֵל	235	God
אֵם	220	(f) mother
אַמָּה	248	(f) cubit
אַף	277	nostril, nose, face, anger
אָרוֹן	201	chest, ark
בֶּגֶד	215	garment
בֹּקֶר	214	morning
בְּרִית	283	(f) covenant
בָּשָׂר	270	flesh
גְּבוּל	240	boundary, border
זֶרַע	229	seed, offspring
חַטָּאת	221	(f) sin
חַיִל	244	strength, ability, wealth, army

חֶסֶד	246	goodness, kindness
לֶחֶם	297	bread, food
לַיְלָה	227	night
מִדְבָּר	271	wilderness, desert
מוֹעֵד	223	appointed time, place
מַחֲנֶה	216	(m/f) camp, encampment
מַטֶּה	251	staff, rod, branch, tribe
מַלְאָךְ	212	angel, messenger
מִנְחָה	211	(f) offering, gift, tribute
מַעֲשֶׂה	234	work, deed
נַחֲלָה	221	(f) possession, inheritance, property
נַעַר	240	lad, youth
עָוֹן	229	iniquity, guilt, punishment for iniquity

213

עוֹלָה 286 (f) whole burnt offering

עֵת 294 (f) time

צֹאן 273 flock, sheep

קֶרֶב 227 midst, inward part

רֶגֶל 243 (f) foot

שָׁלוֹם 237 peace

תּוֹרָה 220 (f) law, instruction

E. Nouns Occurring 100 to 199 Times

אוֹר 122 light

אֹזֶן 187 (f) ear

אָחוֹת 114 (f) sister

אַחֵר 166 another, other

אַיִל 182 ram

בְּהֵמָה 190 (f) cattle

בְּכוֹר 122 first-born, oldest

בָּקָר 183 herd, cattle

גִּבּוֹר 159 hero, mighty one

דּוֹר 167 generation, period

זֶבַח 162 sacrifice

זָקֵן 187 old one

חוֹמָה 133 (f) wall

חוּץ 164 a place outside the house, the outdoors, a street

חָכָם 138 wise one

חָכְמָה 153 (f) wisdom

חֵמָה 125 (f) heat, rage

חֲצִי 126 half

חָצֵי 190 (m/f) enclosure, court, settlement, village

חֹק 129 statute

חֻקָּה 100 (f) enactment, decree, statute

יַיִן 141 wine

יָמִין 139 (f) right hand, right side, south

יָשָׁר 118 upright one

כָּבוֹד 199 glory, honor

כֶּבֶשׂ 107 lamb

כֹּחַ 125 strength, power

כָּנָף 109 (f) wing, skirt, extremity

כִּסֵּא 135 seat of honor, throne

כַּף 193 (f) hollow of the hand, palm, sole of the foot

לָשׁוֹן 117 tongue

מִגְרָשׁ 110 common-land, open range

מָוֶת 161 death

מְלָאכָה 166 (f) occupation, work

מַמְלָכָה 117 (f) kingdom, dominion, reign

מִסְפָּר 134 number, sum total

מִצְוָה 181 (f) commandment

מַרְאֶה 103 sight, appearance, vision

מִשְׁכָּן 139 dwelling-place, tabernacle

נֶגֶב 110 Negev, dry country, south

נָהָר 117 river, stream

נַחַל	137	torrent valley, wadi
נְחֹשֶׁת	133	copper, bronze
נָשִׂיא	129	chief, prince
סוּס	137	horse
סֵפֶר	185	book, document, writing
עֲבוֹדָה	145	(f) labor, service
עֵדָה	149	(f) congregation
עָפָר	110	dust
עֶצֶם	126	(f) bone, substance, self, selfsame
עֶרֶב	135	evening
פַּעַם	115	(f) foot, footstep, time, occurrence
פַּר	133	young bull
פְּרִי	118	fruit

פֶּתַח	164	opening, doorway, entrance
צָפוֹן	153	(f) north
רֹב	151	multitude, abundance, greatness
רֹחַב	101	breadth, width
רֶכֶב	119	chariotry, chariot
רָעָב	101	famine, hunger
שָׂפָה	176	(f) lip, speech, edge
שֵׁבֶט	190	rod, staff, scepter, tribe
שַׁבָּת	111	(m/f) sabbath
שֶׁמֶן	193	oil, fat
שֶׁמֶשׁ	134	sun
שֶׁקֶל	113	shekel, a standard weight of money
תּוֹעֵבָה	117	(f) abomination

F. Adjectives Occurring 50 or More Times

אַחֵר	166	another, other
גָּדוֹל	526	great, large
זָקֵן	187	old
חָדָשׁ	53	new
חָזָק	56	strong, stout, mighty
חַי	239	living, alive
חָכָם	138	wise, skillful
טוֹב	495	good
יָשָׁר	118	straight, right, upright
צַדִּיק	206	righteous

קָדוֹשׁ	116	holy, sacred
קָטֹן	101	small, insignificant
קָרוֹב	78	near
רִאשׁוֹן	140	former, first, chief
רַב	413	many, much, great
רָחוֹק	85	far
רַע	142	evil
רֵק	108	empty, vain
רָשָׁע	263	wicked, guilty
תָּמִים	91	perfect, complete, whole

G. Prepositions/Particles Occurring 50 or More Times

אַחֲרֵי	619	after, behind
אֶל	5464	to, unto
אֵצֶל	61	beside, near
אֵת	938	with
אֵת	10903	sign of direct object
בֵּין	403	between
בִּלְתִּי	111	not, so as not
בַּעֲבוּר	49	on account of, for the sake of
בְּעַד	105	away from, behind
לְמַעַן	271	for the sake of, on account of
לִפְנֵי	1103	in the presence of, before
מִן	1323	from
נֶגֶד	151	in front of, in sight of, opposite to
סָבִיב	334	round about, around
עֵבֶר	90	beyond, across
עַד	1269	until, unto
עַל	5772	upon, above, about
עִם	1091	with
תַּחַת	506	under, instead of

ACCENT TABLES
for Biblia Hebraica Stuttgartensia

In the study of classical Hebrew, students will notice that virtually every Hebrew word receives an accent (called טְעָמִים, "tastes," or נְגִינוֹת, "melodies"). Some of the exceptionally long words may have a secondary accent as well. Words accented on the last syllable are said to be accented מִלְרַע, while words accented on the next to the last syllable are said to be accented מִלְעֵיל. In the *Grammar*, accents are not generally printed unless a word is accented on other than the last syllable (i.e., מִלְרַע). Accents indicate which syllable should receive the stress in pronunciation, and at times they are also important for interpretive reasons (e.g., קָמָה when accented on the first syllable is the Qal perfect third feminine singular, but if accented on the last syllable, it is the Qal active participle feminine singular (cf. *G*, p. 317).

The Hebrew Bible has two systems of accents: one system is for the poetic books (Psalms, Proverbs, and Job) and the other system is employed in the prose books (the balance of the Hebrew Bible). Furthermore, each system is divided into two general types of accents: disjunctive accents and conjunctive accents. Disjunctive accents separate the accented word from the next word in the clause or sentence. Conjunctive accents, on the other hand, establish a connection between the accented word and the word that follows. In the prose books, eighteen disjunctive accents and nine conjunctive accents are employed. In the poetic books, twelve disjunctive accents and nine conjunctive accents appear.

In addition to the two major breaks in a sentence, created by the presence of 'Atnaḥ and Silluq, the other disjunctive accents further divide the sentence into smaller sections. 'Atnaḥ divides the verse into two syntactical divisions. If three such divisions are mandated by the structure of the verse, 'Atnaḥ may be preceded by Segolta, as in Genesis 1:7:

כֵּן : - - - לָרָקִיעַ - - - הָרָקִיעַ - - - -

Both the 'Atnaḥ and the Silluq sections of the verse may be further divided by such disjunctives as Zaqef (qaton or gadol), Reviaʿ, Ṭifḥa, etc.

(Gen. 3:5) אֱלֹהִים - - - מִמֶּנּוּ - - - עֵינֵיכֶם - - -

וָרָע : - - - כֵּאלֹהִים

In the following lists of accents, those marked as *prepositive* stand at the beginning of the word, either over or under the initial consonant. Those marked as *postpositive* stand at the end of the word, either over or under the final consonant. Consequently, in both cases the tone-syllable in the word may be other than that marked with the accent. In the case of a word accented by Pašta, a *postpositive* accent, Pašta is written over the final consonant in the word and is then repeated over the tone-syllable if it is other than the final syllable in the word (cf. מֶלֶךְ).

217

Prose Accents

(A. Disjunctive)

(1)	⋮	דָּבָר׃	Sof pasuq accompanied by Silluq
(2)		דָּבָר	ʾAtnaḥ
(3)		דָּבָר	Segolta (*postpositive*)
(4)		דָּבָר׀	Šalšelet
(5)		דָּבָר	Zaqef qaton
(6)		דָּבָר	Zaqef gadol
(7)		דָּבָר	Reviaʿ
(8)		דָּבָר	Ṭifḥa
(9)		דָּבָר	Zarqa (*postpositive*)
(10)		דָּבָר or מֶלֶךְ	Pašṭa (*postpositive*)
(11)		מֶלֶךְ	Yeṭiv (*prepositive*)
(12)		דָּבָר	Tevir
(13)		דָּבָר	Geresh or Ṭeres
(14)		דָּבָר	Garshayim
(15)		דָּבָר	Pazer
(16)		דָּבָר	Pazer gadol or Qarnê fara
(17)		דָּבָר	Telisha gedolah (*prepositive*)
(18)		דָּבָר׀	Legarmeh

(B. Conjunctive)

(19)		דָּבָר	Munaḥ
(20)		דָּבָר	Mahpakh or Mehuppakh
(21)		דָּבָר	Merekha
(22)		דָּבָר	Merekha khefula
(23)		דָּבָר	Darga
(24)		דָּבָר	ʾAzla

(25)	.... ⁹	דָּבָר	Telisha qeṭanna (*postpositive*)
(26)	.... ᵛ	דָּבָ֫ר	Galgal or Yeraḥ
(27)	......	בְּשִׁבְעֹתֵיכֶם	Ma'yela

Poetic Accents

(A. Disjunctive)

(1)	....	דָּבָ֑ר׃	Sof pasuq accompanied by Silluq
(2)	.... ˂	דָּבָ֫ר	ʿOleh weyored
(3)	.... ᴧ	דָּבָ֖ר	ʾAtnaḥ
(4)	....	דְּבָ֗ר	Reviaʿ gadol
(5)	....	דְּבָ֗ר	Reviaʿ mugraš
(6)	....	דְּבָ֓ר׀	Šalšelet gedolah
(7)	.... ᵓ	דָּבָ֮ר	Ṣinnor or Zarqa (*postpositive*)
(8)	....	דְּבָ֔ר	Reviaʿ qaton (before ʿOleh weyored)
(9)	....	דָּבָ֪ר	Deḥi or Ṭifḥa (*prepositive*)
(10)	....	דָּבָ֟ר	Pazer
(11)	׀ .... ˂	דְּבָ֤ר׀	Mehuppakh legarmeh
(12)	׀	דְּבָ֨ר׀	ʾAzla legarmeh

(B. Conjunctive)

(13)	....	דָּבָ֣ר	Munaḥ
(14)	.... /	דָּבָ֥ר	Merekha
(15)	....	דָּבָ֢ר	ʿIlluy or Upper munaḥ
(16)	....	דָּבָ֖ר	Ṭarḥa
(17)	.... ᵛ	דָּבָ֪ר	Galgal or Yeraḥ
(18)	.... ˂	דְּבָ֤ר	Mehuppakh or Mahpakh
(19)	....	דְּבָ֨ר	ʾAzla or Qadma
(20)	....	דְּבָ֓ר	Šalšelet qeṭannah
(21)	דְּבָ֞ר or דְּבָ֬ר		Ṣinnorit

219

SOURCES FOR FURTHER STUDY

Concordances

Even–Shoshan, A., ed. *A New Concordance of the Old Testament Using the Hebrew and Aramaic Text*. 2nd. ed. Grand Rapids: Baker Book House, 1989.

Lisowsky, G. *Konkordanz zum Hebräischen Alten Testament*. 2nd. ed. Stuttgart: German Bible Society, 1981.

Hebrew Language and Script Development

Joüon, P. and T. Muraoka. *A Grammar of Biblical Hebrew*. Vol. 1. Rome: Pontifical Biblical Institute, 1991, pp. 2–12 (a good, brief, useful discussion).

Naveh, J. *The Early History of the Alphabet*. Jerusalem: Magnes Press, 1982, pp. 23–30.

Schmitz, P. C. "Linguistic Affiliation." In *The Anchor Bible Dictionary*. Vol. IV. New York: Doubleday, 1992, pp. 204–206.

Schramm, G. "Hebrew as a Language Name." In *The Anchor Bible Dictionary*. Vol. IV. New York: Doubleday, 1992, pp. 203–204.

Accentuation of the Masoretic Text

Joüon, P. and T. Muraoka. *A Grammar of Biblical Hebrew*. Vol. 1. Rome: Pontifical Biblical Institute, 1991, pp. 61–69.

Wickes, W. *Two Treatises on the Accentuation of the Old Testament* טעמי אמ״ת *on Psalms, Proverbs, and Job;* טעמי כ״א ספרים *on the Twenty-one Prose Books*. New York: KTAV Publishing House, Inc., 1970 (in-depth, research-level resource).

Yeivin, I. *Introduction to the Tiberian Masorah*. Trans. and ed. E. J. Revell. Missoula: Scholars Press, 1980, pp. 157–174 (very good on relationships between accents).

Masoretic Studies

Scott, W. R. *Simplified Guide to BHS*. 2nd. ed. Berkeley: Bibal Press, 1990.

Weil, G. E. *Massorah Gedolah*. Rome: Pontifical Biblical Institute, 1971.

Yeivin, I. *Introduction to the Tiberian Masorah*. Trans. and ed. E. J. Revell. Missoula: Scholars Press, 1980, pp. 157–174.

Text Criticism of the Hebrew Bible/Introduction to BHS

Scott, W. R. *Simplified Guide to BHS*. 2nd. ed. Berkeley: Bibal Press, 1990.

Tov, E. *Textual Criticism of the Hebrew Bible*. Minneapolis: Fortress Press, 1992.

Weingreen, J. *Introduction to the Critical Study of the Text of the Hebrew Bible*. New York: Oxford University Press, 1982.

Wonneberger, R. *Understanding BHS: A Manual for Users of Biblia Hebraica Stuttgartensia*. Rome: Biblical Institute Press, 1984.

Würthwein, E. *The Text of the Old Testament: An Introduction to the Biblia Hebraica*. Rev. ed. Grand Rapids: William B. Eerdmans Publishing Co., 1994.

Advanced Grammars

Gesenius, W. *Gesenius' Hebrew Grammar*. Edited and enlarged by E. Kautzsch. 2nd. ed. revised by A. E. Cowley. Oxford: Clarendon Press, 1910.

Joüon, P. and T. Muraoka. *A Grammar of Biblical Hebrew*. 2 Vol. Rome: Pontifical Biblical Institute, 1991.

Waltke, B. K. and M. O'Connor. *An Introduction to Biblical Hebrew Syntax*. Winona Lake: Eisenbrauns, 1990.

Ben Zvi, Ehud, Maxine Hancock, Richard Beinert, *Readings in Biblical Hebrew: An Intermediate Textbook*. New Haven: Yale University Press, 1993. (Cross-referenced throughout to Kelley's *Grammar*)

SUBJECT INDEX*

*The subject index is keyed primarily to the footnotes of the *Handbook*. For example, 14(d) refers to page 14, footnote (d).

222